AF477156

How to Make
Your Own Roguelike
With TypeScript

Jakob Gaardsted

How to Make Your Own Roguelike with TypeScript

Copyright © 2023 Jakob Gaardsted

1. edition 2023

By Jakob Gaardsted

Cover Illustration Copyright © 2023 Jakob Gaardsted

Printed by IngramSpark

Published by Jakob Gaardsted

Windelsvej 75, 5000 Odense C, Denmark

https://github.com/pylgrym/roguelike/blob/main/README.md

ISBN 9788797439012

Contents

1 What Are Roguelikes   **3**
  1.1   A Roguelike Timeline   6

2 Language Tooling   **7**
  2.1   Typescript Build-Tools   8
  2.2   TL,DR - Where Is All the Code 16
  2.3   Summary 17

3 Term - Drawing Output   **19**
  3.1   Colored Letters 20
  3.2   Testing our Terminal 24
  3.3   Adding Automatic Resizing 25

4 Input - Events & Screens   **29**
  4.1   Keyboard Input 30
  4.2   Input-Output Screens Plan 30
  4.3   Implementation 31
  4.4   Running the Screens 31

5 Stack of Screens   **33**
  5.1   Screens Stacked on Each Other 34
  5.2   Design 34

6 ScreenMaker Factory   **37**
   6.1   Dynamic Screen Maker 41

7 Dungeon Map Model   **45**
   7.1   Data Model for Our Game State Parts 46

8 Game Model & Builders   **57**
   8.1   Game Model 58
   8.2   Builder 58

9 Creatures in the Dungeon   **63**
   9.1   Moving Mobs Taking Turns 64
   9.2   Player & Monsters as Mobs 65
   9.3   Turn Queue, Whose Turn Is It 67
   9.4   Screen for Mob & Player Turns 70
   9.5   Moving the Player 74
   9.6   Updated Builder Builds Player 79
   9.7   Running the Game Screen 80
   9.8   Testing the Combined Features 81

10 AI Sheep Monsters   **85**
   10.1   A Simple Enemy Monster 86
   10.2   AI, More Art Than Int 86
   10.3   Implementing so-called AI 87

11 Conflict, Cat Combat   **93**
   11.1   Attacking 94
   11.2   More Dynamic Combat 98
   11.3   Hit Points Dashboard 99
   11.4   Player Death 100
   11.5   Monster Death 100
   11.6   Player Attack 102

12 Combat Log   **105**
   12.1   Intent 106
   12.2   Plan 106
   12.3   Model to Hold the Log 107

12.4 Displaying the Log Messages 110
12.5 Log Archive Viewer 114

13 Stairs & Levels **117**
13.1 A Way Out.................................... 118
13.2 Making Stair Travel Work........................ 120
13.3 What Walking Down Stairs Does 121
13.4 Designing Our Stairs............................ 123
13.5 Implementing Stairs............................. 124
13.6 Testing Our Stairs 127

14 Next Level Ants **129**
14.1 A Different Level 130
14.2 A Wellbehaved Enemy 130
14.3 Picking Different Levels 132
14.4 Placing Enemies Reasonably 132

15 Better Dungeon Layout **135**
15.1 Level Map Generator 136
15.2 Plan 136
15.3 Implementation 138
15.4 Doors 143

16 Making It Prettier **153**
16.1 We Can Change How We Draw.................... 154
16.2 Colouring Our Map Tiles 154

17 Healing **157**
17.1 Restoring Our Player's Hit Points................. 158
17.2 Implementation 158
17.3 Integration.................................... 161
17.4 Trying Out Autoheal 162

18 b - Better Balanced Bats **163**
18.1 Balanced Chase 164
18.2 Combat Balance 165
18.3 Balance Principles 165

18.4 Order of Implementation 168
18.5 Making Mood & Proximity 169
18.6 Erratic Movement 170
18.7 Visibility Aspects 172

19 Combat Difficulty Dynamics   **183**
19.1 Neither Too Easy Nor Too Hard 184

20 Monster Difficulty Progression   **187**
20.1 Enemy Progression Structure, Why 188
20.2 Plan for the Progression Structure 188
20.3 The Monster Progression Structure 189
20.4 Building the Progression Monsters.................. 189
20.5 Scaling the Monster Qualities 191
20.6 An Updated AI 193
20.7 Testing the Progression Monsters 194

21 Items in the Dungeon   **197**
21.1 Plan for Items Support 198
21.2 Holding Items in the Model 198
21.3 Defining the Items 199
21.4 Sensing the Items 204
21.5 Gaining Loot When Killing an Enemy.............. 205

22 Player Bag Inventory   **207**
22.1 Somewhere to Put Your Stuff....................... 208
22.2 Plan 208
22.3 Implementation 209
22.4 Looking at Our Bag Inventory 212
22.5 Dropping Stuff Again 214

23 Equipping Items on Player   **219**
23.1 Some Use for Items 220
23.2 Intent & Motivation 220
23.3 Plan for Implementing Equipment 221
23.4 Worn Model 221

CONTENTS

23.5 Equip & Unequip Commands 224
23.6 Equip Integration.......................... 228
23.7 Testing Worn-Items Features 229
23.8 Worn Equipment Display 230
23.9 Unequipping Command Included 233
23.10 Combat Effects of Worn Equipment................. 233
23.11 Armor Mechanics Background 236

24 Spells, Buffs I   241
24.1 Monsters Different Through Spells................. 242
24.2 Intent 242
24.3 Plan 243
24.4 Making AIs Use Spells 244
24.5 The Buff Command 247
24.6 Storing Buffs on Mob 248
24.7 Mob Buffs Lifecycle 250
24.8 Buffs on Dashboard 252
24.9 Effects of Confusion 253

25 Spells, Buffs II   255
25.1 Spell Effects 256
25.2 Implementing Buff Effects 258
25.3 Impaired Mechanism....................... 259

26 Digging   281
26.1 Mr Gorbachev, Tear Down This Wall 282
26.2 Digging Cost 282
26.3 Interface Design 283

27 Ranged Missile Spells   287
27.1 Motivation.............................. 288
27.2 Balance and Limits 288
27.3 Possibilities 288
27.4 Plan 289
27.5 Approach & Mechanism 289
27.6 Design 290
27.7 A Bullet Spell 291

27.8 Timing Mechanism 297

28 Item Spells for Player   **299**

28.1 Player Power Through Items 300
28.2 Constraining Player's Spell Use 300
28.3 Our Choice of Cost: Items 301
28.4 Potion & Scroll Items 301
28.5 A Menu to Use Items 302
28.6 Implementing Item Spell Use 303
28.7 Add Zap Wand for Zap Spell 306
28.8 Spell Charges 310

29 Generic Spell Interface   **313**

29.1 Intent 314
29.2 Spell Enumeration 314
29.3 Plan 315
29.4 Player Spell Access 316
29.5 SpellFinder for the Screen 318
29.6 The New Spell Commands 320
29.7 Reusable Payload Missile Spell 322
29.8 Item Spells, Version 2 324
29.9 Rare Wands 326
29.10 Distinguishing Item Qualities 327
29.11 Updating the Items in Builder 329
29.12 Enemy Spell Access 329
29.13 Shooting AI 331

30 An End, How to Win   **339**

30.1 A Way to Win 340
30.2 A Means to an End - Design 340
30.3 Plan 344
30.4 Implementation 345
30.5 So, Is the Game Balanced Now? 356
30.6 The End of the End 357
30.7 What Now? 357

31 Features We Didn't Do ..Yet   **359**

31.1   Just One More Feature, I Promise 360
31.2   Hunger Clock.. 360
31.3   Light/Torch Clock 361
31.4   Proper Field of View/Vision 362
31.5   Item Identification 362
31.6   Weight Limit Effects 363
31.7   Secret Traps & Areas 364
31.8   Crafting... 366
31.9   Trading & Merchants 366
31.10   Town Levels 367
31.11   Character Stats 367
31.12   Skills 367
31.13   Mana Magic 368
31.14   Levels & XP 368
31.15   Schools of Magic 368
31.16   Resistance & Weakness 369
31.17   Deities 369
31.18   Classes 369
31.19   Mini-Map 370
31.20   Game Persistence, Save & Load 370
31.21   Time/Speed Movement Systems 371
31.22   Dynamic Terrain 371
31.23   Visiblity & Sound 372
31.24   Pets 372
31.25   Artifact Weapons & Armor 372

32 Just Make a Small Program?   373
32.1   Maybe 374
32.2   Should I Code in This Book's Style? 378

33 Making better maps   381
33.1   Rooms & corridors 382
33.2   Map-Builder's workshop 382
33.3   Starting Out 385
33.4   Broken Columns 386
33.5   Alternating Walls Maze 388
33.6   Placing Random rooms 391

33.7 Grid of boxes 394
33.8 Basic mazes 402
33.9 Improving ordinary mazes 406
33.10 Removing dead-ends from mazes 409
33.11 Growing Box-seeds 412
33.12 Sprouter 419
33.13 Binary space partition 429
33.14 Thoughts on Making Dungeon Layouts 435
33.15 Connecting Corridors, Basic Algorithm Outline 439
33.16 Connecting Corridors, Advanced Algorithm Outline 441
33.17 Using Builders in `MapBuilder` 443

34 About   **445**

CONTENTS

F 1: Make Your Own Roguelike With TypeScript

1   WHAT ARE ROGUELIKES

We are going to build a game. What kind of game? It will be turn-based, like chess is. The player will not need twitchy trigger-fingers. He can consider his next turn, his choices, for as long as he likes.

The player is represented by an @-sign, in a top-down grid representation of a dungeon, facing enemy **monsters** represented by moving alphabet letters, and fighting back using other ascii-character **items** he finds there.

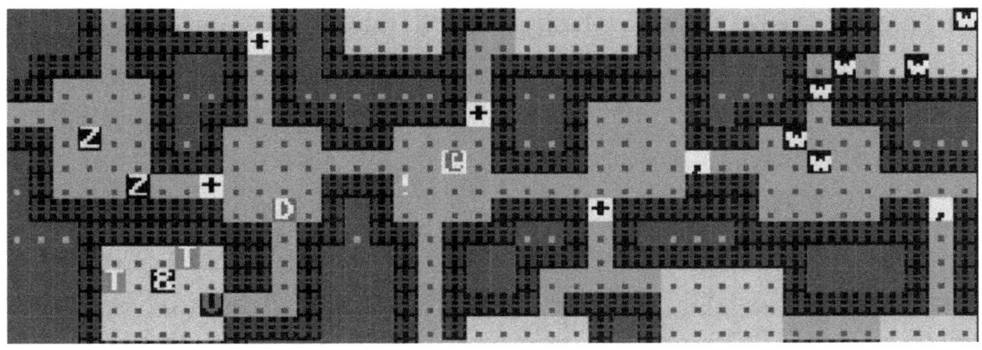

F 1.1: A roguelike playing area

I first encountered roguelike games when I was about 16 years old, having launched some of them by accident, while searching for interesting or useful *software* (what you might call *games*). I stared at them for a bit, thinking there had to be some sort of misunderstanding. They seemed to have misplaced their graphics, their sound effects, their action, and even their user-interface? I figured out how to *close* the programs again, then promptly forgot about them.

Little did I know that I had been sitting with a drug syringe in my hand, wondering where to insert the batteries. A few years later, now at university, I encountered roguelikes **again**. Strange.. Why wouldn't those weird misunderstandings stay away? This time, I had some boring assignment to do, but the computer I was sitting at also had MORIA installed. Some time passed, then I looked up at the wall clock. A few years had gone by, and suddenly I had better get back to work finishing that assignment and my studies.

Elsewhere in the world, a subsidiary of a company called Blizzard cloned another roguelike - actually, also here a variant of Moria. They added isometric graphics to it, hooked its turn-loop up to a regular timer-interval, and released it under the name 'Diablo'.

This time around I was no longer clueless regarding what those weird games with ASCII letters were all about. In the meantime I had learned, that those ugly-looking games were made of highly concentrated **game essence**. Other games might have 10 or 20 mechanics. Those games, without thinking too deeply about it, would routinely have 50 or 100 different mechanics, many of them interacting with each other.

Now in the 2020's, Diablo might be a dated game. You may instead have heard of a game called *Minecraft*. Minecraft is a roguelike in 3d. There are even people who have created old-school 2d Minecraft clones in ASCII.

Roguelike games may not look like much. Instead their focus is on building fun and intricate game mechanics. To the extent they succeed at this, you are free to embellish them with better graphics and animations, sound effects and music, to make them "look like much".

In their roots, they offer tactical gameplay with outset in their symbolic 'chess board playing field' of letters, and turn-based freedom to think carefully about your next move and options. If you try to convert them into twitchy fast-paced real-time 3d action, some nuances may be lost in translation. Or not - consider Minecraft and Diablo, which succeed competently in doing just that.

If you switch perspective from that of the player, to that of the game developer, roguelike games offer something else: The opportunity for a single person, or just a few persons, to become *kings of their own game* - or lost in the game development jungle for years, as happens to some of us. Either way, you'll have an adventure, and might live to tell the tale (and some will get lost already on their way to the airport before departing, but avoiding that will be your responsibility).

This opportunity is unique, as most modern games are too huge for a single individual to undertake. So if you ever speculated about creating your own computer game, all by yourself, roguelike games offer you a unique chance to do this.

A quick tip for the impatient: The proper game parts only start from chapter 7 and 9 onwards. The first six chapters deal with "boring" foundations which are either required, or a hassle to add in afterwards. Chapter 7 introduces the game map (the playing area), and chapter 9 finally lets the player move his avatar around.

1.1   A ROGUELIKE TIMELINE

Obviously and arguably the first roguelike, Rogue itself appeared around 1980. A couple of similar games appeared around the same time, but none of these had the scope of rogue. One of the major inspirations for Rogue was the d&d roleplaying games of the 1970's. Soon, similar games appeared. Hack in 1982 (later nethack in 1987), Moria in 1983 (later UMoria in 1988). Moria also begat Angband (1990), which then led to the 'Band derivatives.

In the 90's, Diablo (1997) and ADOM (1994) appeared, and in 2011, Minecraft arrived.

Along the way, countless others roguelikes have been created. Those mentioned above are just some of the major lighthouses of the genre.

The classic category of roguelikes is the dungeon crawler, where your roleplaying activities are focused on gaining power by killing monsters and searching dungeons for loot. But roguelikes can be very different from this and anything you want, depending on who you are arguing with.

2 Language Tooling

(In which we set up our development environment with the typescript language)

F 2.1: Tools we need but don't understand

2.1 Typescript Build-Tools

2.1.1 Setting up Our Programming Language Environment to Code Our Game in

Some prerequisites for this book, and **for you**. You will be expected to program.

This book is *not a programming language tutorial*. If you are not already a programmer, you must either be following other materials that teach you the TypeScript language, or otherwise be on your way to learn programming. You must either be a (beginner) programmer, or working to become one.

That said, the subjects in this book are good material to cut your teeth on, as you strive to improve your programming abilities. Becoming a good programmer is, above all, about **doing actual programming**.

We are about to set up our computer environment for programming. This will require two things: A so-called **editor** to create and edit source code files (which are files that contain code as plain text). And the so-called **command prompt** or **terminal**, aka **shell**, for executing and running commands.

The command-prompt, if you are working under Windows, is aptly named `Command Prompt`. Under linux, it is called a terminal or shell, often the `bash` shell.

For the editor, I recommend either `SublimeText` or `VSCode`, but any editor will do.

The details of how to create and work with files is outside the scope of this book, but be advised that you are expected to use a text editor to work with the source code files that appear in the following.

2.1.2 LET'S GO!

We will run our game in a web browser window, and we will program it with javascript code - almost. We will actually program in the language **typescript**, which is a practical way to write javascript. As its name suggests, it adds **types** to javascript, and types are a wonderful aid when making **larger** programs, and when making **changes** to larger programs. And as you build a large program, you **will** make *changes* to your existing parts.

If we stuck with plain javascript, we wouldn't need setup - we could just open up a text editor, and start plopping in javascript code (we'd still need some *webserver* to get that code into a web-browser though). But trust that I have tried doing that, and it was so painful, I refused to make any more javascript games, unless typescript was there to help me.

The problem is not when you write smaller javascript programs with maybe a few hundred lines of code. There, you can reasonably assume you can keep it all in your head. The problem is, your programs will grow to thousands of lines, and even bigger. By then, you'll invariably discover that you lose track of all the places you need to adjust, when you update some parts.

The way typescript and types help us, is that they keep track of all the rules and promises we make to ourselves, as we build our game. It will helpfully tell us *"remember that you promised, that you would always specify an (x,y) position for the monsters in your game. Well, in line 187 and 453 of file* `somefile.ts`*, it seems you forgot to include the (x,y) values? Can you fix that?"*

Having such a nit-picker may *sound* like a nuisance, but a *real* nuisance is, when you have played for 3 hours, and your hero suddenly dies on level 7, because you forgot to specify a comma somewhere. I say all this to motivate, why we now spend the following efforts to get our hands on typescript, when we instead could have started straight into javascript in 60 seconds.

To get our typescript setup, we will set up a kind of bottle-ship. Our end goal is to get javascript into a web **browser**. But web browsers show stuff they get from web **servers**. And also, we have typescript, which must be **translated** to javascript. And web browsers don't really show javascript, they show **web pages with** javascript. So we need 3 things - our typescript into javascript, our javascript into a web page, and our web page into a web server (and from there, finally into a browser).

Luckily for us, there are systems that **do just that**, made by and for people with similar needs. The foundation is **nodejs**, a javascript engine and environment, which you can download and install. Once you have node.js, it can do two things for you: It can run javascript (big surprise there), and it can install, manage and run javascript **modules**. This means we can install a bunch of **node modules** that do those three things we need.

The central module for us is a system called **webpack**. It interfaces to all the things we need, and need taken care of. Webpack will orchestrate turning typescript to **javascript**, getting that javascript into a **web page**, and even run a tiny and clever **webserver** to deliver our page and scripts to the browser.

With those goals, let's see what we need. We'll name and make a folder for **our** node module, where we'll build our game:

```
mkdir mygame
cd mygame
npm init
```

npm is the **node package manager**, and controls everything about nodejs javascript **modules**. Now with a module of our own, we can install the packages we need. Our node module shopping list is as follows. You can go ahead and install them all.

```
npm install -D typescript
npm install -D webpack-cli
npm install -D webpack@^5
npm install -D ts-loader
npm install -D @types/jquery
npm install -D jquery
npm install -D webpack-dev-server
npm install -D html-webpack-plugin@^5
npm install -D file-loader
```

What are all those parts, actually? Well,

- The **typescript** module is the general engine that can translate typescript to javascript.
- **webpack** and **webpack-cli**, is the 'forklift' that integrates all these parts we are bringing in.
- **ts-loader** lets webpack operate the typescript module (it's the interface between those two).
- The two **jquery** things, are the definitions for JQuery, and JQuery itself (if you forego JQuery, you can leave these out).
- **webpack-dev-server** is the test-webserver built into webpack - it means you don't need to get hold of a 'real' webserver - you can think of it as 'batteries-included'.
- The **file-loader** lets the dev-server serve ordinary files as well, which 'is a thing it just needs' (hint: favicon.ico).

In this chapter, we won't explain in depth what all those moving parts do. There are up-to-date thorough resources on the web, that explain what you need to know about flavor-of-the-month webpack and typescript. Our focus is on getting a typescript environment up and running, without getting bogged down by all the tiny wheels and gears within webpack.

With this excuse, I dump the following incomprehensible heap of steaming `webpack.config.js` on your head:

```
const HtmlWebpackPlugin=require("html-webpack-plugin");
const webpack = require("webpack");
module.exports = {
  entry: './src/index02_hello.ts',
  module: { rules: [
    { test:    /\.ts$/,
      use: 'ts-loader', exclude: /node_modules/ },
    { test: /\.(ico)$/,
      use: 'file-loader?name=src/[name].[ext]' }
  ] },
  mode: 'development',
  resolve: {
      extensions: [ ".js", ".ts" ],
      modules: [ 'src', 'node_modules' ]
  },
  plugins: [
    new HtmlWebpackPlugin(
    { template: './src/index0.html',
      favicon: './src/favicon.ico' } ),
    new webpack.ProvidePlugin(
      {$: 'jquery',jquery: 'jquery'}
    )
  ],
  devServer: { static: './dist' }
}
```

To allow us to run, we need a `tsconfig.json`, which must contain
the following. `baseUrl` lets us import our types from our module
source root. Without it, we would get those weird '../..' paths
when we import our own stuff. The rest are good defaults, which
protects us against cutting ourselves. You could leave out most
of them, but it will just allow you to have more undetected bugs.

```
{ "compilerOptions": {
    "baseUrl": "./src",
    "target": "ES2020", // or stick to "ES6",
    "strict": true,
    "alwaysStrict": true,
```

```
    "strictFunctionTypes": true,
    "strictBindCallApply": true,
    "strictPropertyInitialization": true,
    "noImplicitThis": true,
    "noImplicitAny": true,
    "noUnusedLocals": true,
    "noImplicitReturns": true,
    "noFallthroughCasesInSwitch": true,
    "forceConsistentCasingInFileNames": true
} }
```

And then, we need a sprinkle of source code. We need some
definite typescript, which you'll put in a subfolder `src`. First,
we'll do these commands:

```
mkdir src
cd src
```

Inside the `src` folder, we can then make `src/index02_hello.ts`:

```
let test:string = 'Hello Typescript!';
console.log(test);
document.body.textContent = test;
```

And a webpage `src/index0.html` to host it in. We could make do
with this tiny bit:

```
<!DOCTYPE html>
<html> <body id="body1">
  Hello!
  <canvas id="canvas1"></canvas>
</body> </html>
```

But we'll use this more complete version, which includes stuff
we want to be there. There is a graphics canvas we are going to
draw on, and some sensible default settings (getting rid of
default margin, setting proper encoding, and a background color
that lets us see how the canvas is doing).

```html
<!DOCTYPE html>
<html>
  <head>
    <style>
      body { margin: 0px; }
      html { background: black; color:cyan;
             overflow: hidden; }
      canvas { background: lightblue; }
    </style>
    <meta charset="utf-8">
  </head>
  <body id="body1">
    <canvas id="canvas1"></canvas>
  </body>
</html>
```

We need one extra thing. We must provide our website with a
`favicon.ico`, the site bookmark icon. We can do so in a cheating
manner, by editing the file `src/favicon.ico`, and type a single 'a'
letter into it. It is cheating, as it won't actually function as a
proper icon. But it's enough to trick the dev-server and the
browser, which require it to have at least one byte. If it irks you
we are cheating, you are welcome to procure a proper
`favicon.ico` . Or you may use the html syntax `<link
rel="icon"..>` to control favicon behaviour - the details of which
are not covered here.

We are almost ready to type `npm start`. For that, we have to **add**
the `start` script to our `package.json`, so the script section will
look like this:

```json
"scripts": {
    "start": "webpack serve --open",
    "test": "t"
},
```

With this done, you can type `npm start` (back in the root of your
`mygame` folder). As it runs, it should look something like this:

```
> webpack serve --open

<i> [webpack-dev-server] Project is running at:
<i> [webpack-dev-server] Loopback: http://localhost:8080/
<i> [webpack-dev-server] On Your Network (IPv4): http://192.168.0.99:8080/
<i> [webpack-dev-server] Content not from webpack is served from './dist' directory
<i> [webpack-dev-middleware] wait until bundle finished: /
asset main.js 243 KiB [emitted] (name: main)
asset index.html 374 bytes [emitted]
asset favicon.ico 1 bytes [emitted]
runtime modules 27.3 KiB 12 modules
modules by path ./node_modules/ 160 KiB
  modules by path ./node_modules/webpack-dev-server/client/ 55.8 KiB 12 modules
  modules by path ./node_modules/webpack/hot/*.js 4.59 KiB
    ./node_modules/webpack/hot/dev-server.js 1.88 KiB [built] [code generated]
    ./node_modules/webpack/hot/log.js 1.34 KiB [built] [code generated]
    + 2 modules
  modules by path ./node_modules/html-entities/lib/*.js 81.3 KiB
    ./node_modules/html-entities/lib/index.js 7.74 KiB [built] [code generated]
    ./node_modules/html-entities/lib/named-references.js 72.7 KiB [built] [code generated]
    + 2 modules
  ./node_modules/ansi-html-community/index.js 4.16 KiB [built] [code generated]
  ./node_modules/events/events.js 14.5 KiB [built] [code generated]
./src/index02_hello.ts 103 bytes [built] [code generated]
webpack 5.75.0 compiled successfully in 3870 ms
```

F 2.2: running the npm command in the commandline console

As a result, your tiny web page with typescript code should hopefully compile and run, and show up in your web browser looking like this:

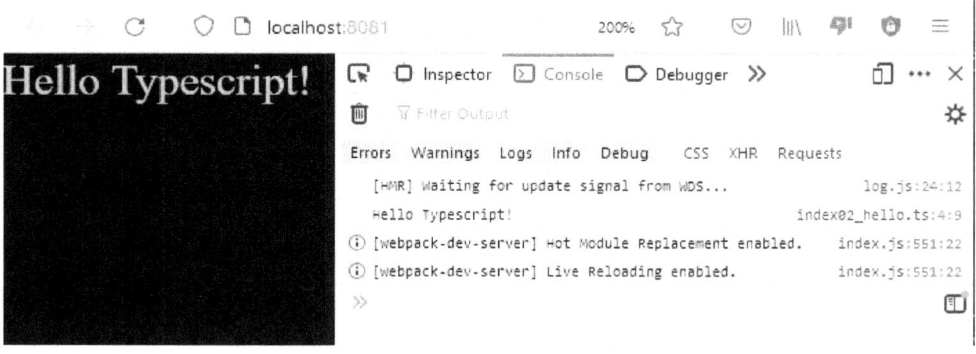

F 2.3: Typescript running in the web browser

Typically, if you press the key F12 in your web browser, it will show the **javascript console** visible here on the right, where you can see the output 'Hello Typescript!'.

(For the curious: Only the `start` script has that special `npm start` shorthand for `npm run start`. Any other script requires the full `npm run other` syntax.)

Normally, the **entry** to run must be specified - and updated - in the `webpack.config.js` file. If you prefer to manually specify which `indexN.ts` to run, on the command-line, you can instead do this:

```
npx webpack serve --open --entry ./src/index02_hello.ts
```

or even shortened to this: (depending on your webpack config)

```
npx webpack serve --open --entry index02_hello.ts
```

2.2   TL,DR - Where Is All the Code

The code for all the chapters is available as branches in a git repository on github - `https://github.com/pylgrym/roguelike`. For example, the code for chapter 2 is at `https://github.com/pylgrym/roguelike/tree/ch02` .

If you clone that git repository, you should be able to `git switch ch02` to a given branch, run `npm install` and then run it with whatever runner applies to it, e.g.

```
npx webpack serve --open --entry index02_hello.ts
```

Note that you *should* be able to enter the entire program from the listings in this book - I have done so several times myself, during proofreading. I'm not suggesting that you should type it all in by hand. The point I'm making is that you should be able to **read** the entire program from this book, without wondering "is there some special extra hidden code he is not showing us?"

That said, I have excluded a lot of extraneous "plumbing" code. In particular, every typescript file will contain a lot of tedious `import` declarations at the top. I have excluded those, because they tell the reader nothing. If you use a modern code editor like `VS Code`, it should help you configure those imports automatically.

2.3 SUMMARY

To sum up what we have accomplished in this chapter: We can now launch and run a small web page, which will execute a piece of typescript that we point it towards (the `indexNNN.ts` file).

When you want to compile and run a given `indexN.ts` file, you run this phrase in your commandline prompt:

```
npx webpack serve --open --entry indexN.ts
```

Typically, you can **interrupt** that running npm process again, by pressing Ctrl-C on your keyboard.

Pressing F12 in your web browser, should show you the javascript console for your running browser program, and thus allow you to see log messages, and any errors and stack traces.

3 TERM - DRAWING OUTPUT

(In which we get to draw some stuff on the screen)

F 3.1: Some sort of screen with coloured letters on it

3.1 Colored Letters

3.1.1 Drawing Game Graphics on Our Screen with Term

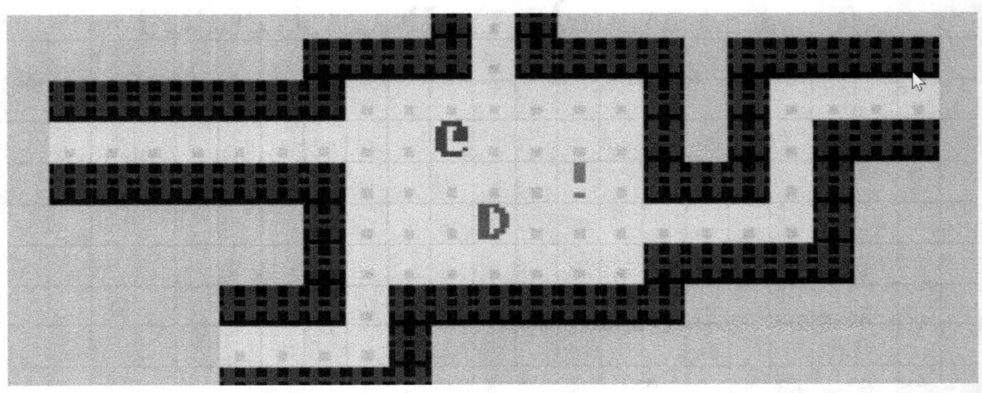

F 3.2: Player near violet potion & mature red dragon

Let us consider what we are going to do. Our game is supposed to look something like the picture above here. So we must figure out how to draw ..that. What is it? Well, it's a grid of letters - so-called **characters**. And they are colored. So we have to *draw colored letters, in a grid.* And it looks like we are drawing their *backgrounds* in various colors, as well.

This approach does not come out of the blue. Roguelike games used to be played on so-called text-terminals, named so because they could not draw 'proper' graphics. From this legacy, we talk of drawing to a **terminal**, and we will code ourselves a terminal interface, which we will affectionately name Term.

Our terminal interface will be brief:

- It will have width and height **dimensions**, holding the number of cells on each side of the grid.

- It will have a method at() for setting a given character cell at a given x and y coordinate (within the dimensions), with a given foreground and background color.

- Allowing ourselves a bit of luxury, it will also have a method
  `txt()`, working like `at()`, but printing a whole text string.

We can place such an interface in file `src/01term/03TermIF.ts`:

```
export interface TermIF {
  dim: TPoint;
  txt(x:number, y:number, c:string,
      fg:string, bg:string):void;
  at( x:number, y:number, s:string,
      fg:string, bg:string):void;
}
```

```
export class TPoint {
  constructor(public x:number=0,
              public y:number=0) {}
}
```

`TPoint` is a helper class for `TermIF`. We will put it in its own file
`03TPoint.ts`. It denotes any point on the terminal surface.
However in `at` and `txt`, we will use direct x and y instead of
`TPoint`, as this will be more practical for us.

```
export class TPoint {
  constructor(public x:number=0,
              public y:number=0) {}
  static StockDims = new TPoint(32, 16);
}
```

We then **implement** the terminal. We add a class `Term` to
`03Term.ts`, and begin by making `txt()` and `at()`:

```
export class Term implements TermIF {
  txt(x:number, y:number, s: string,
      fg:string, bg:string
  ) {
    for (let i=0; i<s.length; ++i) {
      this.at(x,y,s.charAt(i), fg,bg);
      ++x;
```

```
      if (x >= this.dim.x) {
        x=0; ++y;
        if (y >= this.dim.y) { y=0; }
      }
    }
  }
}
```

`txt()` works by delegating to `at()`, to draw each single letter in
the string to be printed. `at()` looks like this:

```
at(x:number,y:number,char:string,fg:string,bg:string){
  let fx = (x      )*this.hside,
      fy = (y      )*this.vside;
  let px = (x+0.5)*this.hside,
      py = (y+0.5)*this.vside;

  this.ctx.save();
  {
    this.ctx.fillStyle = bg;
    this.ctx.fillRect(fx,fy,this.hside,this.vside);

    this.ctx.beginPath();
    this.ctx.rect(fx,fy,this.hside, this.vside);
    this.ctx.clip();

    this.ctx.fillStyle = fg;
    this.ctx.fillText(char, px, py);
  }
  this.ctx.restore();
}
```

The details here are not important to understand precisely (in a
roguelike context, of course. They must still work!) The salient
points are:

- `fillRect` will draw a square or rectangle, in the fill color
  style of `bg`, our background color.
- `fillText` draws the specified letter `char` on top of that

> square, in the `fg` (foreground) color.
> * the `path/rect/clip` restricts the drawn text to not draw
>   outside the colored square, into neighbouring squares.

There was a bit of cheating again: We need that `ctx` and `hside`
stuff. `ctx` is a drawing-context for the HTML canvas, and the
`side` variables are the sizes of the square letter tiles we draw. So
with the final parts, class `Term` looks like this:

```
export class Term implements TermIF {
  ctx: CanvasRenderingContext2D;
  hside: number = 1; // ie undef.
  vside: number = 1;
  side:  number = 40; // (pixels)
  scale: number = 0.8;


  constructor(public dim:TPoint) {
    this.ctx = this.initCtx();
  }


  initCtx(): CanvasRenderingContext2D {
    let cnv = <HTMLCanvasElement>
      document.getElementById("canvas1");
    let ctx = <CanvasRenderingContext2D>
        cnv.getContext("2d");
    // controls how non-square:
    this.hside = this.side*1.0;
    this.vside = this.side*1.0;

    let squeeze:number=this.side*this.scale;
    ctx.fillStyle = "#110";
    ctx.strokeStyle = "red";
    ctx.textAlign = "center";
    ctx.textBaseline = "middle";
    ctx.font = `${squeeze}px sans-serif`;
    return ctx;
  }
  public static StockTerm():Term {
      return new Term(TPoint.StockDims);
```

```
      }
      // here follows txt() and at():
      ..
```

3.2   TESTING OUR TERMINAL

Now it would be nice to see all that code run, and **do** something.
We need some code to use and exercise our terminal - this test
class 03TestTerm.ts will do:

```
export class TestTerm {
  static test(term:TermIF) {
    term.at(0,0,"a","white", "gray");
  }
  static test2(term:TermIF, str:string) {
    for (let y=0; y<term.dim.y; ++y) {
      for (let x=0; x<term.dim.x; ++x) {
        let n = (5*y*x+3*x);
        let nc = (n%26) + 'a'.charCodeAt(0);
        let c = String.fromCharCode(nc);
        let bg = '#' + ((n+ 0)%16).toString(16)
                     + ((n+ 5)%16).toString(16)
                     + ((n+10)%16).toString(16);
        term.at(x,y, c,"white", bg );
      }
    }
    term.txt(2,1,'##.##','white','black');
    term.txt(2,2,'#@.k!','white','black');
    term.txt(2,3,str,'yellow','red');
  }
}
```

You can go with test() if you are in a hurry, or use test2() if
you want some pay-off. Finally, we'll need an entry-point to run
it all: index03_drawterm.ts

```
TestTerm.test2( Term.StockTerm(), 'Hi!' );
```

Remember to update the `webpack.config.js` setting `entry` from `index02_hello` to `index03_drawterm`! Then, `npm start`.

Alternatively, you may pass the desired entry point directly to the `webpack` command as an argument , like this:

```
npx webpack serve --open --entry ./src/index03_drawterm.ts
```

If it worked, it should look something like akin to

F 3.3: Our drawn grid of coloured letters

3.3 ADDING AUTOMATIC RESIZING

That is pretty much what we need! Its main defect is that it doesn't resize, so let's fix that. We will create a new `Term` class called `ResizingTerm`, which will build on `Term`, and extend it with some features. We put this into `03ResizingTerm.ts`:

```
export class ResizingTerm extends Term {
  public reinitCtx() { this.ctx = this.initCtx(); }
  public resize(w_px:number, h_px:number) {
    let tx = Math.floor(w_px / this.dim.x);
```

```
      let ty = Math.floor(h_px / this.dim.y);
      let side_cand = (tx > ty ? ty : tx);
      this.side = side_cand;
      this.reinitCtx();
    }
    public onResize() {
      let w = window.innerWidth; let h = window.innerHeight;
      $('#canvas1').prop('width',  w);
      $('#canvas1').prop('height', h);
      this.resize(w,h);
    }
    public static StockTerm():ResizingTerm {
        return new ResizingTerm(TPoint.StockDims);
    }
}
```

(This split-up into two classes using inheritance was artificial. It allowed us to examine drawing, and now resizing, as separate isolated features. Normally, the methods of both `Term` and `ResizingTerm` could just go into a single class.)

We are about to create a new `index03_resize.ts` entry point, to try out our resize. Note that from now on, we will regularly create a fresh `indexN+1.ts` entry point to try out new features as we introduce them. Whenever this happens, you must either update `entry` in `webpack.config.js`, or specify it explicitly when you run `npm`, like this: `npx webpack serve --open --entry ./src/index03_drawterm.ts`

We hook up our resizing to the browser window's resize event. With JQuery, `index03_resize.ts` looks like this:

```
let term = ResizingTerm.StockTerm();
function onResize() {
  term.onResize();
  TestTerm.test2(term, '-');
}
$(window).on('resize', onResize);
```

```
onResize();
```

And voila! Now our terminal adjusts its tile size, to fit its dimensions inside the current window borders. This involves a compromise with empty borders, as the window may be either too wide or too tall for the tile grid dimensions, which we fixed to 40x25. Believe me, you *would not* want the terminal to stretch or squeeze your font letters wide or narrow to fit your window.

We are quite pleased we got this resizing feature added, because without it, our terminal had a so rigid size that it would never even respect the **grid dimensions** we specified for our term, let alone resize the cell glyph font.

4 Input - Events & Screens

(In which we get to receive user keyboard input)

F 4.1: The cursor keys may move our hero in four directions

4.1   KEYBOARD INPUT

4.1.1   RECEIVE KEYBOARD INPUT
& DRAW ON THE SCREEN

We are now capable of drawing output graphics on the screen,
with the `ResizingTerm` from the previous chapter. Our real goal
is a game where the user can make decisions and give **input**
based on what we have drawn on the screen. We want to build
user interfaces where the user can **interact** with the games we
'draw'. Our game will be built as a series of **screens** that take
input and draw output. That means we must support user input
too, like keyboard, mouse or touch events.

4.2   INPUT-OUTPUT SCREENS PLAN

We devise the concept **RawScreen**, which can **draw**, and receive
keyboard **input**, *somehow*. We will then implement our game as
RawScreens. We define the interface `RawScreenIF` for these
input-output screens - `01term/04RawScreenIF.ts`:

```
export interface RawScreenIF {
  draw(term:TermIF) :void;
  onKey(e:JQuery.KeyDownEvent) :void;
  name:string;
}
```

The `onKey` stuff is about getting user **keyboard input** to the
screens, which we will need in a bit.

4.3   IMPLEMENTATION

We can make the following small test-screen as an example.
`01term/04RawTestScreen.ts`:

```
export class RawTestScreen implements RawScreenIF {
  name='test1';
  key:string='-';
  onKey(e:JQuery.KeyDownEvent){this.key=`?:${e.key}`;}
  draw(term:Term) { TestTerm.test2(term,this.key); }
}
```

The idea is, we store what the user last typed in the field `key`, and use `TestTerm` to draw it on the screen in `draw`.

With this, we have the concept of **Screens**. Each screen will use the `Term` to show the user some specific information. Screens are what people sometimes call **views**. Examples are

- the main **gameplay** screen,
- the **game-over** screen,
- various **sub-menu choice** screens, and
- possibly an **intro** screen or
- a **main game menu** screen.

4.4   RUNNING THE SCREENS

To run the screens, we need a mechanism to **host** them - pass input to them, and ask them to draw on the screen. We will build it out of the parts from the previous chapter. The `ResizingTerm`was a nice resize-feature for our terminal, but its parts were kind of disconnected - just some loose pieces we declared and fitted together directly in our main index file. Instead, we will now combine those parts into a complete class, which we'll name `EventMgr`. `01term/04EventMgr.ts`:

```
export class EventMgr {
  constructor(public term:ResizingTerm,
              public screen:RawScreenIF) {
    $('#body1').on('keydown', this.onKey.bind(this));
    $(window).on('resize', this.onResize.bind(this));
    this.onResize();
  }
  onResize() {
    this.term.onResize();
    this.screen.draw(this.term);
  }
  onKey(e:JQuery.KeyDownEvent) {
    this.screen.onKey(e);
    this.screen.draw(this.term);
  }
  static runRawScreen(rawScreen:RawScreenIF) {
      return new EventMgr(ResizingTerm.StockTerm(),
                          rawScreen); }
}
```

EventMgr ties together the loose bits from `index03_resize.ts`.
Crucially, it doesn't do the actual 'screen' part. Instead, we've
extracted that into the 'generic any-kind-of-screen' `RawScreenIF`.
You can now test it, with `index04_rawscreen.ts`:

```
EventMgr.runRawScreen(new RawTestScreen());
```

F 4.2: The keys you press, printed in red

As you press keys, you should see them displayed on screen.

5 STACK OF SCREENS

(In which we allow multiple screens to be stacked)

F 5.1: The screens stacked on top hide the screens below them

5.1   Screens Stacked on Each Other

*(Note: The **stack screens** introduced here are basically the same thing as the **raw screens** we introduced in the previous chapter. They just include additional 'plumbing' that we will eventually need, and which would be a nuisance to retro-fit later.)*

5.1.1   Motivation

We will support activating other screens while one screen is already being shown. We will have a **Screen Stack** which tracks our screens, and tracks which one of them is currently **active**. It behaves like a stack of playing cards: At any time, the topmost screen (card) is visible. So if you are on a given screen, and activate a sub menu, the menu screen will show up on top, and once you are done with the menu, it will 'pop' back off the stack, so the earlier screen once again is visible.

5.2   Design

The screens that our screen-stack will contain, will not exactly be the raw-screens from the earlier chapter. The interface of these **stack screens** will be a tiny bit different from our `RawScreen`. Because they need to start and stop screens themselves, they need direct access to the stack. So their `onKey` handler will get the stack as an extra argument. `01Term/05SScreenIF.ts`:

```typescript
export interface SScreenIF {
  draw(term:TermIF) :void;
  onKey(e:JQuery.KeyDownEvent, stack:StackIF) :void;
  name:string;
}
```

The `ScreenStack` needs a number of operations. You can remove (`pop`) the topmost card, ask what the topmost card is (`cur`), and

add a new topmost card (push). Its interface becomes this -
`01term/05ScreenStackIF.ts`:

```
export interface StackIF {
  pop():void;
  push(screen:SScreenIF):void;
  cur():SScreenIF;
}
```

We can whip up our implementation of
`01term/05ScreenStack.ts`:

```
export class Stack implements StackIF, RawScreenIF {
  name='stack';
  s:SScreenIF[] = [];
  pop(){ this.s.pop(); }
  push(screen:SScreenIF) { this.s.push(screen); }
  cur():SScreenIF { return this.s[this.s.length-1]; }
  draw(term:TermIF) {
    let s = this.cur();
    if (s) { s.draw(term); }
  }
  onKey(e:JQuery.KeyDownEvent) {
    let s = this.cur();
    if (s) { s.onKey(e,this); }
  }
}
```

It combines two things. It implements the stack part of push, pop,
cur. It also implements RawScreenIF, so EventMgr can host it. The
last part is clever, in that it forwards drawing and keyboard
events to the current **stack screen**.

We will add a helper to `05ScreenStack.ts` for using it:

```
  static run_SScreen(sScreen:SScreenIF) {
    let stack = new Stack();
    stack.push(sScreen);
    EventMgr.runRawScreen(stack);
  }//If you want to manually push a specific screen.
```

We can now test it, with this: `index05_stack.ts`:

```
ScreenStack.run_SScreen( new StackTestScreen() );
```

`01term/05StackTestScreen.ts`:

```
export class StackTestScreen implements SScreenIF {
  name='test2';
  onKey(e:JQuery.KeyDownEvent, s:ScreenStackIF){}
  draw(term:TermIF) { TestTerm.test2(term,'-'); }
}
```

It will look just the same as `index04_rawscreen.ts` did, but now
we support nested screens.

6 ScreenMaker Factory

(In which we allow screens to be used together without knowing each other)

F 6.1: In the middle ages, roguelike screens were assembled by masterful craftsmen

6.0.1 Combining several screens to be used together, without tying those screens directly to each other.

(The motivation for the ScreenMaker, which is the subject of this chapter, is just tooling. It is a factory mechanism that will allow us to easily swap which combinations of screens our game is composed of. You can very well build a full game with ZERO screen makers, by just directly hardcoding the screens you use, in various places. But for our tutorial approach, the screen-maker makes it much easier to swap out and update pieces as we go. If you feel screenmaker is 'too much red tape', you are welcome to avoid it.)

We now support multiple screens. But to switch between them, it appears our screens will have to reference each other directly. Doing so would tie everything hard to each other. For example, our `GameScreen` will need to activate our `GameOverScreen`, and the `GameOverScreen` similarly needs the `GameScreen` to start a new game. Coupling everything directly is annoying when you are developing (modifying) a game, because it is inflexible, and requires you to do a lot of manual changes, every time you want to recombine things differently.

We can address it by extracting the relevant bits out into separate code through an interface. Then you can supply different implementations of that interface, to vary those bits. We won't do it for all screens; that would defeat the purpose, and the interface itself would become rigid. But we will do it for two fundamental screens - the **main** game screen, and the **game-over** screen.

They hold a crucial role. When we create a main-game screen, we need to build up a full fresh game state, and this requires access to special resources. When we create a game-over screen, we also require specific things. We again need the game-state of the lost game passed (to show the game-over status). And we need those same special resources mentioned for creating the game-screen, because the game-over screen must be able to restart the game.

We extract creation of the special screens into its own module. It can't be the screen stack itself, otherwise we'd need to create new screen stacks for every variation. So we need an interface for creating the special screens: 06screen/06ScreenMakerIF.ts:

```typescript
export interface MakerIF {
  new_Game():SScreenIF;
  gameOver():SScreenIF;
}
```

Let's make some screens for it: 06screen/06OverScreen.ts:

```typescript
export class OverScreen0 implements SScreenIF {
  name='gameover';
  constructor(public make:MakerIF) {}
  draw(term:Term) {
    term.txt(1,1,' GAME OVER! ', 'yellow', 'red');
  }
  onKey(e:JQuery.KeyDownEvent, s:StackIF) {
    s.pop();
    s.push(this.make.new_Game());
  }
}
```

06screen/06DummyScreen.ts:

```typescript
export class DummyScreen implements SScreenIF {
  name='dummy-game';
  constructor(public make:MakerIF) {}
  draw(term:Term) {
    term.txt(1,1,' Press Key! ', 'cyan', 'blue');
  }
  onKey(e:JQuery.KeyDownEvent, s:StackIF) {
    s.pop();
    s.push(this.make.gameOver());
  }
}
```

That is enough so we can populate a `ScreenMaker` in
`06ScreenMaker_Fixed.ts`:

```
export class ScreenMaker0_Fixed implements MakerIF {
  new_Game():SScreenIF { return new DummyScreen(this); }
  gameOver():SScreenIF { return new OverScreen0(this); }
}
```

To be able to run it, let's add some helper methods to
`06ScreenMaker_Fixed`:

```
export class ScreenMaker0_Fixed
  ..

  static run_GOfirst(m:MakerIF) {
    Stack.run_SScreen(m.gameOver());
  }
  static StockMaker():MakerIF {
    return new ScreenMaker0_Fixed();
  }
  static GOfirst() {
    this.run_GOfirst(this.StockMaker());
  }

  ..
```

Of course, you could combine all 3 parts in a single statement,
but separating and naming them like this, allows you to declare
why you do them, and to re-use them. Here we only did the
game-over-first variant. A main-game-first works the same way.

`index06_maker_fixed.ts`:

```
ScreenMaker0_Fixed.GOfirst();
```

As you run this, you should be able to toggle between the two
screens, by pressing keys.

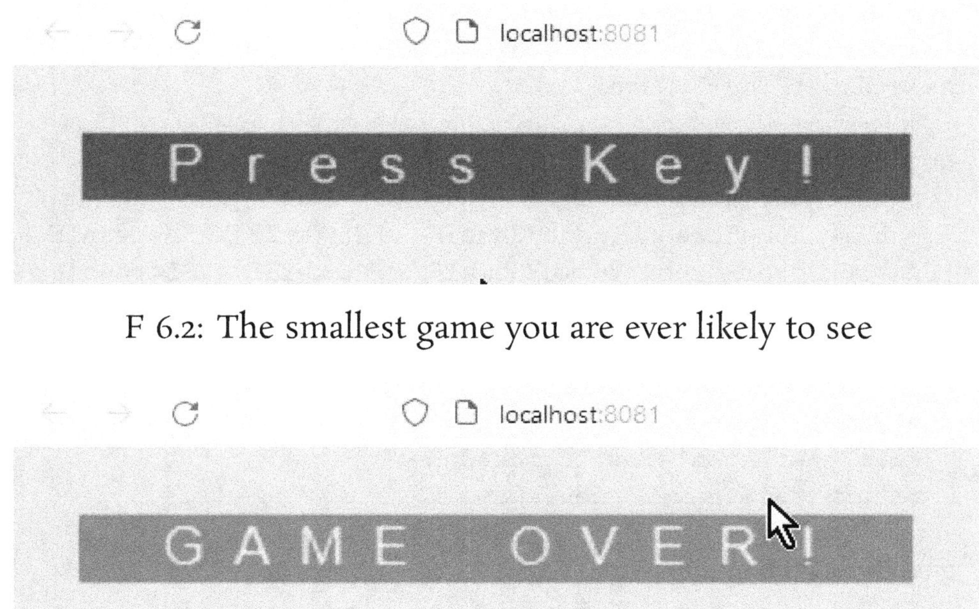

F 6.2: The smallest game you are ever likely to see

F 6.3: The most advanced game-over screen you'll ever see

6.1 DYNAMIC SCREEN MAKER

We just demonstrated the game-maker concept working. But `ScreenMaker0_Fixed` is itself hardcoded. It is not a big problem - we can solve what we need, just by making such similar tiny 'factory classes' to instantiate the screen combinations we need. However, we can actually also make a parameterized `ScreenMaker`. **We won't use this actively yet**, but we will illustrate the mechanism.

You can ignore the details of `GameIF` and `BuildIF1` here. They represent the eventual game to be passed between the screens, and the 'crucial resources' needed to restart a game, respectively. `06Screen/06ScreenMaker_Dyn.ts`:

```
export interface GameIF {}
export interface BuildIF1 {makeGame():GameIF}
```

```
export class ScreenMaker1_Dyn implements MakerIF {
  game:GameIF|null = null;

  constructor(
    public build:BuildIF1,
    public gameScreen:(game:GameIF,sm:MakerIF)=>SScreenIF,
    public overScreen:(game:GameIF,sm:MakerIF)=>SScreenIF,
    public init:(sm:MakerIF)=>SScreenIF
  ) {}

  new_Game():SScreenIF {
    this.game = this.build.makeGame();
    return this.gameScreen(<GameIF>this.game, this);
  }
  gameOver():SScreenIF {
    return this.overScreen(<GameIF>this.game, this);
  }
}
```

The idea is, that we pass the construction code as lambdas. So
gameScreen here is a function that constructs and returns a game
screen, and overScreen a function that provides a game-over
screen. Further, with the function init, we can control how we
start, i.e. which screen is placed initially. Typically, init is used
to call either gameOver() or new_Game().

To use it, we can extend ScreenMaker1_Dyn with these helpers:

```
export class ScreenMaker1_Dyn {
..

  static runDyn(dyn_gs:ScreenMaker1_Dyn) {
    Stack.run_SScreen(dyn_gs.init(dyn_gs));
  }
  static runBuilt_GOfirst(build:BuildIF1) {
    let dyn_gs:ScreenMaker1_Dyn = new ScreenMaker1_Dyn(
      build,
      (g:GameIF,sm:MakerIF) => new GameScreen(g, sm),
      (g:GameIF,sm:MakerIF) => new OverScreenO(sm),
```

```
      (sm:MakerIF) => sm.gameOver()
  );
  this.runDyn(dyn_gs);
}
..
```

In the upcoming chapters, we will get to use `ScreenMaker1_Dyn`.

7 Dungeon Map Model

(In which we get a dungeon map playing area)

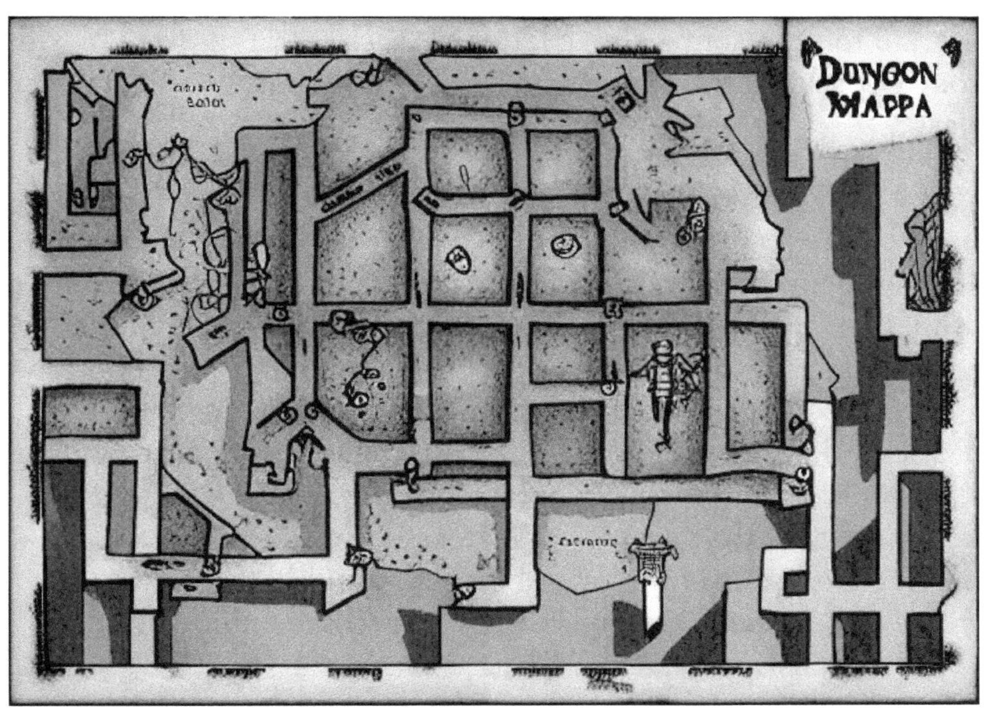

F 7.1: The dungeon map model will define and track what is in the dungeon from moment to moment, while the game is running

7.1 Data Model for Our Game State Parts

With our terminal screens, we can **draw**. Our intention was to draw a dungeon map, but we intend **more** than that. We want to have the **player**, and monsters, **moving** about inside that map. And if something **happens** in our dungeon - say a wall is broken down, a door is opened, a treasure is dropped, or some lava flows - we want to draw that **change** too. So it is not enough to **draw** the dungeon. We have to **track** what the dungeon currently looks like - we need a **model**, a dungeon model. In this model, we will track what is inside each (x,y) cell tile in the map grid.

Our game map model is a two-dimensional grid of **map cells**. So we will have a class `DMap` to hold the entire map grid, which will use another class `MapCell` for each cell. `MapCell` might seem overkill to represent a single letter for each cell. But `MapCell` will soon get several things to handle, so it really needs to be its own class.

7.1.1 Glyph Enumeration for Map Cell Types

Having seen how our game screen is supposed to look, we might think that we should put the screen characters directly in the map and map cells. That is, a '#' for walls, and a ' . ' for floors, and so on. That approach is possible, but **not recommended**. It has several problems: One problem is, that we have to remember what we are using each symbol for. Another problem is, we might upgrade the graphics to instead draw images. Or we might change our mind about how walls should be drawn - **not** with a #. So, we need a third thing - a map-tile enumeration `Glyph` type, listing what can appear in map tiles, which we will put in `02Model/07Glyph.ts` .

It is tempting to make the enum values be character strings directly, like this:

```
// (We will NOT do this!)
export enum Glyph_Sketch {
  Bad ='§',
  Rock ='%',
  Wall='#',
  Floor='.',
  Unknown ='?'
}
```

However, string-based enums in typescript behave differently from integer-based enums and are not as powerful, so we will resist the temptation and stick with an integer-based enum. Another benefit of this approach is, that it will allow us to use the same character to draw two similar but distinct glyphs (for example a wall, and a hidden-door wall segment). If we stuck with character-based enums, that would not work.

O2Model/07Glyph.ts:

```
export enum Glyph {
  Bad, // will be numbers 0,1,2 etc.
  Rock,
  Wall,
  Floor,
  Unknown
}
```

It will have more than those five kinds, but you get the idea. This way, our code will talk about `Floors` and `Walls`, instead of '.' and '#'.

7.1.2 MAP OF MAP CELLS

Our map will be a grid of these `MapCells`. O2Model/07MapCell.ts:

```
export class MapCell {
  constructor(public env:Glyph) {}
  glyph():Glyph { return this.env; }
}
```

We can define an interface for maps. `O2Model/07DMapIF.ts`:

```
export interface DMapIF {
  dim:WPoint;
  cell(p:WPoint):MapCell;
  legal(p:WPoint):boolean;
  level: number;
}
```

The `WPoint` there is a **world point**, which is `O2Model/07WPoint.ts`:

```
export class WPoint {
  constructor(public x:number=0, public y:number=0) {}

  static StockDims = new WPoint(
    TPoint.StockDims.x,TPoint.StockDims.y);
}
```

And a first sketch for `DMap`: (with a critical piece missing.)
`O2Model/07DMap.ts`

```
export class DMap implements DMapIF {
  cells:MapCell[][];
  constructor(public dim:WPoint, public level:number){}
  cell(p:WPoint):MapCell {
    return this.cells[p.y][p.x];
  }
  legal(p:WPoint):boolean {
    return p.x >= 0 && p.x < this.dim.x
        && p.y >= 0 && p.y < this.dim.y;
  }
}
```

The missing piece is the setup of the cells grid array, which here
is uninitialized and undefined. So let's specify how to initialize it:

```
// change ctor to this:
constructor(public dim:WPoint, g_empty:Glyph,
            public level:number) {
  this.cells = this.allocMap(g_empty);
}
```

```
allocMap(g_empty:Glyph) {
  let cells = new Array(this.dim.y);
  let p:WPoint = new WPoint();
  for (p.y=0; p.y<this.dim.y; ++p.y) {
    cells[p.y] = new Array(this.dim.x);
    for (p.x=0; p.x<this.dim.x; ++p.x) {
      cells[p.y][p.x]=new MapCell(g_empty);
    }
  }
  return cells;
}
```

With this, we have enough pieces to **create** and initialize our
`DMap` with `MapCells` specifying `Glyphs`, indexed by `WPoints`.

7.1.3 DISPLAYING THE MAP

We must also **draw** it. Let us put the draw mechanism by itself,
because we'll need it from several places. `02model/07DrawMap.ts`:

```
export class DrawMap {
  static drawMap0(term:TermIF, map:DMapIF, vp:WPoint) {
    let tdim = term.dim;
    let t=new TPoint();
    let w=new WPoint();
    for (t.y=0, w.y=vp.y; t.y<tdim.y; ++t.y, ++w.y) {
      for (t.x=0, w.x=vp.x; t.x<tdim.x; ++t.x, ++w.x) {
        let cell:MapCell =
            (map.legal(w) ? map.cell(w) : this.outside);
        let i:GlyphInf0 = GlyphMap0.inf(cell.glyph());
        term.at(t.x, t.y, i.c,'gray', 'lightgray');
      }
    }
  }
  static outside:MapCell = new MapCell(Glyph.Unknown);
}
```

Most of this code is obvious - it runs through the rectangle of map cells, the outer loop handling each row of the map, and the inner loop taking care of the cells in each horizontal line. For each cell character, it transfers and draws the map letter from the cell to the terminal with `at()`. Notice that we try to handle gracefully, when the terminal and the map have different dimensions.

7.1.4 VIEWPORT

There is one tricky part though, the `vp` argument. It is the **viewport**, which is an offset, that controls at which part of the world map we start drawing from. If you consider a huge world map - larger than the screen terminal - then we obviously couldn't fit all of that world map on to the screen at the same time. Instead, we'll want to draw the nearest rectangle centered around the player, which would have the same dimensions as the smaller terminal rectangle. At the moment, we don't even have a player, so we'll just pass (0,0) as viewport offset for now. But later, this will allow us to scroll around the map, and keep the player in the center of the screen.

7.1.5 GLYPHMAP

For the above `drawMap0()` method to work, we need that `GlyphMap0`, which will translate the `Glyph` enums to the ASCII characters we want to draw. Its two crucial parts are the map `glyphs`, which hold a `GlyphInf` for each Glyph, and the method `inf()`, which safely does the lookup into `glyphs`. Note that `initGlyphs()` and `add()` are used to populate the glyphs map.

```
export class GlyphInf0 {
  constructor(public glyph:Glyph,public c:string){}
}


export class GlyphMap0 {
  static glyphs: Array<GlyphInf0> = [];
```

```
static bad:GlyphInf0 = new GlyphInfo(Glyph.Bad,'?');
static inf(glyph:Glyph):GlyphInfo {
  return (glyph in GlyphMap0.glyphs)
    ? GlyphMap0.glyphs[glyph]
    : GlyphMap0.bad;
}
static ensureInit:number = GlyphMap0.initGlyphs();
static initGlyphs():number {
  var add = GlyphMap0.add;
  add('§',Glyph.Bad);
  add('%',Glyph.Rock);
  add('#',Glyph.Wall);
  add('.',Glyph.Floor);
  add('?',Glyph.Unknown);
  return GlyphMap0.glyphs.length;
}
static add(c:string, g:Glyph) {
  let inf:GlyphInfo=new GlyphInfo(g,c);
  GlyphMap0.warn(g);
  GlyphMap0.glyphs[g] = inf;
}
static warn(g:Glyph) {
  if (GlyphMap0.glyphs.length == g) { return; }
  console.log(g, 'differs from',
    GlyphMap0.glyphs.length
  );
}
}
```

7.1.6 RUNNING THE MAP CODE

We will need a **screen** that can display a map.
`01term/07MapScreen.ts`:

```
export class MapScreen implements SScreenIF {
  name='map';
  constructor(public map:DMapIF) {}
  onKey(e:JQuery.KeyDownEvent, stack:StackIF){}
```

```
draw(term:TermIF) {
    DrawMap.drawMap0(term,this.map,new WPoint());
}

static runMapScreen(map:DMapIF) {
  Stack.run_SScreen(new MapScreen(map));
}
}
```

Also, a small class that will provide us with a test map - we'll expand on that class later. `02model/07TestMap.ts`:

```
export class TestMap {
  static test0():DMapIF {
    let wdim = new WPoint(14,8);
    let level = 0;
    return new DMap(wdim,Glyph.Wall,level);
  }
}
```

We can run and test our map with this `index07_map.ts` .. but it will look **boring**, as the map is boring:

```
MapScreen.runMapScreen( TestMap.test0() );
```

7.1.7 MAKING RANDOM

We can make a more interesting **random** map. We first need something that can provide **randomness** - a random number generator.

First, a core that **makes** random numbers. `02model/07Rnd.ts`:

```
export class RndRoot {
  constructor(public seed:number){}
  getSeed():number { return this.seed; }
  setSeed(newSeed: number) { this.seed = newSeed; }
  srand():number {
    this.seed = (this.seed * 9301 + 49297) % 233280;
    var rn = this.seed / 233280;
```

```
      return rn;
  }
}
```

Then a small engine on top that makes it possible to use it: (we still put these in `02model/07Rnd.ts`)

```
export class RndBase extends RndRoot {
  rnd(lower:number,higher:number=0):number {
    var range, draw, roll;
    if (!higher) {
      // If you only specify first arg,
      // it's 0-N (N not included.)
      higher = lower;
      lower = 0;
    }
    if (lower > higher){
      let swap = lower; lower = higher; higher = swap;
    }
    range = (higher-lower);
    draw = this.srand()*range;
    roll = Math.floor(draw) + lower;
    return roll;
  }
  // Includes upper limit:
  rndC(lower:number,higher:number):number {
      return this.rnd(lower,higher+1);
  }
  oneIn(N:number):boolean { return (this.rnd(N) == 0); }
}


// (We must present it as the name Rnd,
// which will later become a more complete version.)
export class Rnd extends RndBase { }
```

7.1.8   Making a Less Boring Map

Now, with our random module, we can make our less boring map - we add this method to our existing `02model/07TestMap.ts`:

```typescript
export class TestMap {
  static test(dim:WPoint, rnd:Rnd, level:number):DMapIF {
    let m = new DMap(dim, Glyph.Wall, level);
    for (let p=new WPoint(); p.y<dim.y;++p.y) {
      for (p.x=0; p.x<dim.x;++p.x) {
        let edge = !( p.x > 0 && p.x < dim.x-1
                   && p.y > 0 && p.y < dim.y-1);
        let chance = rnd.oneIn(4);
        let wall = (edge || chance);
        m.cell(p).env = (wall ? Glyph.Wall : Glyph.Floor);
      }
    }
    return m;
  }

  static fullTest():DMapIF {
    let wdim = new WPoint(32,16);
    let rnd = new Rnd(42);
    return TestMap.test(wdim,rnd,0);
  }
}
```

Then a test with `index07_maptest.ts`:

```typescript
MapScreen.runMapScreen( TestMap.fullTest() );
```

It may not look like the greatest thing in the world, but it **is a map**, and **we** made it. If we can make this, surely we can make anything!

```
# # # # # # # # # # # # # #
#  .  # #  .  .  #  .  .  .  .  #  .  #
#  .  #  .  .  #  .  #  .  .  .  #  .  #
#  .  .  .  # #  .  .  .  .  .  #  .  #
#  .  .  .  .  .  .  .  .  .  .  #  #
# #  .  .  .  .  #  .  .  .  .  # # #
#  .  .  .  .  .  .  # #  .  .  .  # #
# # # # # # # # # # # # # #
```

F 7.2: Not the most advanced map you are ever likely to see

8 Game Model & Builders

(In which we define a structure for building and combining the parts of the game model)

F 8.1: The tiny imps inside your computer responsible for assembling your dungeons, going about their work

8.1 GAME MODEL

We have now designed a dungeon map `DMap`, and also initialized an instance with `fullTest()`. However, the dungeon map is not the full game model. We expect to add more parts to the model. Like we saw with the resizing terminal, it's not preferable to handle a collection of things as a bunch of separate parts - it got easier to manage by combining those parts together in `EventMgr`. The same goes for our game model parts. We will create a class `Game` to hold it all, to be our **game model**. Some additional pieces we will store there, are:

- the player himself
- the `Rnd` random number generator
- the `Dungeon`
- a builder, which we will explain in the following.

8.2 BUILDER

8.2.1 A CLASS DEDICATED TO THE COMPLEX TASKS OF CREATING AND ASSEMBLING THE PARTS OF OUR GAME, AS WE NEED THEM DURING PLAY

The `GameModel` will **hold** our data. But we also need to **construct** the model, to compose its pieces together. Instead of doing that piece by piece, we can make an interface and a class for a **builder**. The builder will know how to make a player, a whole dungeon, a dungeon level, monsters, and items.

Constructing and composing our (eventually) complex game world model is not a simple task. Because of this, we make this dedicated class to handle it - the Builder or Game Builder.

Having builders and a toolbox for it, will allow us to quickly and easily spin up small test scenarios, with specific combinations of walls, rooms, monsters and objects. E.g. 'what happens if I fight a monster while standing on an item? What happens if I kill a monster while we are both standing on items?'. (Maybe this causes a problem, if the killed monster tries to drop loot on top of the existing item.)

Similarly, testing out relative power in combat is quick, if it's easy to spin up a micro-dungeon with you trapped between two kobold warriors. Or to test a given spell or attack on a given group of monsters - either attacking them with it, or seeing what happens when they attack **you** with it.

In general, troubleshooting is easier, if we make it quick and painless to spin up complete or minimal alternate environments, including or excluding specific features, or including specific alternative implementations of features (e.g. a different way to draw the map).

Another reason we need a builder, is to handle **Game Over**. Once the player has lost the previous game, we need to create a fresh `GameModel`, in which he is again alive. Maybe the next fresh dungeon layout is easier to survive than the previous one he died in?

Our initial builder interface will start out as `03build/08BuildIF0.ts`:

```typescript
export interface BuildIF0 {
  makeGame():GameIF;
  makeLevel(rnd:Rnd, level:number):DMapIF;
  makeMap(rnd:Rnd, level:number):DMapIF;
}
```

and `03build/08GameIF.ts`:

```typescript
export interface GameIF {
  rnd:Rnd;
  curMap():DMapIF|null;
}
```

If we have one of these builders, we can ask it to provide us with a game, and to provide a map of a given level. For now, we'll ignore the level number, but later it will control how difficult the level will be.

8.2.2 BACKGROUND ON MAKING BUILDERS

There is a design choice in builders, about who creates what. We need to create things twice. Once, to **allocate** the empty 'container object', and a second time, to **populate** that same object. In one design choice, the same party (that is, the builder) handles both. In the opposite design, the owning/receiving part (the game model) handles the empty-allocation part, and the builder only handles the populating/filling part. Whoever handles the initial empty-allocation, gets to control the actual types we end up using, and in particular what we will need to do, if we want to switch to a different/newer type with support for more stuff.

A related choice is the ordering of combining smaller and larger things. In one approach, you construct the big thing first, then gradually stuff the smaller parts inside it (**top-down** approach). In the opposite approach, you construct the smaller pieces first, then pass them immediately to the larger item upon construction (**bottom-up** approach). Neither approach is 'more correct'. But they have different properties. Bottom-up has a nice safety-property: Because its tinier parts are constructed up front, you have a guarantee it is always correctly constructed (since you are forced to supply the necessary components immediately when creating it). But this guarantee has a cost in rigidity, as you are forced to construct everything in a "correct" order. In comparison, top-down is flexible, but so flexible you risk screwing it up, e.g. leaving parts uninitialized you were supposed to fill out. For example, top-down would let you decide if you want to place enemies or player first, whereas bottom-up might require you to supply the player first (however, maybe you could still *adjust* the player's position later).

8.2.3 BUILDING THE BUILDER

We need a Game class for the `GameIF`, `02model/08GameModel.ts` :

```
export class Game0 implements GameIF {
  constructor(public rnd:Rnd) {}
  map:DMapIF|null = null;
  curMap():DMapIF|null { return this.map;}
}
```

Now we can implement the builder: `03build/08Builder0.ts`

```
export class Builder0 implements BuildIF0 {
  makeGame():GameIF {
    let rnd = new Rnd(42);
    let game = new Game0(rnd);
    game.map = this.makeLevel(rnd,0);
    return game;
  }
  makeLevel(rnd:Rnd, level:number):DMapIF {
    return this.makeMap(rnd, level);
  }
  makeMap(rnd:Rnd, level:number):DMapIF {
    let wdim = WPoint.StockDims;
    return TestMap.test(wdim, rnd, level);
  }
}
```

This may look like a lot of unnecessary structure. But as we continue to add more features and details to our game, it will be useful having this dedicated module to handle all that configuration. In particular, it will be clear where to place additional configuration. We will later make more complete `Builder1` and `Builder2`, which has more complex and fleshed-out ideas for dungeon layouts, monster types and placements. For now, it's enough to have `BuildIF0` in place with `Builder0`, so we have the proper structure for injecting a map and a game.

We will not be running an `indexN.ts` for our builder yet. We need something to use it in.

9 CREATURES IN THE DUNGEON

(In which our player character walks around the dungeon map for the first time)

F 9.1: The player, so far sole inhabitant of our dungeon

9.1 Moving Mobs Taking Turns

9.1.1 First Moving Player

We have reached a pivotal part of the game to make. By now we have our dungeon map, the playing area. We have so far used our drawing capabilities to make a pretty picture of a dungeon. But it is very static, and nothing is **happening** yet.

To arrive at a game, something must be able to **move** around and make choices. What we lack, are moving monster **creatures** in there, that are able to take turns executing their chosen actions. The player will be such a creature, and so will his computer-controlled NPC enemies. The player should be able to move his @-sign, and monsters of some kind should walk around and act in the dungeon as well, otherwise the player will be quite alone in there, and lack opponents to challenge him.

Creating the supports for such moving action-taking creatures is a major undertaking. It requires a number of mechanisms in place, and can only function with their full combination. This means we have to create and complete this entire set of features, before we get to see them do anything. The feature set we are about to build, consists of these parts:

- a `Mob` class, to track each creature (its position, name, etc.)
- a `TurnQueue` - a list of all alive mobs, to track their turn order
- integrating `Mob` and `TurnQueue` into `MapCell` and `Map`, so we can draw the monsters with the map, and know where they are in the map
- a `GameScreen` that draws the map, and executes the player and creature turns
- a `ParsePly` helper class, that maps player input to game turns
- an upgraded `Builder`, that builds players and monsters, not just the dungeon map

- a screen-maker to combine our new screens

In principle we **could** 'hack it early', and for example demo a solo player walking around the map, before we had all the parts above made, maybe without the `TurnQueue`. But it wouldn't be useful for anything, because most of that 'try-it-out' work would have to be thrown away again and replaced with the later proper mechanisms. We would not be able to reuse the effort for anything.

So prepare yourself for building six features in a row, which we can only try out once all six are in place.

9.2   PLAYER & MONSTERS AS MOBS

For our moving bits, we introduce the concept 'mob' - from 'mobile' or 'mobile object'. The *player* will be a mob, and the *monsters* will also be mobs. Let's consider some properties mobs will need:

- An (x,y) coordinate **position**

- A **glyph** or character to draw it as, in the dungeon map

- A **name**, so we and the player can tell what is going on

- Some way to know if it's the player or not

- a way to tell if the mob is alive or dead

`02model/09Mob.ts:`

```
export class Mob {
  constructor(g:Glyph, x:number, y:number) {
    this.isPly = (g == Glyph.Ply);
    this.g = g;
    this.name = Glyph[g];
    this.pos.x = x; this.pos.y = y;
  }
```

```
  pos:WPoint = new WPoint();
  g:Glyph = Glyph.Unknown;
  name:string = '?';
  isPly:boolean = false;

  alive():boolean { return true; }
}
```

We need to expand `Glyph` a bit, to also represent mobs:

```
export enum Glyph {
  Ply,
  Ant,
  Bat,
  Cat,
  Sheep,
  ..
```

Also, `GlyphInfO.initGlyphs` must get

```
  ..
  add('@',Glyph.Ply);
  add('a',Glyph.Ant);
  add('b',Glyph.Bat);
  add('c',Glyph.Cat);
  add('S',Glyph.Sheep);
  ..
```

9.2.1 INTEGRATING MOB WITH MAPCELL

Our mobs should walk around in the map, and thus appear in our `MapCells`. So we add a reference to `Mob` in our existing `MapCell.ts`. For a given cell, its `mob` property will either contain any present mob, or else have the value `undefined`. This means only a single mob can occupy a map cell at a time. Notice how we change `glyph()` to show the glyph of any present mob, so that `DrawMap` now automatically shows any mobs too.

```
export class MapCell {
  constructor(public env: Glyph) {}
  mob:Mob|undefined;
  glyph():Glyph {
     return this.mob ? this.mob.g : this.env;
  }
}
```

9.3   TURN QUEUE, WHOSE TURN IS IT

What we did above will enable us to represent, hold, and display
mobs. But it is still just passive description. To get our mobs
active in the game, we introduce another concept - a Turns
Queue, or "Mob Queue". It will be a sorted list representing the
order in which the mobs take their turn.

It works like this: We will let the first mob in the queue take his
turn. Then we'll remove him from the front, and re-add him at
the back of the queue. That is all!

We will just repeat this sequence until the game ends. Whenever
the front mob is the **player**, we will ask the computer for
keyboard input to decide his turn. If the front mob is a computer
monster, our code will decide a turn for it.

02model/09TurnQ.ts:

```
export class TurnQ {
  mobs: Mob[] = [];
  curMob():Mob { return this.mobs[0]; }
  pushMob(m:Mob) { this.mobs.push(m); }
  popMob():Mob { return <Mob> this.mobs.shift(); }
  removeMob(m:Mob):boolean {
     let ix = this.mobs.indexOf(m);
     if (ix < 0) { return false; }
     this.mobs.splice(ix,1);
     return true;
```

```
  }
  frontPushMob(m:Mob) { this.mobs.unshift(m); }

  next():Mob {
    this.pushMob(this.popMob());
    return this.curMob();
  }
}
```

9.3.1 INTEGRATING TURN QUEUE INTO DMAP

We will place the turn queue inside the dungeon map. We do so, as the map already keeps track of the mobs inside the map cells. To keep it all consistent, this secondary tracking of the monsters is best kept in the map as well. So class DMap gets these additional parts: (02model/07DMap.ts)

```
Q: TurnQ = new TurnQ();

..

moveMob(m:Mob, p:WPoint):void {
  this.cell(m.pos).mob = undefined;
  m.pos.x = p.x; m.pos.y = p.y;
  this.cell(m.pos).mob = m;
}
addNPC(m:Mob):Mob {
  this.cell(m.pos).mob = m;
  this.Q.pushMob(m);
  return m;
}
removeMob(m:Mob):void {
  this.Q.removeMob(m);
  this.cell(m.pos).mob = undefined;
}
enterMap(ply:Mob, np:WPoint):void {
  ply.pos.set(np);
  this.cell(ply.pos).mob = ply;
  this.Q.frontPushMob(ply);
}
```

We extend the interface DMapIF with these new methods:

```
  Q:TurnQ;
  addNPC(m:Mob):Mob;
  enterMap(ply:Mob, np:WPoint):void;
  moveMob(m:Mob, p:WPoint):void;
  removeMob(m:Mob):void;
```

enterMap is a bit special. We use it to let the **player** arrive on a map. The player is the only mob who will be able to travel between levels, which means his position needs special care - we will need to provide a reasonable and correct position for him, whenever he arrives on a level (e.g. not inside a wall). Also, we want the player to 'cut in line' and always get in front of the turn queue, so we add him with frontPushMob instead of pushMob.

For the above to work, we must add the set() method to WPoint.ts:

```
set(n: WPoint) { this.x = n.x; this.y = n.y; }
```

9.4   SCREEN FOR MOB & PLAYER TURNS

We need a screen for this - a game screen which will handle turns for the player, as well as for the NPC enemy mobs. Here, a raw **draft** of 06screen/09GameScreen.ts:

```
export class GameScreenDRAFT implements SScreenIF {
  name='game';
  game:GameIF;
  constructor(public game:GameIF, public make:MakerIF) { }
  draw(term:Term) {
    DrawMap.drawMap0(term,this.game.curMap(),new WPoint());
  }
  onKey(e:JQuery.KeyDownEvent, s:StackIF) {
    this.plyKeyTurn(s, ParsePly.keyPressToCode(e));
  }
  plyKeyTurn(s:StackIF, c:string):void {
      if (this.plyTurn(s,c)) { this.npcTurns(s); }
      return true;
  }
  plyTurn(s:StackIF, c:string):boolean { return true; }
  npcTurns(s:StackIF) {
    let ply = <Mob> this.game.ply;
    let map = <DMapIF> this.game.curMap();
```

```
      let q = map.Q;
      var m:Mob;
      for (m=q.next(); !m.isPly && !this.over(); m=q.next()) {
        this.npcTurn(m,ply);
      }
    }
  npcTurn(m: Mob, ply:Mob) {}
  over(s:StackIF):boolean {
    let over = !this.game.ply.alive();
    if (over) {
      s.pop();
      s.push(this.make.gameOver());
    }
    return over;
  }
}
```

This is just a draft, because neither the player nor the enemy mobs actually **do** anything here. But the main needed mechanism is present: Whenever we receive keyboard input in `onKey()`, `plyKeyTurn()` asks `plyTurn()` whether this can be parsed into a **turn** for the player (e.g. "go north one step", or "hit monster east of me"). If it can, the player's turn is completed, and `npcTurns()` then processes turns for the rest of the mobs in the queue, until the player is once again in front.

The whole while, we'll watch whether the player has been killed. Otherwise, once the player died, the other mobs would continue playing forever among themselves, without ever returning back from `npcTurns()` to the event loop (i.e. where the player could again solicit keyboard input).

The game-over method `over()` handles that: In case of death, it discards the game screen and activates the game-over screen - this is where our earlier `ScreenMaker` effort comes into play. It knows how to create that screen, and how to pass it the necessary resources.

To support the sketched approach, we must add the player property `ply` to `GameIF` and `Game0`:

```
export interface GameIF {
  rnd: Rnd;
  curMap(): DMapIF | null;
  ply: Mob;
}
export class Game0 implements GameIF {
  ..
  ply:Mob = <Mob><unknown> undefined;
  ..
}
```

Before we get too far with the game-screen draft above, we'll refactor it and split it into two classes. We will make a base class called `BaseScreen`, which will handle all the NPC stuff, and derive a class `GameScreen` from it, where we put the player's main turn mechanism. We will eventually get a number of screens that do different kinds of player turns, and they all need to handle that same NPC stuff, which we conveniently keep in the `BaseScreen`. In general, `BaseScreen` will hold common features we need across many screens.

Here a second attempt at `06screen/09GameScreen.ts`, and now `09BaseScreen.ts` (still no `indexN` to test it, as we need more bits before it can actually **do** anything).

```
export class BaseScreen implements SScreenIF {
  name='base';
  constructor(public game:GameIF, public make:MakerIF){}
  draw(term:TermIF) {
    DrawMap.drawMap0(
      term, <DMapIF> this.game.curMap(), new WPoint()
    );
  }
  onKey(e:JQuery.KeyDownEvent, s:StackIF) {}
  npcTurns(s:StackIF) {
    let ply = <Mob> this.game.ply;
```

```
    let map = <DMapIF> this.game.curMap();
    let q = map.Q;
    var m:Mob;
    for (m=q.next();
         !m.isPly && !this.over(s);
         m=q.next()
    ) {
      this.npcTurn(m,ply);
    }
  }
  npcTurn(m:Mob, ply:Mob) {}
  over(s:StackIF):boolean {
    let over = !this.game.ply.alive();
    if (over) {
      s.pop();
      s.push(this.make.gameOver());
    }
    return over;
  }
}

export class GameScreen extends BaseScreen {
  name='game';
  constructor(game:GameIF,make:MakerIF) {
    super(game, make);
  }
  onKey(e:JQuery.KeyDownEvent, s:StackIF) {
    this.plyKeyTurn(s, ParsePly.keyPressToCode(e),e);
  }
  plyKeyTurn(s:StackIF, c:string,
             e:JQuery.KeyDownEvent|null):void {
    if (this.plyTurn(s,c,e)) { this.npcTurns(s); }
  }
  // (plyTurn is a DRAFT, proper version comes below.)
  plyTurn(s:StackIF,c:string,
          e:JQuery.KeyDownEvent|null):boolean {
    return true;
  }
```

```
}
```

9.5   Moving the Player

For a while we can tolerate that the NPC monsters don't yet do
real turns, but we do need a basic implementation of
plyKeyTurn(), to try out the moving-monsters-in-the-map
mechanism. We want four direction-keys to move the player
north, south, east and west. We will make a class ParsePly,
which decodes keyboard input into a possible turn, and executes
that turn. First, fix plyTurn above to be this:

```
plyTurn(s:StackIF, c:string,
        e:JQuery.KeyDownEvent|null):boolean {
  let parser = new ParsePly(this.game, this.make);
  return parser.parseKeyCodeAsTurn(c,s,e);
}
```

Then 06Screen/09ParsePly.ts is

```
export class ParsePly {
  public ply:Mob;
  public map:DMapIF;
  constructor(public game:GameIF, public maker:MakerIF) {
    this.ply = <Mob> game.ply;
    this.map = <DMapIF> game.curMap();
  }
  static keyPressToCode(e:JQuery.KeyDownEvent):string {
    let c:string = e.key;
    switch (e.code) {
    case 'ArrowUp':
    case 'ArrowDown':
    case 'ArrowLeft':
    case 'ArrowRight':
      c = e.code; break;
    }
    return c;
```

```
}
parseKeyCodeAsTurn(c:string, ss:StackIF,
                   e:JQuery.KeyDownEvent|null):boolean {
  let cmd = this.parseKeyCmd(c,ss,e);
  return (cmd ? cmd.turn() : false);
}
parseKeyCmd(c:string, ss:StackIF,
            e:JQuery.KeyDownEvent|null):CmdIF|null {
  let dir = new WPoint();
  switch (c) {
  case 'ArrowLeft':  case 'h': case 'H': dir.x-=1; break;
  case 'ArrowRight': case 'l': case 'L': dir.x+=1; break;
  case 'ArrowDown':  case 'j': case 'J': dir.y+=1; break;
  case 'ArrowUp':    case 'k': case 'K': dir.y-=1; break;
  case '.': return this.waitCmd(); break;
  }
  if (!dir.empty()) { return this.moveCmd(dir); }
  return null;
}
moveCmd(dir:WPoint):CmdIF {
  return new MoveCmd(dir,this.ply,this.game);
}
waitCmd(): CmdIF {
    return new WaitCmd(this.ply,this.game);
}
}
```

That was quite a mouthful, let's explain its various parts.

We used an `empty()` on `WPoint`, which we'll add as:

```
empty():boolean { return this.x == 0 && this.y == 0; }
```

9.5.1 GAME TURN COMMANDS

We foresee that the player will, eventually, have a lot of commands at his disposal, so we set up this separate class (`ParsePly`) for that.

Then there is some stuff about a `CmdIF`. This is for all our fancy game moves. All the spells and kinds of play-turns we can do, we will put into **command** classes, which share a common `CmdIF` interface - `04cmds/09CmdIF.ts`. This way, all our mobs - the player as well as the enemy mobs - can use the same spells.

```
export interface CmdIF {
  exc():boolean;

  me:Mob;
  g:GameIF;
}
```

Naïvely, we'd just expect to `exc()` to execute a command. However, we foresee we would like to distinguish between when we execute as a full **turn**, and when we instead just execute to **compose** as part of a bigger command. For this, we give `CmdIF` a couple of aliases for `exc`. We'll then call those aliases, and **they** will call `exc` for us. Thus, the full `CmdIF` becomes

```
export interface CmdIF {
  exc():boolean;

  turn():boolean;     // as a turn.
  raw():boolean;      // in composing.
  npcTurn():boolean;  // as a turn.
  me:Mob;
  g:GameIF;
}
```

We will also make a base class `CmdBase` that implements `CmdIF`. Deriving all our commands from `CmdBase` instead of `CmdIF` will later allow us to change `CmdIF` , without having to fix-up each of our many commands. Instead, we then only need to adjust `CmdBase` to accommodate the new `CmdIF`.

```typescript
export abstract class CmdBase implements CmdIF {
  exc(): boolean { throw 'no exc'; }
  constructor(public me:Mob, public g:GameIF){}

  public turn():boolean { return this.exc(); }
  public raw():boolean  { return this.exc(); }
  public npcTurn():boolean { return this.turn(); }
  // (when using commands to move npcs)
}
```

As mentioned, all three aliases just lead to calling `exc`. Similarly, `npcTurn` is really just `turn`, but reminds us why we are calling.

9.5.2 Move Command

We used a `MoveCmd` out of thin air, which we need to provide:
`04cmds/09MoveCmd.ts`

```typescript
export class MoveCmd extends CmdBase {
  constructor(
    public dir:WPoint, public me:Mob, public g:GameIF
  ) { super(me,g); }
  exc():boolean {
    let map = <DMapIF> this.g.curMap();
    let np = this.dir.plus(this.me.pos);
    map.moveMob(this.me,np);
    return true;
  }
}
```

`MoveCmd` calculates the new position np, by adding the direction to the player's current position. We used a `plus()` method, which we can append to `WPoint`:

```typescript
plus(p:WPoint) { return this.copy().addTo(p); }
copy():WPoint { return new WPoint(this.x, this.y); }
addTo(b:WPoint):WPoint {
```

```
    this.x += b.x; this.y += b.y; return this;
}
```

Beware if you use `addTo`, that you will be modifying an existing point directly! For example, if you used it on `dir` above, that `dir` would suddenly contain a full point, and not just an offset anymore. Similarly, if you use it on a `Mob`'s embedded point, that could cause trouble for `map.moveMob()`! (Because `moveMob` needs the old mob position in order to clear the old cell). That is why we have both `plus` and `addTo`.

You might consider `MoveCmd` to be an awful lot of red tape for moving a monster a single step. The idea behind it is that movement will eventually get a lot more complicated, and `MoveCmd` is where we put all that.

9.5.3   USING YOUR TURN TO WAIT

Finally, we have a `WaitCmd`, which is a turn that on purpose does nothing. The player might use this, for example if he is waiting for a monster to move closer to him, in order to attack it - maybe the player is standing in an advantageous position. Again, it may appear silly to use that much code to 'do nothing'. But as our game becomes more complicated, waiting in place may also become more complicated. Maybe a resting player will have gathered extra strength for a powerful attack, or heals faster, or other kinds of side effects. Having an explicit `WaitCmd` gives us a natural place to put such stuff.

Apart from that, it is a good principle that all legal game moves - even the wait command - are expressed with the same structure, i.e. the command interface `CmdIF`. This makes it explicit we intend 'wait your turn' as a proper move.

04cmds/09WaitCmd.ts:

```
export class WaitCmd extends CmdBase {
  exc(): boolean { console.log('wait..'); return true; }
}
```

9.6 UPDATED BUILDER BUILDS PLAYER

To get started testing it, we first need a builder. We made a
Builder0 in the previous chapter, but it was a 'map-only' builder,
which did not add a player - it didn't **know** about players and
mobs. Our updated builder will look like this:
O3Build/09BuildIF1.ts, O3Build/09Builder1.ts

```
export interface BuildIF1 extends BuildIF0 {
  makePly():Mob;
}
export class Builder1 implements BuildIF1 {
  makeGame():GameIF {
    let rnd = new Rnd(42);
    let game = new Game0(rnd);
    game.ply = this.makePly();
    game.map = this.makeLevel(rnd, 0);
    this.enterFirstLevel0(game);
    return game;
  }
  makeLevel(rnd:Rnd, level:number):DMapIF {
    let map = this.makeMap(rnd, level);
    return map;
  }
  makeMap(rnd:Rnd, level:number):DMapIF {
    let dim = TPoint.StockDims;
    let wdim = new WPoint(dim.x, dim.y);
    return TestMap.test(wdim, rnd, level);
  }
  enterFirstLevel0(game: Game0) {
    let map = <DMapIF> game.map;
    let np = this.centerPos(map.dim);
```

```
    map.enterMap(game.ply,np);
  }
  centerPos(d: WPoint):WPoint {
    return new WPoint(Math.floor(d.x/2), Math.floor(d.y/2));
  }
  makePly():Mob { return new Mob(Glyph.Ply,20,12); }
}
```

Notice we use `enterMap` and `enterFirstLevel0` to place the player
into the map, outside of `makeLevel` and `makeMap`. This is a
deliberate choice. It keeps us in control of how and where the
player appears when he enters a dungeon, through the
`enterFirstLevel` method and its variants. The goal is to keep
player placement out of level creation and map creation. This
frees us to let gameplay concerns control how the player should
move around and arrive. If instead `makeLevel` would place the
player, we could not change this.

9.7   RUNNING THE GAME SCREEN

9.7.1   COMBINING OUR SCREENS WITH SCREENMAKER

We will need a `ScreenMaker` that uses our `GameScreen`.
`06Screen/09ScreenMaker2.ts` is:

```
export class ScreenMaker2_Fixed implements MakerIF {
  game:GameIF|null = null;
  constructor(public build:BuildIF1) {}
  gameOver():SScreenIF { return new OverScreen0(this); }
  new_Game():SScreenIF {
    this.game = this.build.makeGame();
    return new GameScreen(<GameIF>this.game, this);
  }
}
```

To run that, we'll extend it with a few helper methods:

```
export class ScreenMaker2_Fixed ..
  ..
  static run_Gfirst(m:MakerIF) {
    Stack.run_SScreen(m.new_Game());
  }
  static StockMaker(build:BuildIF1):MakerIF {
    return new ScreenMaker2_Fixed(build);
  }
  static Gfirst(build:BuildIF1) {
    this.run_Gfirst(this.StockMaker(build));
  }
}
```

9.8 TESTING THE COMBINED FEATURES

With that, we should be ready to test it out. There are no enemies yet, but we'll be able to move the player around the map. Let's whip up a `index09_builder.ts` file to test it:

```
ScreenMaker2_Fixed.Gfirst( new Builder1() );
```

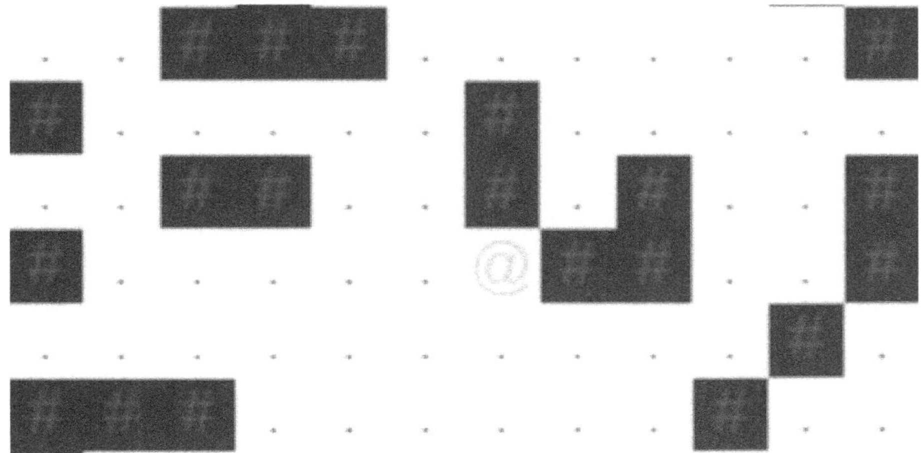

F 9.2: Moving orange @-you next to #-walls

9.8.1 Blocking Walls, Blocked Tiles

The good news is that we can finally move around the map. The bad news is that neither walls nor the edge of the map is stopping us - we can walk right through everything. We need some mechanism so we can't walk through walls. We can update `exc()` on `MoveCmd`, to be

```
exc():boolean {
  let map = <DMapIF> this.g.curMap();
  let np = this.dir.plus(this.me.pos);
  let legal = !map.blocked(np);
  if (legal) { map.moveMob(this.me,np); }
  return legal;
}
```

So `DMap`, and `DMapIF`, must get

```
blocked(p:WPoint):boolean {
  if (!this.legal(p)) { return true; }
  let c = this.cell(p);
  return c.blocked();
}
```

And `MapCell` must get

```
blocked():boolean {
  return (!!this.mob || this.env == Glyph.Wall);
}
```

This change means that attempts to move into an illegal tile will **not** count as a turn, but be ignored. We do not need a new `indexN` for this - if you run `index09_builder.ts` again, you should see the change.

9.8.2 Viewport

Because we have a player walking around now, we can do a clever adjustment to the map drawing: We can center it on the player, so the screen scrolls around as he moves. All it takes, is this adjustment to `07DrawMap.ts`, and then a small adjustment to `BaseScreen`.

```
static drawMapPly(term:TermIF, map:DMapIF,
                  plypos:WPoint, g:GameIF) {
  if (!plypos) { plypos = new WPoint(); }
  let vp:WPoint = new WPoint( // Must get viewport:
    -Math.floor(term.dim.x*0.5)+plypos.x,
    -Math.floor(term.dim.y*0.5)+plypos.y,
  );
  this.drawMap0(term,map,vp);
}
```

`09BaseScreen.ts` gets `draw` changed to this:

```
draw(term:TermIF) {
  DrawMap.drawMapPly(
    term, <DMapIF>this.game.curMap(),
    this.game.ply.pos, this.game
  );
}
```

And, voila! If you run `index09_builder.ts` again, the map and camera should follow the player around as he moves.

9.8.3 Some Thoughts on Mob Positions

Consider that we **could** let Mob inherit from `WPoint`, instead of having position as a property. It would be a bit dirty, but quite practical for programming, since all our mobs will have a position, and a lot of our code with mobs will deal with their **positions**. It would make a lot of our code simpler to *write*, but less obvious to *read*.

We could also do the opposite, sort of: To disentangle mobs from WPoint. That is really about separating positions from point calculations. When we are **calculating** with points, we want that to be easy - easy to change stuff. When we are concerned with **positions**, we want it to be **difficult** to actually change them. Think about it: We only want mob positions to **change**, when we are correctly moving the mob in the map. In all other cases, accidentally changing a mob's position would probably cause bugs, since the map would not be correctly updated. A first step to avoid that, would be to stop using the WPoint type directly for positions. We will do neither here, but be aware that the ways you process points, will affect the kinds of bugs you can make.

10 AI Sheep Monsters

(In which the first enemy mobs choose their turns in the map)

F 10.1: Feral underground sheep. Strength in numbers

10.1   A Simple Enemy Monster

10.1.1   Adding NPC Monsters to the Game, Mainly With AI

Our player can finally move around, but is alone. We haven't added any monsters yet. To do so, we must make them **decide what to do**. How to take their turns. We need to create some monster action-picking logic, so-called **AI**, artificial intelligence. Here, "intelligence" is a generous term, given that a lot of game AI involves little if any actual intelligence.

Once we have AI code to decide the **actions** of our monsters, getting monsters into the game is almost as simple as throwing a `new Mob(..)` into the turns queue - the AI will do the rest. Monsters are 95% their AI, the rest being 4% mob-turns-queue and 1% empty mob husk.

Naively and ideally, the monsters should have all kinds of ideas for being sneaky and deceitful and aggressive, choosing between attacking, hiding, moving about, and casting spells. However, we'll start with more modest ambitions, just getting our monster to chase the player, in a primitive way.

10.2   AI, More Art Than Int

This may reveal itself to be a good thing. As you get a feel for monster AI, you may find most players prefer enemies that are not all-powerful fiends. What often makes for a better game, is monsters behaving a bit like chess pieces. Each recognisable monster having some different specific qualities, which requires the player to deal with them as separate kinds of threat to balance, and against which to employ specific tactics.

- One monster might explode if he ever gets close to you, like the creeper in Minecraft.
- One monster might prefer to keep a distance, shooting arrows at you unless you are at close range - your tactic might be to hug him.
- Another monster might steal some of your stuff if he gets next to you.
- Yet another monster might cause confusion effects on you - a tactic might be to fight him in a hallway.
- Another monster may have a habit of teleporting you to himself.
- Some monsters might summon or wake up other monsters.
- Some might multiply if left unchecked.

In short, the possibilities and variations are endless. If **all** monsters did **all** of these things **all** of the time, most tactics would go out the window, and revert to 'hide in the cellar, or run for the hills'. However, there **are** people who prefer really hard enemies; those kinds of players may especially like playing against other *human* opponents, which one might reasonably expect to match their skill level.

10.3 IMPLEMENTING SO-CALLED AI

We are about to make one of our simplest 'chess pawns', which will be s, the hunting feral **sheep**. We will later have a's for ants, b's for bats and c's for cats, as we make the game more complex. But for now, let's focus on sheep. First, we need an interface for AIs: `05ai/10MobAiIF.ts`

```
export interface MobAiIF {
  turn(me:Mob, enemy:Mob, game:GameIF):boolean;
}
```

Then we may create AI classes for various behaviours. Our first 'hunt the player' AI is: `05ai/10MobAi1_sheep.ts`

```
export class MobAI1_sheep implements MobAiIF {
  turn(me:Mob, enemy:Mob, game:GameIF):boolean {
    let dir = me.pos.dir(enemy.pos);
    let cmd = new MoveCmd(dir,me,game);
    return cmd.npcTurn();
  }
}
```

which requires a `dir()` helper on `07WPoint.ts`. We will add
distance calculator methods, while we are at it:

```
dir(p:WPoint):WPoint {
  return new WPoint(Math.sign(p.x-this.x),
                    Math.sign(p.y-this.y));
}
dist(b:WPoint):number { return Math.sqrt(this.sqDist(b)); }
sqDist(b:WPoint):number {
  let d = this.minus(b);
  return (d.x*d.x + d.y*d.y);
}
minus(b:WPoint):WPoint {
  return new WPoint(this.x-b.x, this.y-b.y);
}
```

For our AI to take effect, we need it in the NPC turn loop, so we
need it in `BaseScreen`. We will not create it directly in
`BaseScreen`, because we have plenty of ideas for different kinds
of AI, and therefore we must be able to substitute them. Instead,
we will add the AI to our builder. And the builder must also start
creating the enemy monsters for us. The interface
`03build/10BuildIF2.ts` becomes this:

```
export interface BuildIF2 extends BuildIF1 {
  makeAI(): MobAiIF | null;
}
```

And `GameIF` and `Game0` must get an AI attribute:

```
// in GameIF:
ai: MobAiIF | null;

// in Game0:
ai:MobAiIF|null = null;
```

So we make `03build/10Builder2a.ts` by cloning and renaming
our `Builder1.ts`, and update it to look like this (only new and
changed parts listed here):

```
export class Builder2a implements BuildIF2 {

  makeGame():GameIF {
    let rnd = new Rnd(42);
    let game = new Game0(rnd);
    game.ply = this.makePly();
    game.map = this.makeLevel(rnd, 0);
    this.enterFirstLevel0(game);
    game.ai = this.makeAI();
    return game;
  }
  makeLevel(rnd:Rnd, level:number):DMapIF {
    let map = this.makeMap(rnd, level);
    this.makeSheepRing(map,rnd);
    return map;
  }

  makeAI():MobAiIF|null{ return new MobAI1_sheep(); }
  makeSheepRing(map:DMapIF, rnd:Rnd) {
    this.makeMobRing(Glyph.Sheep, map, rnd);
  }
  makeMobRing(g:Glyph, map:DMapIF, rnd:Rnd) {
    let dim = map.dim;
    let c = new WPoint(Math.floor(dim.x/2),
                       Math.floor(dim.y/2));
    let p = new WPoint();
    for (p.y=1;p.y<dim.y-1;++p.y) {
      for (p.x=1;p.x<dim.x-1;++p.x) {
        let d = c.dist(p);
```

```
        if (d<7 || d>9) { continue; }
        if (map.blocked(p)) { continue; }
        this.addNPC(g,p.x,p.y, map,0);
      }
    }
  }
  addNPC(g:Glyph, x:number, y:number,
         map:DMapIF, level:number) {
    let mob = new Mob(g,x,y);
    map.addNPC(mob);
    return mob;
  }
}
```

In `BaseScreen`, we update the method `npcTurn()` to use the AI:

```
npcTurn(m: Mob, ply:Mob) {
  let ai = this.game.ai;
  if (ai) { ai.turn(m,ply,this.game); }
}
```

We can run it with this `index10_ai_sheep.ts`:

```
ScreenMaker2_Fixed.Gfirst(new Builder2a());
```

If all our bits worked out OK, we should now have monster
sheep running around after us. Because we improved `MoveCmd` in
the player chapter, the monsters will not walk through walls, nor
through each other.

We placed the monsters in a **circle**, to set a scene for some action.
If we had just placed the monsters immediately next to the
player, he would be blocked in before anything could happen.
(`Builder2a.makeSheepRing`)

We placed the player in the **middle** of the screen, to distance him
from the enemies, but still in **trouble**, **surrounded** by them.
(`Builder2a.centerPly`)

The monsters now chase us. Because our monsters are **hunters**, they should soon **swamp** us. Mobs block each other's way - we cannot step onto a tile occupied by another mob. This blocks us in so we can't move, and prohibits the game from going further. So eventually we are blocked in by our opponents, with no way out, and no way to fight back. We can just annoy each other by **blocking**. Arrgh.. If only we could **fight back**!

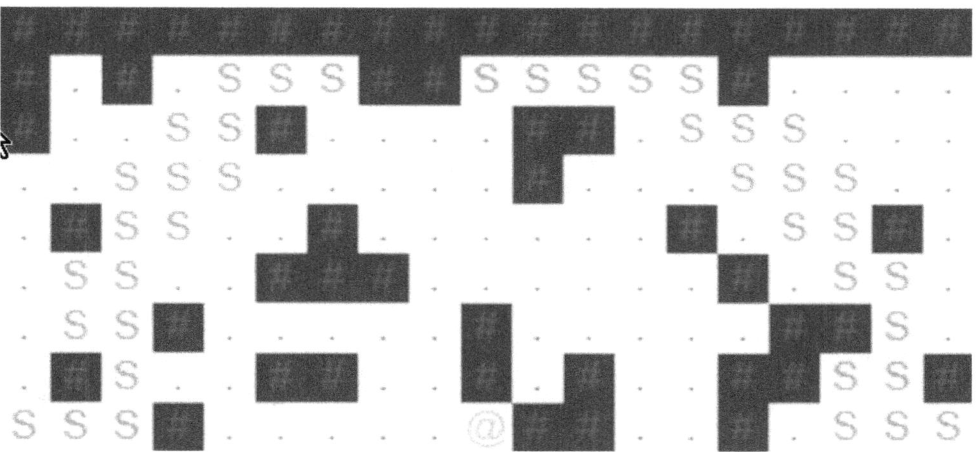

F 10.2: Our in-game sheep differ from the earlier illustration

F 10.3: But this is what you should imagine in your mind

11 Conflict, Cat Combat

(In which our mobs get to damage and defeat each other)

F 11.1: Cats are vicious merciless hunter-killers

11.1   Attacking

What if attempting to move into a tile occupied by another mob, instead would **attack** the mob in that square? We could make it, so that mobs can **hit** each other. But what **happens** when they hit?

Should a monster die and disappear, as soon as someone hits it? That seems a bit too abrupt. It would also kill **us** in a single hit. If you think about it, arcade games often work that way - everybody has to avoid being hit by bullets, and dies if they are hit. Typically, you then restart the current level, having 3 such lives in total. Some games instead operate with a shield, where you can take between 1 and 3 hits before your spaceship is destroyed.

But our game is not a real-time arcade game, it's more like a kind of "chess game". Chess is strange too - in chess, your king only has one life, and you lose the game as soon as he takes any hit. The reason this works is, that 'the king is not the game'. In chess, all your **other** pieces take hits, and once enough of your pieces have been hit, they are unable to further protect your king from being hit.

We could introduce the concept of a mob's **hit points**, which means you can take as many hits as you have hit points. Once you are reduced to 0, you have lost. Some attacks might hit for several points at once.

Let us add a hit point counter `hp:number` to all the mobs, and initialize this counter to start out with e.g. 3. We also need a `maxhp:number`, because if we regain lost hit points by healing, we need to stop if we reach our **maximum hit points**, otherwise a winning strategy would just be to keep on healing, to get a million hit points and be invincible. `02model/09Mob.ts`:

```
hp:number = 3;
maxhp:number = 3;
```

If **we** are going to hit, it's only fair the NPC enemies can **hit us** too. We could update our old `AI1_sheep` to use a hit command, but instead we will create a new monster AI, `O5ai/11MobAI2_cat.ts`:

```
export class MobAI2_cat implements MobAiIF {
  turn(me:Mob, enemy:Mob, game:GameIF) {
    let r = game.rnd; // slows hunting a bit.
    if (r.oneIn(3)) { return false; }

    let dir = me.pos.dir(enemy.pos);
    let cmd = new MoveBumpCmd(dir,me,game);
    return cmd.npcTurn();
  }
}
```

We will not need our old sheep-AI after this point, so we will clone our `Builder2a` into `Builder2b`, and change the parts that made sheep, into cat-making parts instead (this just switches to `Glyph.Cat` instead of `Glyph.Sheep`. There is nothing deeper behind it). Behold `O3build/11Builder2b.ts`:

```
export class Builder2b implements BuildIF2 {

  makeLevel(rnd:Rnd, level:number):DMapIF {
    let map = this.makeMap(rnd, level);
    //this.makeSheepRing(map,rnd);
    this.makeCatRing(map,rnd);
    return map;
  }
  makeCatRing(map:DMapIF, rnd:Rnd) {
    this.makeMobRing(Glyph.Cat, map, rnd);
  }
  makeAI():MobAiIF|null { return new MobAI2_cat(); }

}
```

The difference to `MobAI1_sheep` is that we now use `MoveBumpCmd`

instead of `MoveCmd`. For that, we need `04cmds/11MoveBumpCmd.ts`.
It checks whether the intended cell already holds a mob, and
diverts to `HitCmd` if it does. Otherwise it **forwards** to the original
`MoveCmd`.

```
export class MoveBumpCmd extends CmdBase {
  constructor(
    public dir:WPoint, public me:Mob, public g:GameIF
  ) { super(me,g); }
  exc():boolean {
    let np = this.dir.plus(this.me.pos);
    let map = <DMapIF> this.g.curMap();
    if (!map.legal(np)) { return false; }
    let cell = map.cell(np);
    let cmd = cell.mob
      ? new  HitCmd(this.me,cell.mob,this.g)
      : new MoveCmd(this.dir,this.me,this.g);
    return cmd.turn();
  }
}
```

So we must provide `04cmds/11HitCmd.ts`. Our first version just
docks the defender one hit point, unconditionally. To show our
good intentions, it also **logs** the perceived event - "someone
hitting somebody for a certain amount of damage". This log, for
now, is just the internal console-log. Later, we will figure out a
proper outlet for such events - a **combat log**.

```
export class HitCmd extends CmdBase {
  constructor(
    public me:Mob, public him:Mob, public g:GameIF
  ) { super(me,g); }
  exc():boolean {
    let me = this.me.name, him = this.him.name;
    let dmg = 1;
    let s = `${me} hits ${him} for ${dmg}`;
    console.log(s);
    this.him.hp -= dmg;
    return true;
```

```
    }
}
```

To run this and try it out, we can make `index11_cat.ts`:

```
ScreenMaker2_Fixed.Gfirst(new Builder2b());
```

There are a couple of things wrong or weird with this initial sketch.

- No one will **know** about this damage. Unless they check the internal log, and have some idea how many hit points people started with.
- There are no real **consequences** to being hit: Your hit points will go to 0. Then to -1. And -2. But passing 0 was supposed to be death?
- Attacks always hit, always for 1. What about attacks **missing**, or hitting extra hard?

The *always-hits* thing could be solved as easily as `rndC(0,2)`. The worst issue is the lack of death. If death worked, the missing status update maybe could be tolerated, given that **death** is a sort of status update. I might not notice when someone has lost 1 or half their hit points, but surely I **will** notice when they have lost **all** their hit points, on account of you (or me) being **dead**.

Still, we'll address the lack of hit-point feedback too. Once we can track the player's current hit points, we can easily tell whether our death-support works: When we see a zero in the player's hit points, we should see some death too. And vice versa - no death unless the hitpoints are at or below zero.

We must deal with two kinds of death: The death of **enemy NPCs** should make them **disappear** from the turns queue and map - hopefully without messing up the turn order. The death of the **player** should instead cause some sort of Game Over. Our plan for the initial version is this:

- We will make hit-damage more interesting.
- We will display the player's hit points on screen, so the player can bite his nails.
- We will address player's death.
- We will address the death of mobs.

11.2　More Dynamic Combat

Let us first fix the 'always-hits-for-1' issue, since it requires so little work. Adjust the first part of `HitCmd.exc` to be

```
exc():boolean {
  let me = this.me.name, him = this.him.name;
  let rnd = this.g.rnd;
  let dmg = rnd.rndC(0,3);
  if (dmg == 3) { dmg = 1; }
  let s=dmg? `${me} hits ${him} for ${dmg}`
          : `${me} misses ${him}`;
  ..
```

With this, we got out of the boring 'let us see who can count down to zero first' situation. We will later make combat more interesting in other ways. Be aware that some might hate the chance for hits to miss. A milder variant could be distinguishing between proper hits and **glancing** blows with reduced damage. Still, there can be value and sense in recognising that some enemies are so much stronger, that physically attacking them with a too-weak character will fail to do any damage.

11.3 HIT POINTS DASHBOARD

We can follow our player's hit points, by adding this to
`02model/07DrawMap.ts` :

```
static renderStats(term:TermIF, game:GameIF) {
  let ply = game.ply;
  let  hp = ` HP:${ply.hp}`
  let mhp = `MHP:${ply.maxhp}`
  let y=1;
  term.txt(0,y++, hp, 'yellow', 'teal');
  term.txt(0,y++,mhp, 'yellow', 'teal');
}
```

Then updating `09BaseScreen.ts` to draw with it:

```
  draw(term:TermIF) {
    DrawMap.drawMapPly(term, <DMapIF> this.game.curMap(),
                       this.game.ply.pos);
    DrawMap.renderStats(term, this.game);
  }
```

For now, the stats panel will simply be drawn on top of the map,
HUD style. We might later make a panelled GUI layout with
different areas dedicated to separate purposes (e.g. log, stats,
map, effects, inventory and so on). For now, with this, we can
keep track of our current hit points, and follow how *low* they dip.

11.4 Player Death

To handle the **player's** death, a number of things must happen.
First, let us update the until now fake `alive()` check in
`02model/09Mob.ts`, to really work:

```
alive():boolean { return this.hp>0; }
```

This will activate a cascade of things. `BaseScreen.npcTurns`
continuously calls `BaseScreen.over`, and now a dying player will
cause it to discard the active game screen, and to activate a
game-over screen. It will also abort the `npcTurns()` loop, and
pass control back to the `ScreenStack`.

This means we now have a game-over mechanism active when
the player dies. Our game-over screen may leave a lot to be
desired, but it works. At a later stage, we'll pass the game model
to the game-over screen, so it can show some kind of
post-mortem, a la 'you died by X, being hit by a Y for N hit
points, after the following happened'.

11.5 Monster Death

Our change to `alive()` means **monsters** can also die now. For
that to work, we must react to such a death, otherwise nobody,
not even the dead monster itself, will notice its death. It would
continue to behave as if still alive - welcome, zombie!

The culprit is `HitCmd.exc()`, which handles health loss with

```
this.him.hp -= dmg;
```

That is insufficient. We need to make **health loss** its own thing,
so it can involve dealing with the consequences - the death.
Death involves a couple of things - the monster must cease to
exist in various ways.

Above all, as a turn-taking entity - it must stop taking turns. This means it must be removed from the turns-queue. Which belongs to the map. Here we focus on consistency for **NPC monsters**. The player himself **may** belong to multiple maps, so to properly clean up a dead player, we might need to remove him from every map. Luckily for us the game ends when the player dies, so we won't address it here. But beware you might have to solve this. If, for example, your game allows respawning your player on the old game world, you would face the problem of cleaning out his old corpses. ..Or maybe you could turn them into evil ghost enemies?

Our `04cmds/11HealthAdj.ts` will start out like this:

```typescript
export class HealthAdj {
  public static adjust(m:Mob,amount:number,
                        game:GameIF,actor:Mob|null) {
    if (amount==0){return;} // do nothing.
    if (amount>0) {return this.heal(m,amount);}
    if (amount<0) {return this.dmg(m,-amount,game,actor);}
  }

  public static heal(m:Mob, amount:number) {
    console.log(`heal .. ${m.hp} += ${amount}`);
    let limit = m.maxhp - m.hp;
    if (amount > limit) { amount = limit; }
    m.hp += amount;
    console.log('h_to', m.hp);
  }
```

The damage part will be:

```typescript
  static dmg(m: Mob, amount: number, game:GameIF,
             attacker:Mob|null) {
    console.log('dmg', amount, m.hp);
    m.hp -= amount;
    console.log('d_to', amount, m.hp);
    if (m.hp <= 0) { this.mobDies(m, game); }
```

```
    }
..
```

and the `mobDies` part will be

```
static mobDies(m: Mob, game:GameIF) {
  let s = `${m.name} dies in a fit of agony`;
  console.log(s);
  let map = <DMapIF> game.curMap();
  map.removeMob(m);
}
```

We can then update `HitCmd` to do this instead:

```
..
  console.log(s);
  HealthAdj.adjust(this.him, -dmg, this.g,this.me);
..
```

11.6 PLAYER ATTACK

We have one more adjustment to make. By now the enemy mobs
can attack **us**, through `MobAI2_cat` and `MoveBumpCmd`, We must
give the **player** similar access to `MoveBumpCmd`. We add this piece
to `06screen/09ParsePly.ts` :

```
..
moveBumpCmd(dir:WPoint):CmdIF {
  return new MoveBumpCmd(dir, this.ply, this.game);
}
..
```

And in `ParsePly.parseKeyCmd`, we replace the `moveCmd` call with
this line:

```
..
// if (!dir.empty()) { return this.moveCmd(dir); }
if (!dir.empty()) { return this.moveBumpCmd(dir); }
..
```

You can now try to run the game again (`index11_cat.ts`), and see what happens when you bump into cats, or cats bump into you..

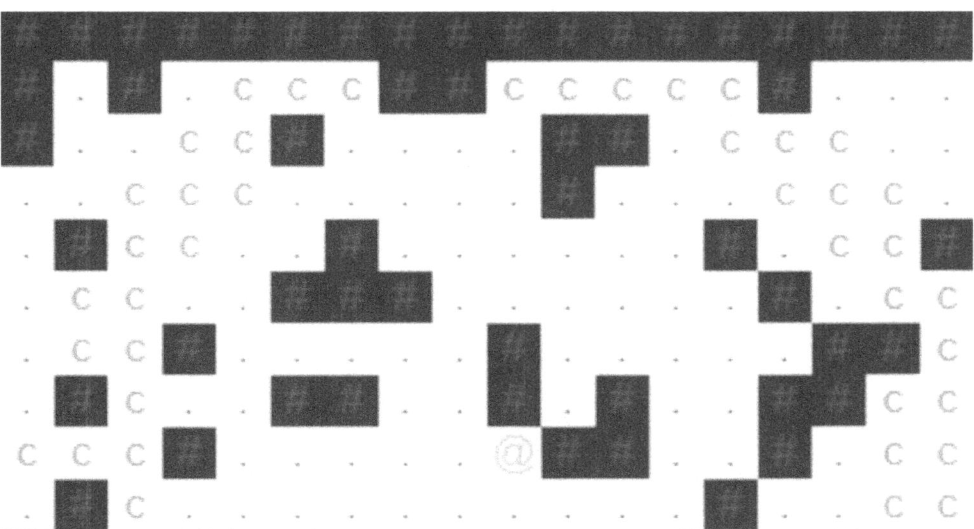

F 11.2: This is a massacre unfolding

With this, the basic mob combat death mechanism works: If someone (e.g. us) hits a mob below 1 hit-point, the mob will be declared dead, and removed from the turns queue. However, it is rather anti-climatic. Apart from the monster character disappearing from the screen, it's hard to tell exactly what happened. Hmm.. maybe we could communicate some details of the fight through the user interface? Maybe some kind of .. **log**?

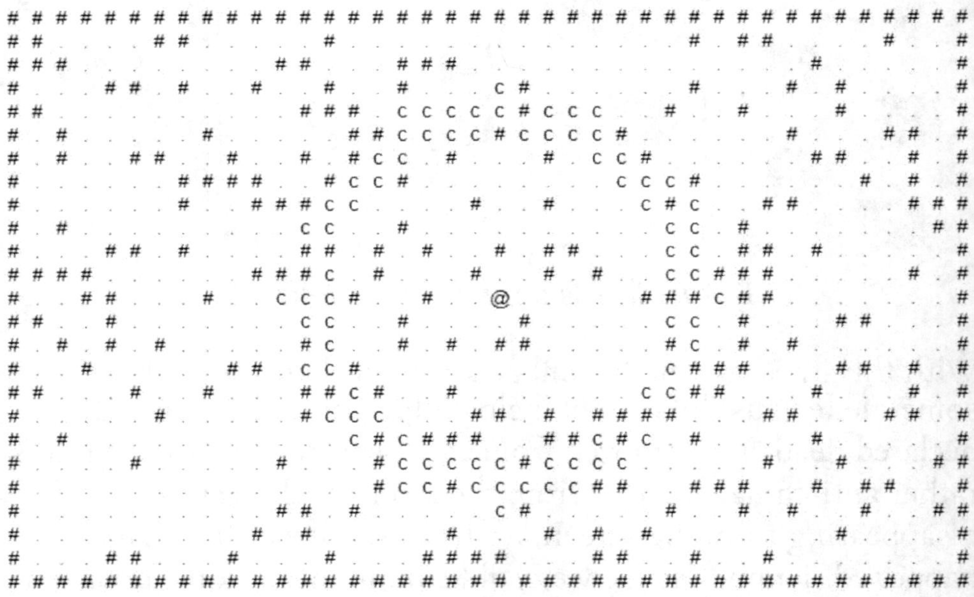

F 11.3: The reality of being fatally surrounded by cats

12 Combat Log

(In which we get told what the mobs do to each other)

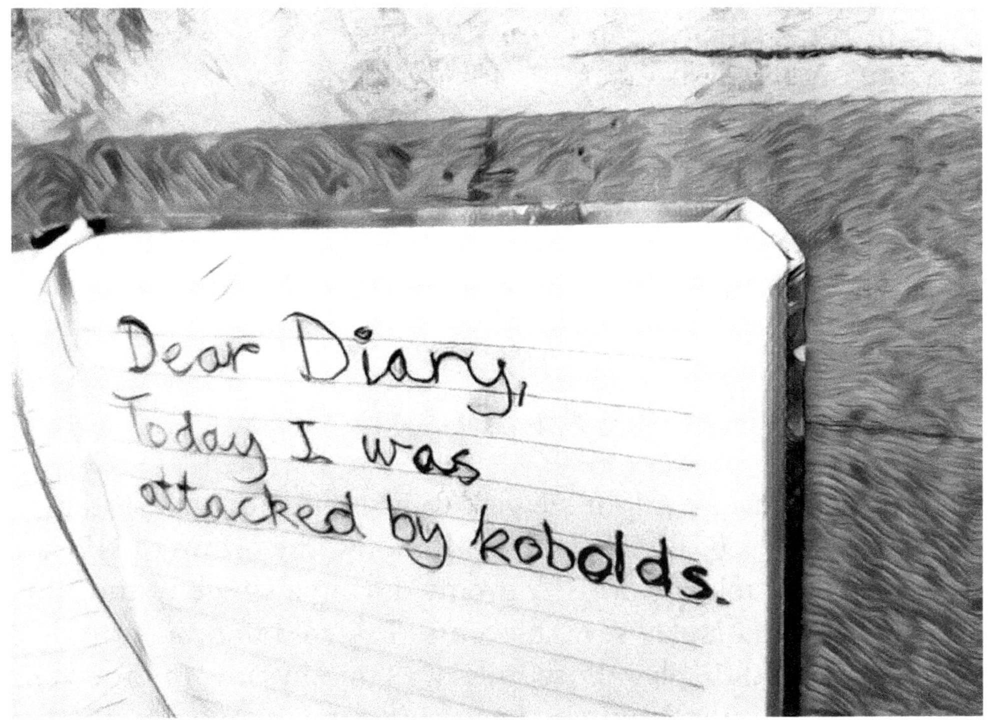

F 12.1: Our journal entries are no walk in the park

12.1 Intent

It would be nice if we could see, what **happened** to cause hit
points to drop. One letter standing next to another letter doesn't
say a lot about that. Though we *could* make the letters blink and
flash and change color, and even cycle the letters, but still.. What
I'm hinting at is that it would be nice to show **messages**, to have
a sort of **message log**. We will not show the entire log on-screen
all the time, it would obscure the map. But we could show the
latest message, and possibly have a player action to temporarily
bring up the rest of the log. The contents of the log messages
would be things like:

- you find 27 coppers.
- the imp drops a wand.
- the orc quaffs a potion.
- the orc looks stronger.
- the worms multiply.
- you hit the orc for 7 damage.
- the orc poisons you.
- you sense the dagger might be cursed.
- you feel weaker.

12.2 Plan

On first thought, we might suggest to just show the latest item
in the message log. But if we think for a bit, the group of NPCs
may cause multiple log-worthy events during a single round. So
we may need to display several events. To avoid flooding our
screen, we could display those messages one by one, in order,
with a number indicating how many still remain. We could
prompt the user to press a key to see each next event. We need
only do so for multiple messages - the last message in each
batch could be displayed directly. (Alternate design idea: You

could also display the full set of monster messages as a single listed news-flash during each round, but that approach might again cover and obscure the playing map it relates to.)

Our next first thought might be to build this complex logging logic directly into `GameScreen`. Our second thought is to instead make a separate `MoreScreen`, whose job it is to display multiple messages. Each time a key is pressed on the `MoreScreen`, the just shown message is discarded, and it proceeds to display the next message. Once the second-last message has finished displaying, the `MoreScreen` is removed again, and we return to the `GameScreen`, which takes care of displaying the remaining message.

For all this to work, the message log must be split into a to-display queue, and a permanent log archive. The `MoreScreen` will work off the display queue. The `npcTurns()` method must help, by activating the `MoreScreen` whenever the queue holds more than one message.

We must ensure single messages are only displayed once. And that messages triggered by the player are correctly included. We handle clean-up after single messages by doing a `clearQueue()` whenever an input event arrives for the `ParsePly` turn. This also satisfies that player-triggered messages will survive and be included, as they happen **after** that point.

12.3   MODEL TO HOLD THE LOG

As seen other times, we need two parts - a model to **hold** the messages we trigger and want to show, and some GUI to **show** those messages. Let's take care of the model first. We'll have a method `msg()` to submit messages, and properties `archive` and `queue` to hold it all. `02model/12MsgLog.ts` is

```
export class MsgLog {
  queue: string[] = [];
  archive: string[] = [];
  msg(s:string) {
    this.archive.push(s);
    this.queue.push(s);
    console.log(s);
  }
  dequeue() { this.queue.shift(); }
  top() {
    return this.empty() ? '-' : this.queue[0];
  }
  clearQueue() { this.queue = []; }
  queuedMsgs():boolean { return this.len()>1; }
  len():number { return this.queue.length; }
  empty():boolean {return !this.queue.length; }
}
```

What is all that? Well, we have two containers, `archive` and
`queue`. `archive` is an archive of all we have logged - later we can
then let the player display all older messages. In the middle of a
fight which is going badly, he may want to inspect the log, to see
exactly what attacks the monsters have used so far.

`queue` holds the messages still to be displayed. At any point we
will display its `top()` message, and we will remove it with
`dequeue()` once finished displaying it.

`queuedMsgs()` lets us check if we have more than one message
queued, which triggers the queue-display mechanism - the
`MoreScreen`.

`clearQueue()` gets rid of any final message after display, during
normal play. We could have handled clear-queue indirectly.
Instead, we've named it to make our design and intention
explicit.

As we put the log into the game model, we'll also add a `msg()`
utility helper on `Game` (and `GameIF`), which forwards to `MsgLog`.

Clone `08GameModel0.ts` into `02model/12GameModel1_Log.ts`, and
rename it from `Game0` to `Game1` :

```
export class Game1 implements GameIF {
  constructor(public rnd:Rnd) {}
  map: DMapIF|null = null;
  curMap(): DMapIF|null { return this.map; }
  ply: Mob = <Mob><unknown>undefined;
  ai: MobAiIF | null = null;
  log: MsgLog = new MsgLog();
  msg(s:string) { this.log.msg(s); }
}
```

And to `08GameIF`, add

```
  msg(s:string):void;
  log:MsgLog;
```

(to fix up `Game0` so it still compiles with the new `GameIF`, you can
add this shim:)

```
  log:MsgLog = <MsgLog>  <unknown> undefined;
  msg(s:string){}
```

To get our updated `Game1` in play, we must clone `Builder2b.ts` to
`03build/12Builder2c.ts`, and change `Game0` to `Game1` in `makeGame`:

```
export class Builder2c implements BuildIF2 {

  makeGame():GameIF {

    //let game = new Game0(rnd);
    let game = new Game1(rnd);

  }
}
```

Then in `HitCmd.exc()` and `HealthAdj.mobDies()`, we change
`console.log(s);` to `this.game.msg(s);` and `game.msg(s);`.

With this, our event messages are forwarded to the game message log. However, we are still logging it to console - so far it does not show up in our GUI.

12.4   Displaying the Log Messages

Once `npcTurns()` in `BaseScreen` has finished with the NPCs, we want it to display the `MoreScreen` whenever necessary. This involves **creating** a `MoreScreen`, but a kink in typescript makes that tricky: Because `MoreScreen` is derived from `BaseScreen`, `BaseScreen` has difficulty making `MoreScreens`! (You need a `BaseScreen` to define a `MoreScreen`. But now you also need a `MoreScreen` to define a `BaseScreen`!)

We can evade that by letting our trusty `ScreenMaker` provide the `MoreScreen`! So to `06ScreenMakerIF.ts` we add

```
    more(game:GameIF|null):SScreenIF;  // ch12
```

Then an implementation in `ScreenMaker2_Fixed`:

```
more(game:GameIF|null):SScreenIF {
    return new MoreScreen(<GameIF>game,this);
}
```

(In the same way, you can add shims to fix up `ScreenMaker0_Fixed` and `ScreenMaker1_Dyn` like this:)

```
more(game:GameIF|null):SScreenIF {
    return new DummyScreen(this);
}
```

With this, we can now modify `BaseScreen`, so that `npcTurns()` will call this `handleMsgs()` method:

```
// 06Screen/BaseScreen.ts:
// At end of npcTurns(), call this.handleMsgs(s);
  ..
    handleMsgs(s:StackIF) {
```

```
    if (!this.game.log) {return;}
    if (this.game.log.queuedMsgs()) {
      s.push(this.make.more(this.game));
    }
  }
```

The display of last queued message must happen in
`BaseScreen.draw()` and `DrawMap`. In `BaseScreen.draw`, we will at
the end call `DrawMap.renderMsg(term, this.game)`, which is

```
static renderMsg(term:TermIF, game:GameIF) {
  let log = game.log;
  if (!log) {return;} //(Let older versions still run.)
  let line = log.top();
  let num = log.len();
  let s = (num > 1)
      ? `${line} (${num} more)`
      : line;
  s = this.extend(s,term);
  term.txt(0,0, s, 'cyan', 'blue');
}


static mask:string='';
static extend(s:String, term:TermIF):string {
    let dim = term.dim; // Extend s to width:
    if (!this.mask) { this.mask = ' '.repeat(dim.x); }
    return s + this.mask.substr(0, dim.x - s.length);
}
```

We use the helper `extend()` to force the log line to fill the entire
width. This ensures we clear the earlier line contents.

`06screen/12MoreScreen.ts` will be

```
export class MoreScreen extends BaseScreen {
  name='more';
  constructor(game:GameIF, make:MakerIF) {
    super(game,make);
  }
  onKey(e:JQuery.KeyDownEvent, s:StackIF) {
```

```
      let log = this.game.log;
      log.dequeue();
      if (!log.queuedMsgs()) { s.pop(); }
   }
}
```

As you can see, it's the same `renderMsg` call that draws queued messages, for both the `MoreScreen` as well as for the normal `GameScreen`. The main difference is that inside `MoreScreen`, it's the `num > 1` case that is drawn.

We need one final adjustment. `GameScreen.plyKeyTurn` must have this clause added:

```
  plyKeyTurn(s:StackIF, c:string):void {
    if (this.game.log) {
      this.game.log.clearQueue();
    }
    if (this.plyTurn(s,c)) { this.npcTurns(s); }
  }
```

This ensures that any single queued message is displayed exactly once, and that it disappears next time we receive any input from the player.

Now we can make an entrypoint, so we can run it. `index12_log.ts` is:

```
ScreenMaker2_Fixed.Gfirst( new Builder2c() );
```

12.4.1 Avoiding Too Many Log Messages

We need to reduce messages, to only those concerning the player. Otherwise we'll get 84 messages regarding 84 monsters bumbling about, for **every turn**. We'll handle it with the following changes. In `HitCmd`, `msg()` is now conditioned:

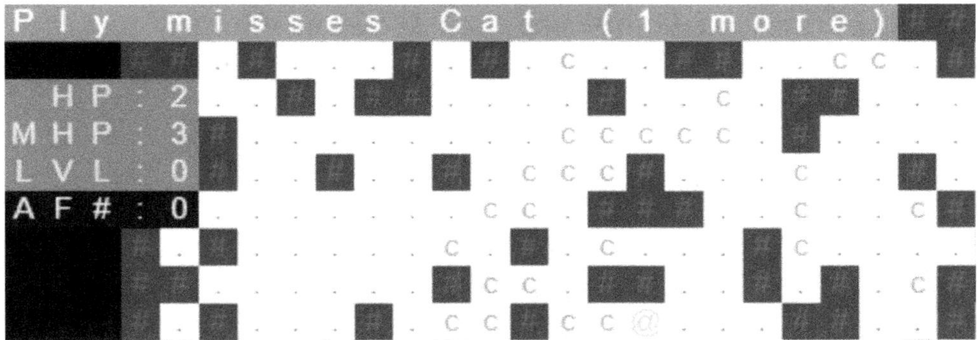

F 12.2: The grim details of how we died

```
if (this.me.isPly || this.him.isPly) {
  this.g.msg(s);
}
```

Similarly, in `HealthAdj`, in `dmg`:

```
let involvesPly = m.isPly ||
      (attacker != null && attacker.isPly);
this.mobDies(m, dung, involvesPly);
```

then

```
static mobDies(m:Mob, game:GameIF, involvesPly:boolean) {
  let s = `${m.name} dies in a fit of agony`;
  if (involvesPly) { game.msg(s); }
  let map = <DMapIF> game.curMap();
  map.removeMob(m);
}
```

This is a balance to keep. We would still like to tell the player about two mobs strengthening each other, or a mob doing something that will later cause trouble ('the orc quaffs a potion of supreme power').

If you run `index12_log.ts`, combat events should now appear at the top of the screen while you play. We can try to play-test the game again. Hopefully you should get a better indication of what is happening during combat.

12.5 Log Archive Viewer

Apart from showing the player event messages as they happen, we can also let him see a historical log of events that happened, with trivial effort. We just introduce a screen that renders a list of recent log messages. The player can activate this view with the Q key.

The log archive can prove useful in battle, if the player suddenly realizes the fight is going much worse that he was prepared for. Often the recent log will reveal hints of what went wrong. Maybe one of the enemies hitting much harder than expected, or being unexpectedly good at avoiding damage, or using an unexpected attack. Or a hidden enemy casting some sort of attack.

06screen/12LogScreen.ts:

```typescript
export class LogScreen extends BaseScreen {
  name:string = 'log';
  msgLog:string[];
  constructor(game:GameIF, maker:MakerIF) {
    super(game,maker);
    this.msgLog = game.log.archive;
  }
  draw(term:TermIF) {
    term.txt(0,0, 'Log:', 'yellow', 'black');
    let log = this.msgLog;
    let range = term.dim.y-1;
    if (log.length < range) { range = log.length; }
    let offset = log.length-range;
    for (let p=0; p<range; ++p) {
      let pos = offset+p;
      if (pos < 0) {continue; }
```

```
      let row = log[pos];
      term.txt(0, 1+p, `${p} ${row}`,'yellow','black');
    }
  }
  onKey(e:JQuery.KeyDownEvent, stack:Stack):boolean {
    stack.pop();
    return true;
  }
}
```

(For now, we only show the latest messages. One might consider
to let the player browse back through the entire archive.)

It fits into parseKeyCmd(), which we change like this:
(06screen/09ParsePly.ts)

```
.. // in parseKeyCmd:
  parseKeyCmd(c:string, ss:StackIF,
              e:JQuery.KeyDownEvent|null):CmdIF|null {
    var s:SScreenIF|undefined = undefined; // ch12
    let dir = new WPoint();
    switch (c) {
    case 'ArrowLeft':  case 'h': case 'H': dir.x-=1; break;
    case 'ArrowRight': case 'l': case 'L': dir.x+=1; break;
    case 'ArrowDown':  case 'j': case 'J': dir.y+=1; break;
    case 'ArrowUp':    case 'k': case 'K': dir.y-=1; break;
    case '.': return this.waitCmd(); break;
    case 'q': s=new LogScreen(this.game,this.maker); break;
    }
    if (s) { ss.push(s); return null; } // ch12
    if (!dir.empty()) { return this.moveBumpCmd(dir); }
    return null;
  }
```

13 STAIRS & LEVELS

(In which we get to navigate between multiple dungeon levels)

F 13.1: Stairs will take our game to a whole new level

13.1 A Way Out

There seems to be no way we can survive the cats assaulting us.
Maybe we could flee down some **stairs**? Stairs look like this: >
(stairs down) and < (stairs up). First, let's add them to `Glyph.ts`:

```
StairsDown,
StairsUp,
```

And for `GlyphInf.initGlyphs`,

```
add('>',Glyph.StairsDown);
add('<',Glyph.StairsUp);
```

We will place stairs next to the player. We'll need a new builder,
so clone `12Builder2c.ts` into `13Builder2d.ts` (remember to
rename the class), and insert this:

```
addLevelStairs(map:DMapIF, level:number, rnd:Rnd) {
    (level == 0) ? this.addStairs0(map)
                 : this.addStairs(map,rnd);
}
addStairs0(map: DMapIF) {
    let pos = this.centerPos(map.dim);
    let p = new WPoint(3,0).addTo(pos);
    map.cell(p).env = Glyph.StairsDown;
}
```

This level-0 special case is tied to 'fleeing from flock of cats'. It
will place the stairs a few squares away from the player. Call
`addLevelStairs()` in `makeLevel`, after the call to `makeMap()`, with

```
this.addLevelStairs(map,level,rnd);
```

On all other levels, we will instead place stairs randomly, both an
up-stair and a down-stair. We do so with `addStairs`:

```
addStairs(map:DMapIF, rnd:Rnd) {
  this.addStair(map, rnd, Glyph.StairsDown);
  this.addStair(map, rnd, Glyph.StairsUp);
}
```

```
addStair(map:DMapIF,rnd:Rnd,stair:Glyph):boolean {
  let p = <WPoint> FreeSpace.findFree(map, rnd);
  map.cell(p).env = stair;
  return true;
}
```

For `addStair` to work, we need the `FreeSpace` tool, which will help us find positions of specific kinds of tiles (e.g. an empty floor tile, or a wall tile). `03build/13FreeSpace.ts`:

```
export class FreeSpace {
  public static findFree(map:DMapIF, rnd:Rnd):WPoint|null {
    return this.find(Glyph.Floor,map,rnd);
  }
  public static find(c:Glyph, map:DMapIF, r:Rnd):WPoint|null {
    let e = new WPoint(map.dim.x-2, map.dim.y-2);
    let s = new WPoint(r.rndC(1,e.x), r.rndC(1,e.y));
    for (let p = s.copy();;) {
      let cell = map.cell(p);
      if (cell.env == c && !cell.mob) { return p; }
      ++p.x;
      if (p.x > e.x) {
        p.x = 1; ++p.y;
        if (p.y > e.y) { p.y=1; }
      }
      if (p.eq(s)) { throw 'freespace not found'; }
    }
  }
}
```

We must add `eq` to `WPoint`:

```
eq(b:WPoint):boolean {
    return b.x ==  this.x && b.y == this.y;
}
```

To test our stairs, we make `index13_stairs.ts`:

```
ScreenMaker2_Fixed.Gfirst( new Builder2d() );
```

13.2   Making Stair Travel Work

Voila, we have stairs! They don't **do** anything yet, though. When a mob steps on them, he should go down (or up) the stairs. Here, we will just let the **player** use the stairs. In theory, we **could** make the enemy monsters react as well when they step on stairs. By default, stepping on stairs should probably make monsters disappear from the level, a bit like a trap. It would be the obvious thing to do, but not very logical - why would an enemy leave by stairs, if he was busy chasing the player? (Note, it **could** make sense, if we wanted enemies to **follow** the player when he flees by stairs, but then fleeing through stairs would be much less useful to us).

We must choose between several possible places to implement stair travel. We could implement it

- directly in `ParsePly`. Here we know we are dealing with the player.
- inside `MoveCmd`.
- with its own command, used from `MoveCmd`.
- (in yet other ways).

We choose an own command, chained from `MoveCmd`. We like commands, because they form our general and reusable spells. A command lets us reuse this 'go to a different level' effect in other cases. Mobs know whether they are the player or not, so that won't cause us trouble. Tying it to `MoveCmd` makes the stair effect general, in case it should affect both NPCs and player in some way. When triggered through `MoveCmd`, it is caused by the stair glyphs. When triggered by calling `StairCmd` directly, no stair glyphs are required.

In `MoveCmd`, we change `exc` to be this:

```
exc():boolean {
  let map = <DMapIF> this.g.curMap();
  let np = this.dir.plus(this.me.pos);
  let legal = !map.blocked(np);
  if (legal) {
    map.moveMob(this.me,np);
    if (this.me.isPly) { this.dealWithStairs(map,np); }
  }
  return legal;
}
```

and we add `dealWithStairs()`:

```
dealWithStairs(map:DMapIF, np:WPoint):void {
  var dir:number;
  switch (map.cell(np).env) {
    case Glyph.StairsDown: dir= 1;break;
    case Glyph.StairsUp:   dir=-1;break;
    default: return; // No stairs here.
  }
  new StairCmd(dir,this.g).raw();
}
```

13.3 WHAT WALKING DOWN STAIRS DOES

We finally have to deal with the actual stair-walking. What should happen when the player walks down a stair? Well, he should arrive **somewhere** on the next level.

This is where roguelike traditions weigh heavily on the game mechanics, and game logic trumps proper logic. A naïve person might assume there would be stairs back up, where the player arrives (connectedness property). A naïve person might also assume the player would arrive in the same place, if he descends the same stairs twice (consistency property).

Nobody can forbid you to implement that behaviour. But here is how the game-logic reasoning goes: Stairs offer a special trade. At first look, they offer an escape, and even a form of reward. If you are being chased by a monster, and are low on hit points, fleeing by the stairs appears to bring you to safety. Given that the game is about progressing forward through the levels, exiting by stairs you have found is also a kind of reward - "you can now proceed to the next level".

Because of the advantages, stairs that were also **consistent** and **connected** might pose a cheating-balance problem. For example, you might handle dangerous monsters by just continuously stepping up and down stairs, alternating between hitting the dangerous monster, and retreating by stairs to heal in safety (arguably, this could be addressed by making monsters **follow** you through stairs, but again, by roguelike tradition, **traditionally** monsters do not follow you through stairs).

Instead, it is tradition to tie some risks to stair traversal. The oldest or most popular tradition dictates that levels are **shuffled** by stair traversal - "you cannot step into the same river twice". This means that every time you go down a level and then back up again, you will arrive at a **new (version of that) level**, not back at that same level you started from.

There are two aspects to this: A long time ago, this spared the (weaker) computers from having to use storage to keep all those levels for later - if you can't ever return to a level, I don't have to keep it in memory for later. The other aspect is that it tightens gameplay. If there is some dangerous but potentially lucrative content on your current level, you must handle it with the resources you have, if you want those rewards - you can't go back for reinforcements to play it safe.

The disadvantage of shuffled levels is that everything becomes temporary. It hurts continuity. You can't find a point of interest (e.g. a shop or a wizard), and then return to it later to sell or buy stuff, or complete a quest. For these reasons, some old games (e.g. Moria) used a limited persistence - you could teleport between town-level and a single current remembered level, but not between the other levels. One perspective on that design is, that town-level never was a 'real' level, it was more like a navigable inventory-bag-shop you could walk around in (the town level is a gaming-system-loop mechanism).

A milder risk version is to keep the levels persistent, but shuffle **where the player arrives**. This gives some of the same design benefits. This way it is still risky to traverse stairs. You don't know where you will arrive - maybe right into a group of dangerous monsters. You can't immediately find stairs back once you arrive, and even if you have successfully been to the level before, you may have to search for the stairs again. You could make it further difficult for the player to reorient himself on an earlier visited level, by clearing his memory of the level map or of the revealed stairs. One advantage of persistent levels is that it inhibits 'scumming play' - you can't continue to replay shuffled versions of the same level to amass loot in an unintended safe way. Instead you are forced to delve deeper to find further loot.

13.4 DESIGNING OUR STAIRS

This background on dungeon stairs informs some of the choices we face when implementing the class which will handle our maps - the Dung class. If we chose to always shuffle level maps, its implementation could be simple - just a *current dungeon level number*, and the ability to generate maps for any given level on the fly.

However, we have chosen persistent level maps, so we will need to track an array of stored level-maps. As we make a new dungeon class `Dung`, it will hold our collection of level-maps, and help us travel between them.

Deterministic stair travel would be easier to implement. But we want the **shuffled** travel, where the player arrives at random locations each time. So we must avoid leaving multiple older copies of the player around the maps. This issue did not exist when we only had one map - the question of exactly how to enter and exit a map level. To formalize our approach, we can give maps the methods `enterMap` and `leaveMap`. (However, `leaveMap` collapses to just `removeMob`) We can then give the dungeon class the method `plySwitchLevel`, which will use those methods in an orderly way.

To sum up our requirements for the dungeon class: - hold a current `level` number (index into the map array) - manage an array of dungeon `maps` - generate maps on the fly, on first reference - deal with `plySwitchLevel`

13.5   IMPLEMENTING STAIRS

`02model/13Dung.ts:`

```
export class Dung {
  level:number = 0;
  maps:DMapIF[] = [];
  curMap(g:GameIF): DMapIF {
    return this.getLevel(this.level,g);
  }
  getLevel(L:number, g:GameIF): DMapIF {
    if (!this.hasLevel(L)) {
      let map = g.build.makeLevel(g.rnd,L);
      this.add(map,L);
    }
    return this.maps[L];
  }
  hasLevel(L:number):boolean {
```

```
      return L<this.maps.length && !!this.maps[L];
    } // && L>=0
    add(map:DMapIF, L:number) {
      if (L >= this.maps.length) { this.extendMaps(L+1); }
      this.maps[L] = map;
    }
    extendMaps(len:number) { this.maps.length = len; }
    plySwitchLevel(newLevel:number, np:WPoint, g:GameIF) {
        let ply = g.ply;
        this.curMap(g).removeMob(ply);
        this.level = newLevel;
        this.curMap(g).enterMap(ply,np);
    }
}
```

We'll have to account for `enterMap` in a bit. To make this work, we must also adjust `Game` and `GameIF`. `GameIF` gets these:

```
dung:Dung;
build:BuildIF0;
```

For the actual game object, we'll clone `Game1` into a new class `Game2`, and adjust it majorly, to look like this:

02model/13GameModel2.ts

```
export class Game2 implements GameIF {
  constructor(public rnd:Rnd, public ply:Mob,
              public build:BuildIF0) {}
  curMap():DMapIF|null { return this.dung.curMap(this); }
  ai:MobAiIF|null = null;
  log:MsgLog = new MsgLog();
  msg(s:string) { this.log.msg(s); }
  dung:Dung = new Dung();
}
```

We have removed the property `map` which `Game0` had, and instead delegate to the dungeon. `ply` has been made a proper constructor member, and we have added `buildIF` as a property.

You can fixup Game0 and Game1 with a shim like this:

```
dung:Dung = <Dung> <unknown> undefined; // ch13
build:BuildIF0 = <BuildIF0> <unknown> undefined; // ch13
```

We must update `Builder2d` to use this `Game2` instead of `Game1`, by changing `makeGame` to this:

```
makeGame():GameIF {
    let rnd = new Rnd(42);
    let ply = this.makePly();
    //let game = new Game0(rnd, ply, this);
    //game.map = this.makeLevel(game, 0);
    let game = new Game2(rnd, ply, this);
    this.enterFirstLevel(game);
    game.ai = this.makeAI();
    return game;
}
enterFirstLevel(game: Game2) {
    let dung = game.dung;
    let map = dung.curMap(game);
    let np = this.centerPos(map.dim);
    game.dung.plySwitchLevel(dung.level,np,game);
}
```

Note the builder no longer directly provides the game object with a built map level. People still call `GameIF.curMap()`, but it now chains from `Dung.curMap()` to the builder. If we ask for a dungeon level that has not been referenced yet, the dungeon uses a builder to construct new map levels. For this, the `Game` must hold a Builder (`BuildIF0`), so additional levels can be built on the fly.

We must scout out the new map beforehand, for a vacant position to put the player in. Beware the player can only manage his position for one map at a time. Assuming our game model has the dungeon design outlined above, our stair command will look like this - `04cmds/13StairCmd.ts`:

```
export class StairCmd extends CmdBase {
    constructor(public levelDir:number, public g:GameIF){
```

```
        super(g.ply,g);
    }
    exc(): boolean {
        let game = this.g;
        let dung = game.dung;
        let newLevel = dung.level + this.levelDir;
        let newMap:DMapIF = dung.getLevel(newLevel, game);
        let newPos = FreeSpace.findFree(newMap, game.rnd);
        let dir = (this.levelDir != -1 ?
                    'descends' : 'ascends');
        this.game.msg(`ply ${dir} some stairs.`);
        dung.plySwitchLevel(newLevel, <WPoint> newPos, game);
        return true;
    }
}
```

13.6 TESTING OUR STAIRS

If you try this out, it should now be possible to flee to different
levels. However, all our levels look the **same**. The only difference
is that the enemies return to their initial starting circle. To help
orient our player a bit, we'll extend `DrawMap.renderStats()` to
also show which level he is currently on:

```
let  hp =  `  HP:${ply.hp}`
let mhp = `MHP:${ply.maxhp}`
let   L = `LVL:${game.dung.level}`


term.txt(0,y++, hp, 'yellow', 'teal');
term.txt(0,y++,mhp, 'yellow', 'teal');
term.txt(0,y++,  L, 'yellow', 'teal'); // ch13.
```

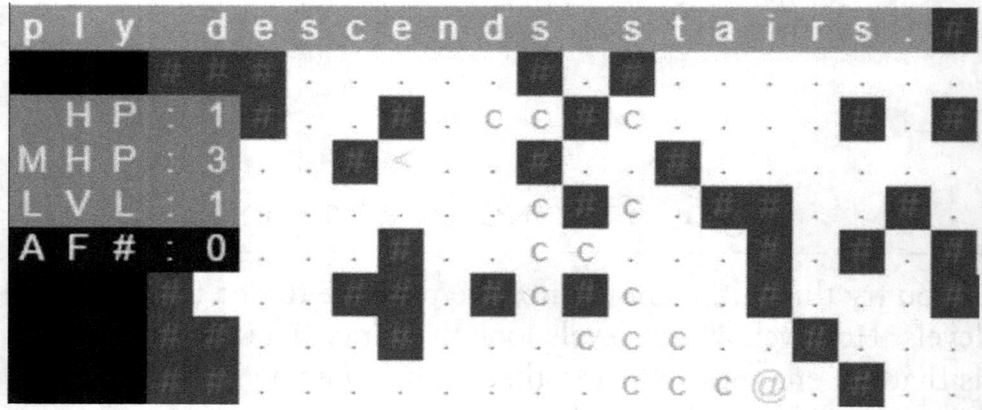

F 13.2: The one who got away

14 NEXT LEVEL ANTS

(In which we make next level ant mobs interesting)

F 14.1: We should be able to survive some ants. In your pants. On
your hands

14.1　A Different Level

In the previous chapter, we found a downwards stair and descended to the next level. Upon arrival, we were sorely disappointed to discover it was **identical** to the previous level. We will address this in a number of ways. We will

- design an appropriate **enemy**
- give those enemies appropriate **behaviour**
- try to **place** the enemies in a reasonable way
- design a different and proper **level** design
- make a mechanism that can **pick** different level designs

14.2　A Wellbehaved Enemy

Right now, when we flee to the second level, we again encounter the same too strong cats we just fled from. We must design an easier and less dangerous starter enemy for this level. We will follow an alphabetical progression for our monster toughness, so these our very easiest monsters will be a for **ants**. Their appropriate and less dangerous **behaviour** will be to move about in a random way, and **not** hunt the player. However, **if** the player is near them, they will probably bite. We will place them **randomly** around the dungeon, so that you sometimes encounter several, but most of the time only one.

Our ant enemy will need an appropriate AI, to behave as described above. `05ai/14MobAi3_ant.ts`:

```
export class MobAI3_ant implements MobAiIF {
  turn(me:Mob, enemy:Mob, game:GameIF):boolean {
    let r = game.rnd;
    let dir = r.rndDir2();
    return new MoveBumpCmd(dir, me, game).npcTurn();
  }
}
```

For this to work, class `Rnd` must get the `rndDir2` method. It will never pick (0,0). This way, we avoid the mob hitting himself! We could instead solve it by checking for it in the AI, before moving. (There is an idea in this problem: Maybe we could attack monsters with a confusion-spell or a compulsion-spell, that would sometimes make them hit itself?)

Add this to `Rnd.ts`:

```
rndDir2():WPoint {  // Never makes zero-zero.
   let a = this.rndC(-1,1);
   let b = this.oneIn(2) ? 1 : -1;
   let h = this.oneIn(2);
   return new WPoint(h ? a : b, h ? b:a);
}
// Two extras you can have for free:
rndDir0():WPoint {
   return new WPoint(this.rndC(-1,1),
                     this.rndC(-1,1));
}
rndDir(p:WPoint=new WPoint()):WPoint {
   return new WPoint(p.x+this.rndC(-1,1),
                     p.y+this.rndC(-1,1));
}
```

To activate the `MobAI3_ant`, we make the switching `AiSwitcher`, which looks like this: `05ai/14AiSwitcher.ts`

```
export class AiSwitcher implements MobAiIF {
  ai2:MobAiIF = new MobAI2_cat();
  ai3:MobAiIF = new MobAI3_ant();
  turn(me:Mob, enemy:Mob, game:GameIF):boolean {
    var ai:MobAiIF;
    switch (me.g) {
      case Glyph.Ant: ai=this.ai3;break;
      case Glyph.Cat: ai=this.ai2;break;
      default:        ai=this.ai2;break;
    }
    return ai.turn(me,enemy,game);
  }
```

```
}
```

14.3 Picking Different Levels

To add our new ants to the level, we once again need a new builder, so we clone `13Builder2d.ts` into `14Builder2e.ts`, with class name `Builder2e`. The AI is included with

```
makeAI():MobAiIF|null { return new AiSwitcher(); }
```

To activate our new mobs, we change `makeLevel` to this:

```
makeLevel(rnd:Rnd, level:number):DMapIF {
  let map = this.makeMap(rnd,level);
  this.addLevelStairs(map,level,rnd);
  this.addMobsToLevel(map,rnd);
  return map;
}
```

and add `addMobsToLevel` as this:

```
addMobsToLevel(map:DMapIF, rnd:Rnd) {
  switch (map.level) {
  case 0: default: this.makeCatRing(map,rnd); break;
  case 1: this.makeAnts(map,rnd); break;
  }
}
```

14.4 Placing Enemies Reasonably

We need some code that will place the enemy ants randomly scattered around the dungeon. We choose to do so by specifying a probability that any given square will contain a monster - the so-called **monster rate**. With a rate of 4, you get 1 in 4, 25% of the squares. With a rate of 50, you get 1 in 50, i.e. 2% of the squares. It could be designed in many other ways, e.g. 1 monster per room, or **clusters** of monsters, in **some** rooms. makeAnts used above here, will be this:

```
makeAnts(map:DMapIF,rnd:Rnd) {
  this.makeMobs(map,rnd,Glyph.Ant,10);
}
```

We then place our random monsters, with this in Builder2e:

```
makeMobs(map:DMapIF, rnd:Rnd, g:Glyph, rate:number) {
  let dim = map.dim;
  let p = new WPoint();
  for (p.y=1;p.y<dim.y-1;++p.y) {
    for (p.x=1;p.x<dim.x-1;++p.x) {
      if (!rnd.oneIn(rate)){ continue; }
      if (map.blocked(p)) { continue; }
      this.addNPC(g,p.x,p.y,map,0);
    }
  }
}
```

And our index14_ants.ts becomes

```
ScreenMaker2_Fixed.Gfirst( new Builder2e() );
```

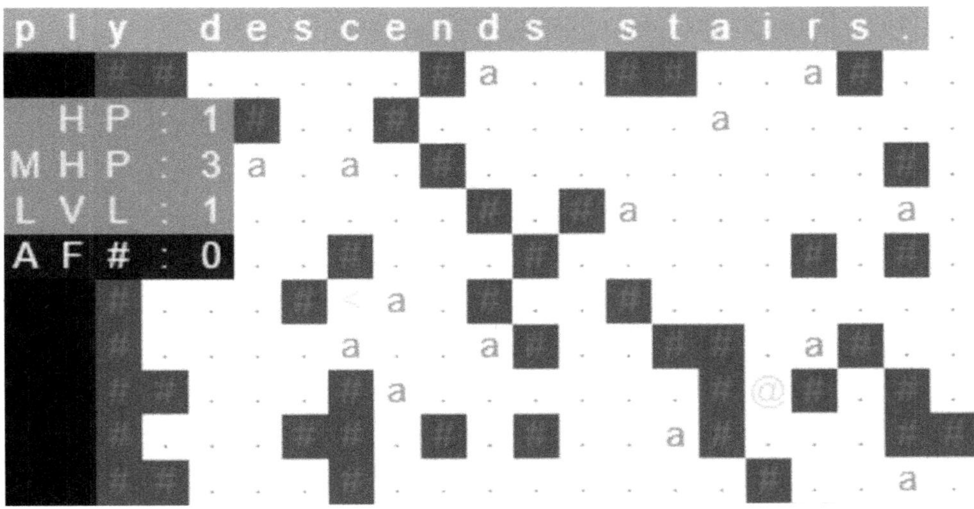

F 14.2: Peaceful coexistence with ants, possible in our lifetime?

You can now test the game again by running `index14_ants.ts`. This time, you actually have a fighting chance against the ants you meet, when you flee to the next level. Eventually the ants will wear you down, as you never regrow your hit points. The **layout** of the second level is also still the same old layout.

15 Better Dungeon Layout

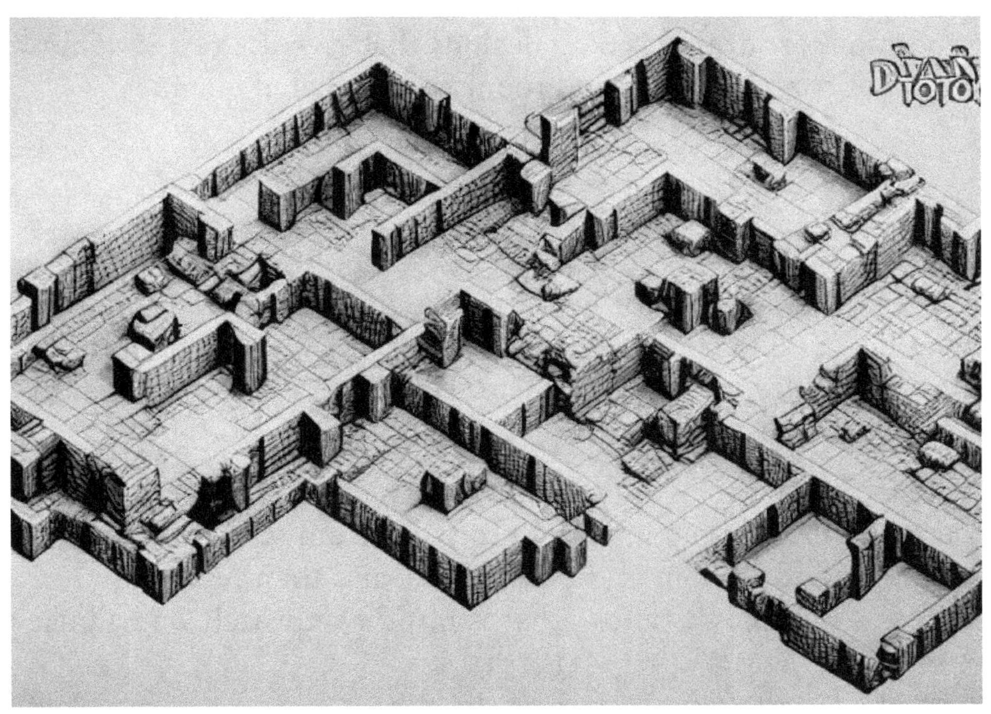

F 15.1: Rooms, Doors & Corridors. Can we do that?

15.1　LEVEL MAP GENERATOR

We have improved the level monsters, but our level layout is still the first simple attempt. We will now build a better map layout. We can surely do better than our initial randomly scattered heap. Our intention is a collection of **rooms** connected by twisting **corridors**. Where some tunnels connect to rooms, we might place **doors**. A door is a barrier which humans can operate, but non-sentient beings cannot.

We shape this design to aid balanced combat. We want to set up an environment for simple combat, with simple enemies. The player should have 'a fighting chance'. Once we have demonstrated that the player can handle and survive combat there, we can then proceed to increase the difficulty. An important part of this is map designs that give the player some degree of control - separated rooms, and isolated enemies.

15.2　PLAN

We need an approach for how to make those connected random room boxes. There are infinite ways to build level maps, and later we will try out more of them. For now, our intention is to get the most result with the least amount of effort.

A classic 'least effort' is alternating between placing a random room, then extending a random corridor from it, then placing another random room at the other end, and then repeating this process a number of times. That is not the approach we will use now.

Instead, we will place a lot of small random rectangles. These rectangles will have an inner center of black wall, and a border rectangle of whitish floor. The trick here is, that the 'floor borders' will always constitute traversable corridors. In this way, their combination will be traversable too.

F 15.2: A,B&C are the walkable corridors:

There is a caveat, in that it is possible to place a disconnected rectangle that doesn't touch the rest of the model. One way to protect against this is to place ..MANY (not a robust fix!). Another way is to run a post-process step which deliberately re-connects any disconnected map parts. A third way is concerned with whether the initial map is all walls or all floor. If it is all floor, the disconnected-issue cannot arise.

We will add a further complication to the mechanism: We initially said that we would make the interior of rectangles be black wall. Well, actually we won't. At random, we'll **sometimes** instead make the inner part be hollow floor. This way, our map will be a mix of open areas and closed-off wall blocks.

We will do a final complication: Instead of only having hollow and solid rectangles, we will have a third variant: The outermost edge is still traversable floor rectangle. We again still give that an inner edge of wall, but now we'll poke 1-2 holes in that wall edge. Further inside, we then leave it hollow. In this way we achieve a

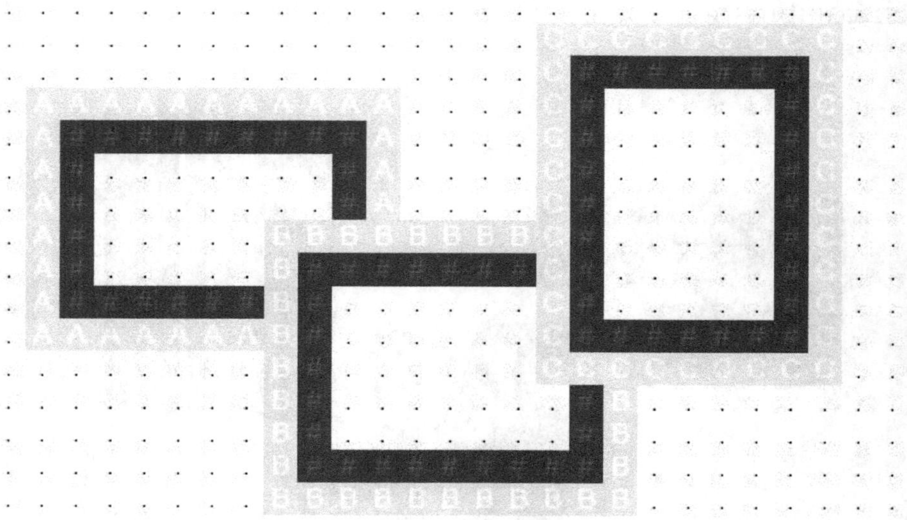

F 15.3: Now there are hollow rooms inside the black walls

kind of room or house, with doorways. We might even make the holes as actual doors, that you could open and close.

15.3 Implementation

The above constitutes our design. It requires a couple of parts. We need a function that can `draw()` the hollow rectangles. We also need a function that can `pick()` such a random rectangle. And we need a **loop** to call the two. An implementation of `loop()` would be `03build/15MapGen1.ts`:

```
export class MapGen1 {
  constructor(public map:DMapIF, public r:Rnd) {}
  public loop(map:DMapIF, r:Rnd) {
    let num = 20;
    let UL = new WPoint(), XT = new WPoint();
    for (let n=0;n<num; ++n) {
      this.pick(UL,XT);
      let filled = r.oneIn(3);
      this.draw(UL,XT,filled);
```

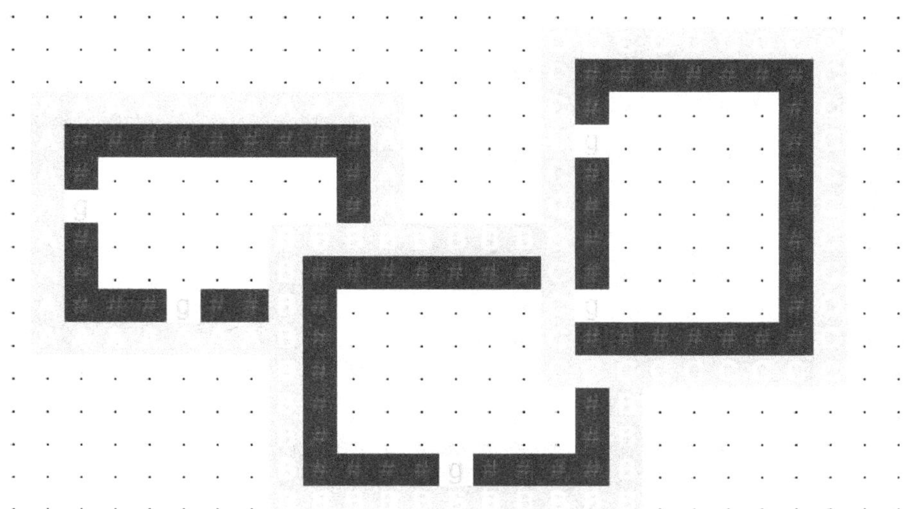

F 15.4: Now door holes punched in the black walls

```
    }
    return map;
  }
```

With `pick()` as

```
  pick(UL:WPoint, XT:WPoint) {
    let r = this.r;
    let dim = this.map.dim;
    XT.y = r.rndC(2,8);
    XT.x = r.rndC(4,12);
    if (r.oneIn(2)) {
      let s = XT.x; XT.x = XT.y; XT.y = s;
    }
    UL.x = r.rnd(1,dim.x-XT.x-1);
    UL.y = r.rnd(1,dim.y-XT.y-1);
  }
```

and `draw()` as

```
draw(UL:WPoint, XT:WPoint, filled:boolean) {
  let center = filled ? Glyph.Wall : Glyph.Floor;
  let x2 = XT.x-1, y2 = XT.y-1;
  let seconds:WPoint[] = [];
  let p = new WPoint();
  let y=0,x=0;
  for (y=0; y<=XT.y;++y) {
    p.y=y+UL.y;
    for (x=0; x<=XT.x;++x) {
      p.x=x+UL.x;
      let edge = (x==0||y==0||x==XT.x||y==XT.y);
      let secs = (x==1||y==1||x==x2  ||y==y2);
      let f = edge
                ? Glyph.Floor
                : (secs ? Glyph.Wall : center);
      this.map.cell(p).env = f;
      if (secs) { seconds.push(p.copy()); }
    }
  }
  if (!filled) { this.makeDoors(seconds); }
}
```

Then `makeDoors()` and a test-caller:

```
makeDoors(seconds: WPoint[]) {
  let r = this.r;
  for (let i=r.rnd(1,3);i>=0;--i) {
    let ix = r.rnd(0,seconds.length);
    let p = seconds[ix];
    this.map.cell(p).env = Glyph.Door_Open;
  }
}


public static test(level:number):DMapIF {
  let dim = TPoint.StockDims;
  let wdim = new WPoint(dim.x, dim.y);
  let map = new DMap(wdim, Glyph.Rock,level);
  // hmm, we should make a stock-map.
```

```
    let rnd = new Rnd(42);
    let gen = new MapGen1(map,rnd);
    return gen.loop(map, rnd);
  }
} // end of class here.
```

Because of `makeDoors()`, we'll have to add door glyphs to `Glyph`:

```
  Door_Open,
  Door_Closed,
}
```

And of course for `GlyphInf.initGlyphs`:

```
  add(',',Glyph.Door_Open);
  add('+',Glyph.Door_Closed);
```

To see it, we can use an `index15_showgen.ts` with

```
MapScreen.runMapScreen( MapGen1.test(0) );
```

Beware that the method `draw()` is more active than its name
might imply. It iterates over all cells in the rectangle. The
outermost 'edge' cells are drawn as **floor**. The **second** inner edge
is always drawn as **walls**, and its points **collected** in the `seconds`
array. We track that inner wall, so we can later punch door holes
in it.

Further cells inside are either drawn as solid wall, or as floor
(depending on `filled` being true a third of the time). Finally,
from the `seconds` array, we then pick 1-3 random points to punch
out as doors. The result looks like *Figure 15.5*

We can activate this through a `15Builder2f.ts`, by making it use
this new level generator for next level. We clone `14Builder2e.ts`
into `15Builder2f.ts`, and change `makeMap` to this:

```
  makeMap(rnd:Rnd, level:number):DMapIF {
    let dim = WPoint.StockDims;
```

```
$ $ $ $ $ $ $ $ $ $ $ $ $ $ $ $ $ $ $ $ $ $ $ $ $ $ $ $ $ $ $ $ $ $ $ $ $ $ $ $
$ $ $ $ $ $ $ $ $ $ $ $ $ $ $ $ $ $ $ $ $ $ $ $ $ $ $ $ $ $ $ $ $ $ $ $ $ $ $ $
$ $ $ $ $ $ $ $ $ $ $ $ $ $ $ $                $ $ $ $ $ $ $ $ $ $ $ $ $ $ $ $
$ $ $ $ $                        $ $  # # # # #   $ $ $ $ $ $ $ $ $ $ $ $ $ $ $
$ $ $ $ $   # # # # # #    $ $   #               $ $ $ $ $ $ $ $ $ $ $ $ $ $ $
$ $ $ $                         #   # # # # # #   $ $ $ $ $            $ $
$ $ $ $   # # # # # # # # #      #   # # # # # #                    # # #   $ $
$ $     # # # # # # # # #          # # # # #   # # # # #     #     #   $ $
$ $   #   # # # # # # # # #     # #             # # #             $
$ $   #   # # # # # # # # #       #       #   # # # # #   # # # # # # #   $
$         # # # # # # # # #       #       #   # # # #   #               #   $
$     #                         #       #                 #           #   $
$   # #   # # # # # #       #       #   # # #             #           #   $
$                                                                     #   $
$ $   # #           # # # # # # #     # # #                 # # # # # # #   $
$ $                 # # # # # # #     #   #
$ $ $ $ $     # # # # # # # #     #   #   # # # # # #   #   $ $ $ $
$ $ $ $ $ $ $   # # # # # # #     #   #         #             #   $ $
$ $ $ $ $ $ $   # # # # # # #     #   #   # #   #           #   # # #   $ $
$ $ $ $ $ $ $   # # # # # # #   #   #   # #   #               #   $ $
$ $ $ $ $ $ $               #   #         #           #       #   $ $
$ $ $ $ $ $ $ $ $ $ $ $ $ $ $       $ $   # # # #   # #       #   $ $
$ $ $ $ $ $ $ $ $ $ $ $ $ $ $ $ $ $ $ $ $                 # # #   $ $
$ $ $ $ $ $ $ $ $ $ $ $ $ $ $ $ $ $ $ $ $ $ $ $ $ $ $             $ $
$ $ $ $ $ $ $ $ $ $ $ $ $ $ $ $ $ $ $ $ $ $ $ $ $ $ $ $ $ $ $ $ $ $
```

F 15.5: It may look weird drawn this way, but it works

```
    var map:DMapIF;
    switch (level) {
      case 0:  map = TestMap.test(dim,rnd,level); break;
      case 1:  map = MapGen1.test(level); break;
      default: map = TestMap.test(dim,rnd,level); break;
    }
    return map;
  }
```

With `index15_mapgen.ts`, you can now test-play the updated
game. It should look like *Figure 15.6*. How does it feel to play?
Beware that you must reach the second level to see it.

```
ScreenMaker2_Fixed.Gfirst( new Builder2f() );
```

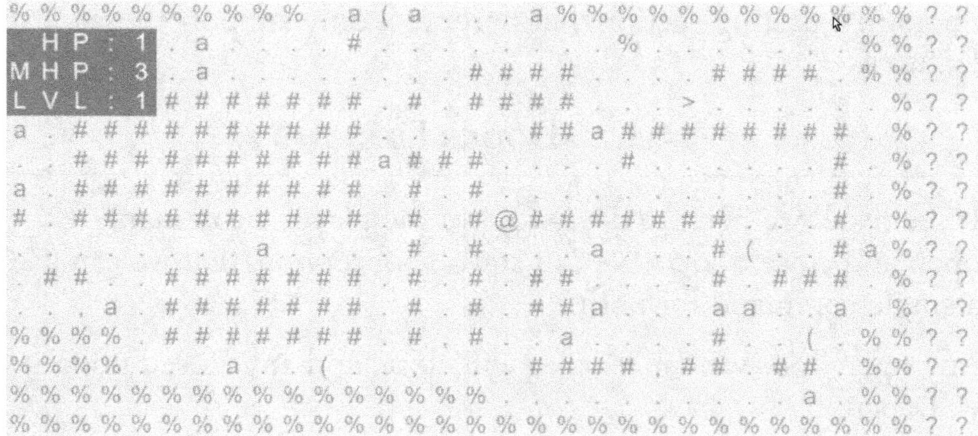

F 15.6: Now we feed the map layout into our playable game

15.4 DOORS

So far, the doorways we generated were always open. They are open empty doorways that everybody can always pass through. We can turn them into actual doors that you can open and close. This could be useful for combat. You could close doors, to block monsters from following you. Some monsters - evil wizards - would be too clever to be fooled by this. But others, like animals and beasts, would not know how to open a door.

15.4.1 DOORS SCOPE

What would it take to support this feature?

- We are already placing (open) doors, so we **might** update that mechanism to place both kinds of doors.
- We must ensure that open doors are passable, and that closed doors are not. This entails updating `blocked` and `opaque` on `MapCell/DMap`.
- We must give the user some actions to open and close doors.

That is pretty much it. We'll discuss further complications of doors in a parting section, but here we'll only support these features.

15.4.2 DOORS DESIGN

It seems all we need to do, is to give the player a command to open and close doors. We can start by observing, that we can use a single command for both:

Any open door we use it on, it will close, and any closed door, it will open.

We need a way to figure out which door we should act on. What if the user stands next to several doors, e.g. in a hallway or intersection?

We could pick the nearest door at random. That is not a good way. In combat, it could be critical that we open or close the correct door. And several doors might be at the same distance.

A naively cool approach would be to simply walk into the door - it clearly indicates what the user intends, and seems like a good 'lazy' UI interaction - just bump into whatever, until you get what you want.. But this does not work when we need to **close** a door - then we would just walk through the doorway instead of closing it. So we'll drop that idea again. Still, in another game with doors that only open, that idea has merit.

Here, we will just let the player specify in which direction he wants to operate a door. So he'll activate the 'door' command, it will then ask for a direction, and if it finds a door in that direction, it will try to toggle that door between open and closed.

15.4.3 DOORS PLAN

We will extend `ParsePly` with a key action to operate doors.

The door action will activate a pick-a-direction **screen**, into which we pass a follow-up command as an argument. That is, **if** the user correctly picks a direction, **then** that follow-up command will be executed with that chosen direction as input. And that follow-up command is of course the actual door open-close command.

We will need to implement that toggle-door command.

Note that the pick-a-direction screen may be generally useful later, for other non-door-related stuff.

Because the door command will sometimes issue user warnings, we must also extend our `MsgLog` with a `flash` method. A flash is a message that we **don't** log.

15.4.4 DOORS IMPLEMENTATION

We'll first take care of the flash feature, so we don't have that to worry about. In `MsgLog`, we change `msg()` to this:

```
msg(s:string, flash:boolean) {
  this.queue.push(s);
  if (!flash) { this.archive.push(s); }
  console.log(s);
}
```

The trick is just, that flashes aren't added to the archive. We then add this method to `GameIF`:

```
flash(s:string):void;
```

And update `Game2` with this:

```
msg( s: string) { this.log.msg(s,false); }
flash(s:string) { this.log.msg(s,true);  }
```

(You can fixup `Game1` and `Game0` with either this or
`flash(s:string){}`).

Our direction-picking screen and our command will need to
communicate. The screen must somehow transfer the chosen
direction to the command. To achieve this, we update
`09CmdIF.ts` to include a `setDir` method, so it now looks like this:

```
export interface CmdIF {
  exc():boolean;
  me:Mob;
  g:GameIF;
  setDir(dir: WPoint):CmdIF;
}
```

On the face of it, this is bad news for all other commands:
Presumably they neither have nor care about directions. And it
seems we are now forcing them to deal with a direction they
don't want.. We handle this by instead updating the base class
for commands - `09CmdBase.ts`:

```
export abstract class CmdBase implements CmdIF {
  exc():boolean{throw 'no exc';}
  constructor(public me:Mob, public g:GameIF){}
  setDir(dir: WPoint):CmdIF {throw 'no setDir';}
}
```

This way, all our commands derived from `CmdBase` will have a
default handler for `setDir`. The downside is, that the compiler
type checks will allow us to call `setDir` on commands that don't
really support it - instead we'll only see the error trigger during
runtime, when `CmdBase` catches it.

With this support for `setDir` in `CmdIF`, we can implement a
direction-picking screen:

`06screen/15CmdDirScreen.ts`

```
export class CmdDirScreen extends BaseScreen {
  name:string = 'dir';
  constructor(public cmd:CmdIF, game:GameIF,
```

```
                maker:MakerIF)
  {
    super(game,maker);
  }
  draw(term:TermIF) {
    term.txt(0,0, 'Which dir?', 'yellow', 'black');
    let R = ['H Left', 'J Down', 'K Up', 'L Right'];
    for (let i=0; i<R.length; ++i) {
      term.txt(0,i+1, R[i], 'yellow', 'black');
    }
  }
  onKey(e:JQuery.KeyDownEvent,
        stack:Stack):boolean
  {
    stack.pop(); // we pop in all cases.
    let dir = new WPoint();
    switch (e.key) {
      case 'h': dir.x = -1; break;
      case 'j': dir.y =  1; break;
      case 'k': dir.y = -1; break;
      case 'l': dir.x =  1; break;
    }
    if (!dir.empty()) { this.actDir(dir); }
    return true;
  }
  actDir(dir: WPoint):boolean {
    return this.cmd.setDir(dir).exc();
  }
}
```

The door command will look like this:

```
export class DoorCmd extends CmdBase {
  dir:WPoint = new WPoint();
  constructor(public me:Mob, public g:GameIF){
    super(me,g);
  }
  setDir(dir:WPoint):CmdIF {
    this.dir = dir; return this;
```

```
  }
  exc():boolean {
    let p = this.me.pos;
    let door = p.plus(this.dir);
    let map = <DMapIF>this.g.curMap();
    let cell = map.cell(door);
    switch (cell.env) {
    case Glyph.Door_Closed:
      cell.env=Glyph.Door_Open;    break;
    case Glyph.Door_Open:
      cell.env=Glyph.Door_Closed; break;
    default:
      this.g.flash(`No door here!`);
      return false;
    }
    this.msg(cell.env);
    return true;
  }
  msg(env:Glyph) {
    let open = (env == Glyph.Door_Open);
    let action = open ? 'opens': 'closes';
    let who = this.me.name;
    this.g.msg(`${who} ${action} the door`);
  }
}
```

It simply inspects the map cell position in the specified direction, relative to the mob that issued the command. If said cell contains an open or closed door, we swap the cell contents to contain the opposite - a closed or open door. If the cell does **not** contain a door, we instead display an error flash.

You might wonder why we pass the monster to the command, instead of simply the **position** of that mob - after all, don't we just need the position to figure out what is going on? This concerns design philosophy. It is a generally good principle that we pass the 'acting entity' to a command. It lets us pass any **effects** of the command on to the player, e.g. a door trap exploding in his face. It also lets us check his **abilities and resources**. Maybe his hands are slippery or freezing numb or shaking from shock, so he can't operate the door handle? Maybe he is encumbered by carrying too much? Maybe he is dazed, confused, or blind? Maybe he is out of mana?

To fit this into `09ParsePly.ts`, we must do this:

```
.. // add this case in parseKeyCmd():
  case 'c': s = this.doorCmd(); break;
..


doorCmd():SScreenIF {
  let cmd = new DoorCmd(this.ply,this.game);
  return new CmdDirScreen(cmd,this.game,this.maker);
}
```

We have one final important thing to do: We must update `blocked/opaque` in `07MapCell.ts`, so `Door_Closed` also blocks movement:

```
..
  opaque():boolean {
    return (
        this.env == Glyph.Wall
     || this.env == Glyph.Rock
     || this.env == Glyph.Door_Closed
    );
  }
  blocked():boolean {
    return (!!this.mob || this.opaque());
  }
..
```

With this, you should be able to open and close doors, by pressing C when standing next to one. You can test it out by running `index15_mapgen` again. Notice how you (and mobs) can hopefully pass through open doors, and hopefully not through closed doors.

15.4.5 DOORS, PARTING THOUGHTS

It is possible to do many further things with doors.

- doors can be **stuck**. Stuck doors cannot be opened. If stuck, it takes violence (kick or bash or shield bash) or magic to force them open, which typically leaves them *broken*.
- you can make a door stuck, by jamming **spikes** into it.
- doors can be **broken**. A broken door cannot be closed. A broken door is a terminally open door, that might as well not even be there.
- doors can be **dissolved**, which means they fully disappear. You can argue that a broken door acts identically to such a disappeared door - the difference is in which game actions will cause it.
- doors can be **locked**, which is akin to being stuck. The difference is that they can be unlocked and relocked, with a key or a lockpick/rogue. They may be so sturdy, that unlocking them is the only thing that works.
- doors can be **hidden** and secret, and must be searched for and discovered.
- doors can be **trapped**, and will be dangerous until you disarm them.
- doors can be **created**, typically with a spell. This allows things like throwing up a tiny protective cage-room of doors around your character, in combat.
- doors, both hidden and normal, can be **revealed** with a spell of **detect doors**,
- depending on your mindset, some doors could also be magical and act in a teleporting way, somewhat like stairs, possibly being one-way affairs, or even one-time use.

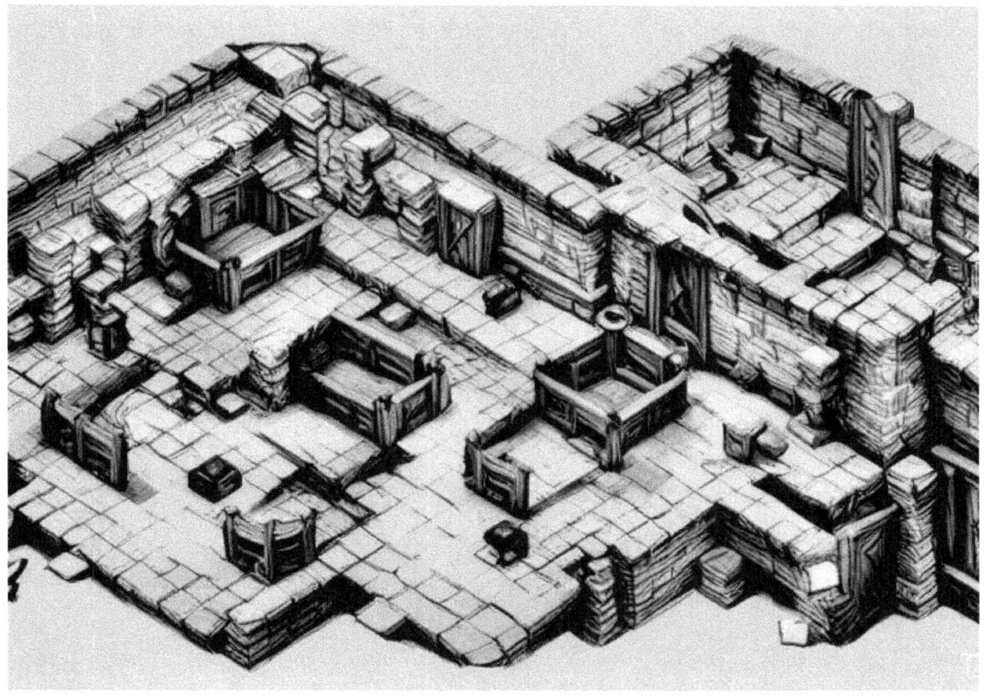

F 15.7: Dungeon architecture doesn't always make logical sense

16 Making It Prettier

F 16.1: Louis Comfort Tiffany briefly dabbled in roguelikes together with Escher, but eventually gave up

(Updates GlyphInf to control colors when drawing glyphs.)

16.1 WE CAN CHANGE HOW WE DRAW

The game maps we have drawn so far are all dullish drab grey colors. We can spice it up with varied colors for background and foreground, to make it easier to see what the various parts are. For example which parts are walls, and which are floor.

16.2 COLOURING OUR MAP TILES

To accomplish this, we clone 07GlyphInf0.ts into an updated 02model/16GlyphInf1.ts. Beware that in 16GlyphInf1.ts, **all references** to GlyphMap0 and GlyphInf0 must be changed to GlyphMap1 and GlyphInf1!

```
export class GlyphInf1 {
  constructor(public glyph:Glyph,
    public fg:string, public bg:string,
    public c:string) {}
}
export class GlyphMap1 {
  static bad:GlyphInf1 =
        new GlyphInf1(Glyph.Bad,'red','yellow','?');
  static add(bg:string, fg:string, c:string, g:Glyph) {
    let inf:GlyphInf1=new GlyphInf1(g, fg, bg, c);
    GlyphMap1.warn(g);
    GlyphMap1.glyphs[g] = inf;
  }
  static ensureInit:number = GlyphMap1.initGlyphs();
  static initGlyphs():number {
    let bg = 1 ? '#fff' : 'black';
    var add = GlyphMap1.add;
    add('red', 'yellow', '§',Glyph.Bad);
    add('#222','#282828','%',Glyph.Rock);
    add('#444','#555555','#',Glyph.Wall);
    add(bg,      '#123',    '.',Glyph.Floor);
    add('#222','#282828','?',Glyph.Unknown);
```

```
add(bg,        'orange',  '@',Glyph.Ply);
add(bg,        '#e2b',     'a',Glyph.Ant);
add(bg,        '#43a',     'b',Glyph.Bat);
add(bg,        '#6c4',     'c',Glyph.Cat);
add(bg,        '#294',     'S',Glyph.Sheep);
add(bg,        'orange',  '>',Glyph.StairsDown);
add(bg,        'orange',  '<',Glyph.StairsUp);
add(bg,        'orange',  ',',Glyph.Door_Open);
add(bg,        'orange',  '+',Glyph.Door_Closed);
.. (etc, specifying colors for remaining glyphs.)
```

We note a background and foreground color for each glyph. To
bring it into play, we change a few lines in `07DrawMap.ts`. The
inner-most loop in `drawMap0()` changes to this:

```
for (t.x=0, w.x=0; t.x<tdim.x; ++t.x, ++w.x) {
  let cell:MapCell =
      (map.legal(w) ? map.cell(w) : this.outside);
  let i = GlyphMap1.inf(cell.glyph());
  term.at(t.x, t.y, i.c, i.fg, i.bg);
} //'gray', 'lightgray'
```

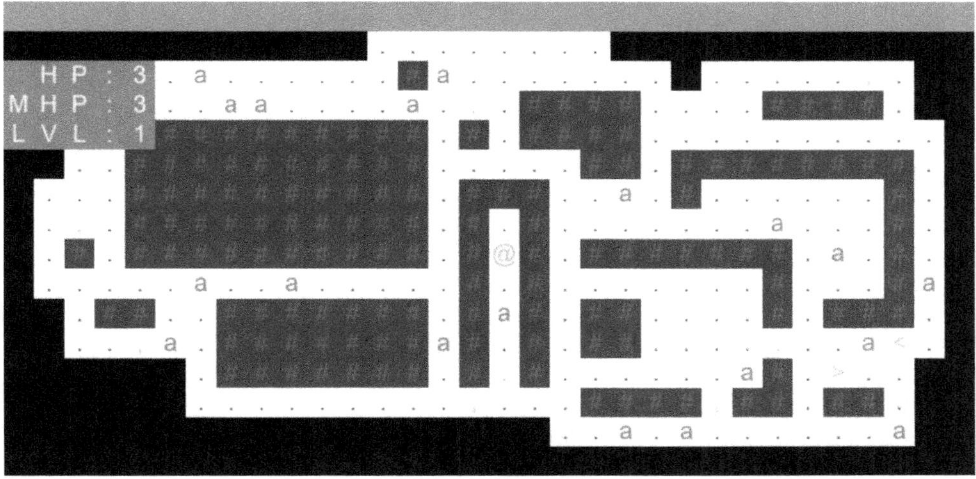

F 16.2: Looks almost, but not quite like nvidia realtime raytracing

17 Healing

(In which our hero gets the ability to heal back up)

F 17.1: Healing is not easy to visualize, so instead of a red health potion, here you have a soothing tranquil garden, which is hard to carry around

(About out-of-combat incremental auto-healing.)

17.1 RESTORING OUR PLAYER'S HIT POINTS

Our short term goal is to **stay alive**. Our long term goal is to locate and reach the **stairs** to the next level. Against the ants on the second level, we can survive for a while, and kill a few. Mainly because they are horrible at fighting back. Still, they hit for 1-2 hit points, and we only have 3 hit points in total. So eventually and invariably, we lose. As is, we'll probably never reach the stairs. We lack a way to heal our player.

There are two game design schools on health and healing. In one approach, the player's health is **long-term** - you are not supposed to lose any of it, and gaining health back is hard. In the other approach, the player's health is short-term, **per-fight**: During combat, it is hard to regain health. But as soon as the current fight is over, you will have relatively easy access to healing. Whichever of these you choose, you will have to stick with your choice, since either choice invalidates the other.

Here, we will go with per-fight health. So we need a mechanism to let the player heal when **out of combat** (OOC).

17.2 IMPLEMENTATION

04cmds/17AutoHeal.ts:

```
export class AutoHeal {
  amountToHealMin:number = 1;
  timeToHealMax:number = 5;
  nextWait:number=0;
  amount:number=0;
  countdown:number=0;
  constructor(){ this.resetHeal(); }
  public static combatReset(mob:Mob, game:GameIF) {
    let ah = game.autoHeal;
    if (mob.isPly && ah) {
```

```
        ah.resetHeal();
    }
  }
  public static combatResets(a:Mob, b:Mob|null,
                                 game:GameIF) {
    this.combatReset(a,game);
    if (b) { AutoHeal.combatReset(b,game); }
  }
  resetHeal() {
    this.nextWait = this.timeToHealMax;
    this.countdown = this.nextWait;
    this.amount = this.amountToHealMin;
  }
  turn(ply:Mob,game:GameIF) {
    if (this.atFullHealth(ply)) { return; }
    this.step_timeToHeal(ply,game);
  }
  atFullHealth(m:Mob):boolean {
    return (m.hp >= m.maxhp);
  }
  step_timeToHeal(ply:Mob,game:GameIF) {
    this.countdown > 0
        ? --this.countdown
        : this.healTick(ply, game);
  }
  healTick(ply:Mob,game:GameIF) {
    game.msg(
`ply feels ${this.amount} better after ${this.nextWait}`
    );
    HealthAdj.heal(ply, this.amount);
    ++this.amount;
    if (this.nextWait>1) {
        --this.nextWait;
    }
    this.countdown = this.nextWait;
  }
}
```

Let's walk through this mechanism. It is a triad of `countdown`, `nextWait` and `amount`.

`countdown` counts down to next heal - if it reaches zero, we heal a bit. `amount` is the size of that heal. `nextWait` holds the number that `countdown` must count down from, in each cycle.

The major idea is that `countdown` counts from `nextWait` to zero, and each time it reaches zero, we heal the player for `amount`. The minor idea is that the countdown **intervals** (`nextWait`) start out long and grow shorter, as we heal more and more. And that the **amount** we heal starts out small and grows bigger, the longer we heal.

But if you are attacked or attack, **all** next-heal values reset back to their defaults. That is, `nextWait` and `amount` also reset to their start values! The in-combat rule cares about last 'combat action' (typically, being hurt and damaged, but maybe even being subjected to an attack that missed). The idea is that you need to remain **out of combat** for a while, to start healing.

The principle is a quickly accelerating heal that starts out slow, but quickly snowballs to full health. This serves two purposes: That a small respite in an ongoing fight can only be (mis-)used to heal us a small bit - keeping tension up. And secondly, that a proper after-fight heal is quickly completed - once the fight is over, we see no benefit in dragging things out.

`step_timeToHeal()` handles the intervening interval countdown. `healTick()` handles the actual heal-effect, shortens the next countdown, and increases the next heal-amount. `resetHeal()` reduces the triad back to the starting point, if our healing is interrupted by trouble.

17.3 INTEGRATION

We must inject the auto-heal into the game. First, adjust `08GameIF.ts` to include

```
autoHeal: AutoHeal|undefined;
```

We'll clone `Game2` to `17GameModel3.ts`, with `Game3` having this bit:

```
autoHeal:AutoHeal|undefined = new AutoHeal();
```

(fixup the earlier `GameN` with this:)

```
  autoHeal:AutoHeal|undefined;
```

In a similar way, clone `Builder2f` to `17Builder2g.ts`, and replace `Game2` with `Game3`:

```
let game = new Game3(rnd, ply, this);
```

To hook `AutoHeal` into the game, we must call it in a couple of places. In `HealthAdj.dmg()`, we must call `combatReset:` (both for attacker and defender).

```
    static dmg(m: Mob, amount: number, game:GameIF,
            attacker:Mob|null) {
    AutoHeal.combatResets(m,attacker,game);
```

Whenever the player does a turn, we need to call `autoHeal.turn()` for his turn-effects. We will update class `BaseScreen`. We introduce `finishPlyTurn`, which we call inside `npcTurns`, just before the `turnQ` loop:

```
.. (in npcTurns:)
this.finishPlyTurn(q);
for (m=q.next(); !m.isPly && !this.over(); m=q.next()) {
  this.npcTurn(m,ply);
}
finishPlyTurn(q: TurnQ) {
  let ply = q.curMob();
  if (!ply.isPly) { throw `${ply.name} not ply?`; }
```

```
if (this.game.autoHeal) {
    this.game.autoHeal.turn(ply, this.game);
  }
}
```

17.4   TRYING OUT AUTOHEAL

To test and run it, we'll make this entry point: `index17_heal.ts`

`ScreenMaker2_Fixed.Gfirst( new Builder2g() );`

Results from play-testing: With a reasonable amount of our ineffectual ants, we have a functioning and feasible but monotonous and tedious setup - it is actually possible to clear the level of ants.

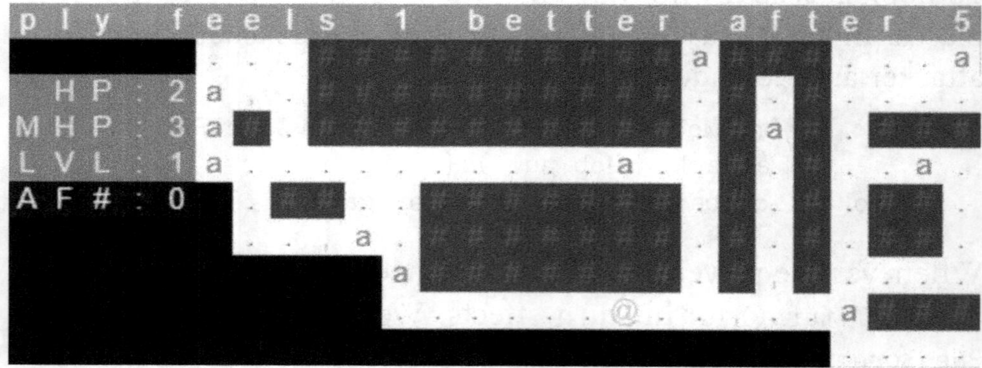

F 17.2: Our man is fit for fight again, now that he has regained 1 hit point

18 b - Better Balanced Bats

(In which we make more interesting and balanced monsters)

F 18.1: Bats in fantasy are something else

(The principles of proximity, visibility, mood, and erratic movement, for interesting and functional enemy gameplay. `MoodAI`, `SleepAI` and `WakeAI` employ those principles.)

18.1　BALANCED CHASE

For a game to be interesting, there must be uncertainty about the outcome, and a belief we can influence it. The **cats** on the first level were too dangerous, we were overwhelmed and our only option was to flee - no chance to win. The **ants** on the second level were rather harmless. They were only a threat because we had tied average damage so tightly to the full hit point pool - after just a single hit, you risked death. These first two attempts were unbalanced. The first was impossibly hard, so you could only survive by fleeing. The mobs in the second attempt technically pose a threat, but are easily handled through careful play, now that we have a way to heal.

Let's consider what middle-ground could provide interesting play. Our hard example highlights an issue with monsters that chase the player:

If all the mobs on a level track the player from any distance and unwaveringly chase him, he will soon be facing 2, 5, then 25 monsters. The player will invariably be forced to face many of them at the same time. To dispatch them as quickly as they close in, he would need a very aggressive way to fight back,

(*Possible challenge to the reader: Make a game where that works!?*)

On the other hand, with our easy-ants attempt, the ants pose **too little** threat because they **don't** chase the player. We seem to have the issue, that we **want** the monsters to chase the player, but we **don't want** the monsters to chase the player..?

What we really want, is some kind of middle ground - for **some** of the monsters to chase the player, **some** of the time. We must give the player influence over how many enemies he takes on at a time. We want to grant the player **some**, but not full, influence over **which** monsters chase him, and **when** they do this. We need mechanisms to avoid enemy attention and awareness. It would help, if enemies only notice us,

- maybe when we get closer,
- maybe when they can see us,
- maybe when we enter specific rooms.

18.2 Combat Balance

For **combat balance** purposes, our initial aim is to balance combat between the player and a **single mob**.

That is, when two mobs fight each other, they should naively have an equal chance of winning. We must however skew this a bit in the player's favor. Because with pure 50/50 odds, the player would almost certainly be dead by his 7th fight - he would only have a 1/128 chance of still being alive!
We also intend to make combat against **two** enemies somewhat difficult to handle. Not to prohibit fighting multiple enemies, but to discourage it, so the player will prefer to avoid it.

18.3 Balance Principles

The principles in the following are intended to help us with these ideas of 'fight one, not two', and balanced chase. There are a myriad of ways to aid this, we will just pick a few.

18.3.1 Proximity Principle, Nearness

A first principle is **proximity**: If you are close to a mob, it might **start** to chase you. If you are far away from a mob, it will not chase you, or may **stop** chasing you. This could be a simple **fixed** rule - once you are closer than 6 tiles, the mob will start to hunt you. It could also be a rule of **chance**: Once you are closer than 6 tiles, there is a high **risk** it will start chasing you. It could even be so that the closer you are, the higher the chance. Similarly, if you are able to **distance** yourself again from a hunter, there'd be a chance he **stops** hunting you. Again, it could either be a fixed rule, or a probability-based rule.

18.3.2   VISIBILITY PRINCIPLE, SIGHT, LOS

A second principle is **visibility**: If you and the enemy can **see** each other, he may **notice** you and start hunting you. If you **can't see** each other, he will probably **not** start hunting you. Again, if you can get out of sight of someone hunting you, he may lose track and **stop** hunting you.

Seeing each other, in game terms, is often termed **Line-of-Sight**, LOS. This is because you can check whether it is possible to draw a connecting **line** between the enemy and you. If the direct line hits a blocking tile (a wall or a closed door), you obviously cannot see each other. Such a **line-of-sight check** could also tell us whether we can hit each other with a magic-missile spell, a cross-bow or a thrown knife.

18.3.3   MOOD PRINCIPLE, MEMORY

A third principle that works well with these two, is **mood**, or state. The idea is that a monster can be in different behaviour states - **moods**. The typical start-mood would be 'asleep', i.e. passive. If we only have one further mood, that second mood would be '**awake**', possibly 'aggressive' . Further possible moods could be 'friendly-ally', or 'hurt-afraid-fleeing'. Together with **proximity** and **visibility**, the mood would **remember** the transition to 'awake-aggressive', and also the transition back to 'asleep-friendly'.

18.3.4 ERRATIC MOVEMENT PRINCIPLE

A fourth principle we may include, is **erratic** movement - the tendency to move randomly. If a monster always chases in a predictable way, the player can exploit this when trying to lure it into a trap, or when deciding how to hide behind a wall. With the risk of random movement, the player must consider his moves more carefully, to account for this. Our existing ant exhibits such erratic movement.

Let us consider what this design may give us, for play balance. The three first principles (nearness, visibility and mood) give us some degree of influence over, **which** monsters, and **how many** monsters, chase us. We can move closer to one monster to wake it up, and keep our distance to other monsters, to avoid waking those up. Once we have defeated one monster, we can try to wake the next one. There can be a challenge in waking one or few monsters, and avoiding waking up too many.

18.3.5 REDUCED-DRAW PRINCIPLE

A fifth principle is the opposite perspective on visibility - whether **the player** can see all enemies at any distance. To be fair, we should really only be able to notice monsters as we get closer to them, or have line-of-sight to them. We are not being fair here only out of kindness to computer monsters, but because it will make the gameplay more interesting. The player will be a bit unsure about where the monsters are, and how many there are.

We can apply visibility constraints on the **player** himself in several ways. One way is to only draw monsters when they are close enough. Another way is to only draw them, if they are in line-of-sight. A third way is to only draw clearly the part of the **dungeon** nearest to the player (e.g. a circle radius of tiles nearer than 7). So not just mobs, but the dungeon in general, would only be drawn for the closer part. Combined with this, the distant parts of the dungeon might still be drawn, but just in vague dark blue shades, and only those parts already visited (i.e. parts the player 'remembers').

The nice thing about this principle of reduced drawing, is that it plays nicely into the idea of the player managing how many monsters he has woken and engaged. If the player can always see the entire dungeon and all its inhabitants, it becomes a bit too clear-cut where to go and not to go, to wake up monsters. But if we keep the dungeon a dark and mysterious place, there is more challenge in keeping track of, where we might run into other monsters.

18.4   ORDER OF IMPLEMENTATION

We have sketched out 5 principles, some of which will also interact with each other. We must figure out an implementation plan, an order in which to make them. We can leave the visibility line-of-sight support for last. We will also postpone a bit the idea of only drawing things close to the player, because we will need our current visibility to test and debug our other distance-related features. Then we have the feature of erratic movement. We can include that with any plan we choose, as it is very simple to do. This leaves the mood-feature and the proximity-feature on the table. The simpler part is proximity. The question then is, whether we want to implement proximity by itself, or we instead should go directly to the combination of mood and proximity. Mood just by itself would not be a very interesting feature. Proximity by itself would be a kind of 'hunting sheep', that ignore the player as soon as he moves away. I decide that we go straight for their **combination**, since the complexity is in the mood mechanism.

Our conclusion is, that we start out by implementing mood,

proximity and erratic movement. Later, we'll then tackle the visibility-check, and the reduced-draw mechanism.

18.5 MAKING MOOD & PROXIMITY

To make a mood mechanism, we'll start out with a `Mood` enum, with the states `Asleep` and `Wake`, and outfit our `Mob` class with such a mood, which we will initialize to `Asleep`.

We will then have a `MoodAI`, which will alternate between a `SleepAI` and a `WakeAI`, depending on the mob's mood. The `SleepAI` will check for distance, and roll a die to wake up whenever the player is close. The `WakeAI` will be our 'Bat AI', with a similar risk to fall asleep, whenever we are far from the player. `02model/18MoodEnum.ts`:

```
export enum Mood { Asleep, Wake }
```

Then to `09Mob.ts`, add this

```
  ..

  mood:Mood = Mood.Asleep;

  ..
```

`05ai/18MoodAI.ts` is

```
export class MoodAI implements MobAiIF {
  constructor(public asleep:MobAiIF,
              public wake:MobAiIF) {}
  turn(me:Mob, enemy:Mob, game:GameIF):boolean {
    var ai:MobAiIF;
    switch (me.mood) {
      case Mood.Asleep: ai=this.asleep;break;
      case Mood.Wake:   ai=this.wake;  break;
    }
    return ai!.turn(me,enemy,game);
  }

  static stockMood(speed:number):MobAiIF {
```

```
      return new MoodAI(new SleepAI(),new WakeAI(speed));
    }
}
```

`05ai/18SleepAI.ts` could be this:

```
export class SleepAI implements MobAiIF {
  turn(me:Mob, enemy:Mob, game:GameIF):boolean {
    if (SleepAI.isNear(me,enemy)) {
      me.mood = game.rnd.oneIn(3)
        ? Mood.Wake : Mood.Asleep;
    }
    return true;
  }

  static isNear(me:Mob, enemy:Mob):boolean {
    let dist = me.pos.dist(enemy.pos);
    return dist < 6;
  }
}
```

18.6 ERRATIC MOVEMENT

`18WakeAI.ts` must be similar to our existing AIs. However, bats
are fast, so we let the bat move twice. It will sometimes move
randomly like the ants, and sometimes target-chasing like the
cats. Right now it will always attempt two moves, but maybe we
should let it randomly do **either** one or two moves.

```
export class WakeAI implements MobAiIF {
  constructor(public speed:number){}

  aiDir:MobAiIF = new MobAI2_cat();
  aiRnd:MobAiIF = new MobAI3_ant();
  turn(me:Mob, enemy:Mob, game:GameIF):boolean {
    let r = game.rnd;
    for (let i=0;i<this.speed;++i) {
```

```
      var ai = r.oneIn(2) ? this.aiDir : this.aiRnd;
      ai.turn(me,enemy,game);
    }
    let far = !SleepAI.isNear(me,enemy);
    if (far) {
      me.mood = r.oneIn(3) ? Mood.Asleep : Mood.Wake;
    }
    return true;
  }
}
```

We update `AiSwitcher` to know about bats as a type. This is how our mood AI becomes active in the game, assuming that any bat **mobs** appear.

```
export class AiSwitcher implements MobAiIF {
  //ai1:MobAiIF = new MobAI1_sheep();
  ai2_cat:MobAiIF = new MobAI2_cat();
  ai3_ant:MobAiIF = new MobAI3_ant();
  ai4_bat:MobAiIF = MoodAI.stockMood(2);
  turn(me:Mob, enemy:Mob, game:GameIF):boolean {
    var ai:MobAiIF;
    switch (me.g) {
      default:
      case Glyph.Cat: ai=this.ai2_cat;break;
      case Glyph.Ant: ai=this.ai3_ant;break;
      case Glyph.Bat: ai=this.ai4_bat;break;
    }
    return ai.turn(me,enemy,game);
  }
}
```

To try it out, we must make the builder **add bats**. Clone `Builder2g` to `Builder2h.ts`. We introduce a and b monsters mixed 50-50 on second level, with the method `makeBatsAndAnts()`.

```
//class Builder2h:

..
```

```
addMobsToLevel(map:DMapIF, rnd:Rnd) {
  switch (map.level) {
    case 0: this.makeCatRing(map,rnd); break;
    case 1: default: this.makeBatsAndAnts(map,rnd); break;
  }
}


makeBatsAndAnts(map: DMapIF, rnd: Rnd) {
  this.makeMobs(map,rnd,Glyph.Bat,15);
  this.makeMobs(map,rnd,Glyph.Ant,15);
}


makePly():Mob {
  let ply = new Mob(Glyph.Ply,20,12);
  ply.hp = ply.maxhp = 5;
  return ply;
}
```

As usual, we make an `index18_bats.ts` ..

```
ScreenMaker2_Fixed.Gfirst(new Builder2h() );
```

We can now try to playtest it. With careful play, it is possible to
defeat both bats and ants. Bats require you to be careful - at
worst, they can take four of your hitpoints in a single round. If
we hadn't increased player's hitpoints from 3 to 5, they would be
too dangerous to fight at all.

18.7   VISIBILITY ASPECTS

With the first 3 principles taken care of, we can now focus on the
remaining two mechanisms which concern **visibility** -
line-of-sight and reduced-drawing.

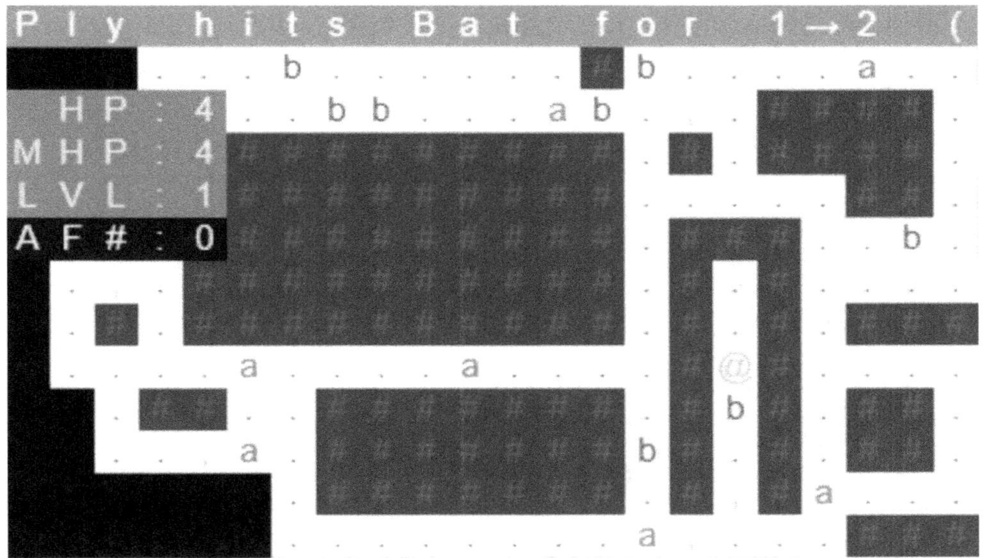

F 18.2: Level 1 is now infested with bats! Who will prevail?

18.7.1 Reduced Drawing

The reduced-drawing mechanism would involve drawing the nearby dungeon parts more clearly than the far parts. Either by not drawing the far parts, or by drawing them indistinctly. Furthermore, we would only draw those distant parts we had earlier visited. We can achieve this with two mechanisms.

We will remember which cells we have seen, by setting a boolean flag `lit` to `true` in them - all cells will start out with a falsy value (either `false` or `undefined`). This provides the **visited** status.

We will determine near and far, by measuring the distance between the player and the given cell. Whenever that distance exceeds our `far` threshold number, that cell is deemed **far**. This provides us the **near-far** status.

Thus to `07MapCell.ts`, we add

```
lit:boolean|undefined;
```

Then to the map-drawing, we make an updated map drawer with these parts (sketch):

```
..
  let  unlit:string = '#001';
  let farlit:string = '#124';
  let farDist:number = 50;
  var fg:string, bg:string;
.. (in x,y loop)
  let dist:number = w.diff(plypos).sqDist();
  let far:boolean = (dist>farDist);
  if (far) {
    bg = unlit;
    fg = (cell.lit ? farlit : unlit);
  } else { // near
    if (!cell.lit) { cell.lit = true; }
..
```

The full version of the updated `drawMap` thus becomes

```
static drawMap18(term:TermIF, map:DMapIF,
                vp:WPoint, plypos:WPoint,
                g:GameIF) {
  let unlit:string='#001';
  let farlit:string = '#124';
  let farDist:number = 50;
  var fg:string, bg:string;
  let tdim = term.dim;
  let t=new TPoint();
  let w=new WPoint();
  for (t.y=0, w.y=vp.y; t.y<tdim.y; ++t.y, ++w.y) {
    for (t.x=0, w.x=vp.x; t.x<tdim.x; ++t.x, ++w.x) {
      let c:MapCell =
        (map.legal(w) ? map.cell(w) : this.outside);
      let dist:number = w.sqDist(plypos);
      let far:boolean = (dist>farDist);
      let g:Glyph = c.glyph();
      let i = GlyphMap1.inf(g);
      if (far) {
        bg=unlit; fg=(c.lit?farlit:unlit);
```

```
    } else { // near
      bg=i.bg; fg=i.fg;
      if (!c.lit) { c.lit = true; }
    }
    term.at(t.x, t.y, i.c, fg, bg);
  }
 }
}
```

18.7.2 PROPER VISIBILITY CRITERIA

We've achieved only-draw-near, with a crude distance-threshold mechanism. There is a more proper and traditional mechanism, commonly referred to as **Field of View**, FoV. It is based on line-of-sight checks in a radius around the player, starting from the player's point of view. There are known solutions to do this, and we may present such mechanisms in a later chapter. For now however, we have demonstrated that a basic similar (but much cruder) effect can be achieved with far simpler means.

Note that such a proper FoV mechanism will behave like a sort of flickering-torchlight visual effect, which may be perceived as either pleasing or annoying, depending on who you ask.

In the meantime, we can add a check for whether monsters can **see** each other. What does 'see' actually mean, here? Well, if there is a brick wall between us, we can't see each other. So we want an unobstructed line of sight between the two creatures. Also just called a **Line of Sight**, or LoS for short.

How can we check that? One approach is to attempt to draw a conceptual 'pixel line' of map tiles between the two creature positions. Then we check whether each of those map tiles is see-through or not. The definition of see-through, is again up to us. We have some leeway or choice there. We will consider a wall or rock tile to **not** be see-through. We will consider empty floor-tiles, floor-tiles with objects, and floor-tiles with monsters on them, to all be see-through. In conclusion, our choice boils down to, that **walls and closed doors are not see-through** (however, you could of course make a game with any weird combination here).

Drawing a (correct) pixel line is not insanely difficult, but it is not trivial either. Luckily for us, a conscientious man called **Bresenham** did the work for us many decades ago, and distilled it into his simple and elegant line drawing algorithm. You can see it below in our `BresIter.ts` file. We have implemented it in a sneaky way, namely as an **iterator**. This allows us to reuse it whenever we need something that involves a line between two points (for example, if we had other spells that would shoot a line of ice at a target, or melt a tunnel through the rock).

We will express our tile see-through check as `opaque()` (i.e. the opposite - **not** see-through). We already have a similar check called `blocked()`. Beware they are not quite the same: A tile may be **blocked**, even though it is still **see-through**. If a cell is blocked by a monster, we still consider it see-through. Similarly, we could have an impassable barred window, which would still be see-through, allowing the player to see whether there is treasure or other items or creatures of interest on the other side.

18.7.3 Line of Sight

Our `LoS` mechanism requires an implementation of Bresenham's line-drawing algorithm. We make `04cmds/18BresIter.ts`:

```
export class BresIter {
  pixels: WPoint[] = [];
  i:number=0; // loop var.
  longest:number=0; shortest:number=0;
  dx1:number=0; dy1:number=0; dx2:number=0; dy2:number=0;
  numerator:number=0;
  x:number=0; y:number=0;
  //The iterator interface - see iterAll2 below as example
```

```typescript
done():boolean  { return !(this.i <= this.longest);  }
iterAll1():void  { // Use this, to fill pixels-vector.
  for (this.i=0; this.i <= this.longest; this.i++) {
    this.next();
  }
}
iterAll2():void {
  var p:WPoint;
  for ( ; !this.done(); ) { p = this.next(); /*Use p*/ }
  do { p = this.next(); } while (!this.done());
  console.log(p);
}
public static BresIter1(p1:WPoint, p2:WPoint):BresIter {
  return new BresIter().init(p1.x, p1.y, p2.x, p2.y);
}
public static BresIter2(x1:number, y1:number,
                        x2:number, y2:number):BresIter {
  return new BresIter().init(x1,y1,x2,y2);
}
init(x1:number,y1:number,x2:number,y2:number):BresIter {
  // Bresenham.
  this.x = x1; this.y = y1;
  let w:number = x2 - this.x;
  let h:number = y2 - this.y;
  this.dx1 = 0; this.dy1 = 0; this.dx2 = 0; this.dy2 = 0;
  if (w < 0) { this.dx1 = -1; }
  else if (w > 0) { this.dx1 = 1; }
  if (h < 0) { this.dy1 = -1; }
  else if (h > 0) { this.dy1 = 1; }
  if (w < 0) { this.dx2 = -1; }
  else if (w > 0) { this.dx2 = 1; }
  this.longest = Math.abs(w);
  this.shortest = Math.abs(h);
  if (!(this.longest > this.shortest)) {
    this.longest = Math.abs(h);
    this.shortest = Math.abs(w);
    if (h < 0) { this.dy2 = -1; }
    else if (h > 0) { this.dy2 = 1; }
```

```
      this.dx2 = 0;
    }
    this.numerator = Math.floor(this.longest*0.5);
    this.i = 0;
    return this;
  }
  public next():WPoint {
    let curPoint:WPoint = new WPoint(this.x, this.y);
    this.pixels.push(curPoint);
    this.numerator += this.shortest;
    if (!(this.numerator < this.longest)) {
      this.numerator -= this.longest;
      this.x += this.dx1; this.y += this.dy1;
    } else {
      this.x += this.dx2; this.y += this.dy2;
    }
    ++this.i;
    return curPoint;
  }
}
```

(Source:

http://tech-algorithm.com/articles/drawing-line-using-bresenham-algorithm/)

The idea with this `BresIter` (Bresenham iterator) is that you supply it with 2 points p1 and p2 that you wish to draw a line between. You can then use it to loop through the series of points lying on the line between the two points.

`iterAll1` and `iterAll2` shows 2-3 ways to do this. They all boil down to calling `next()` and `done()` in a loop - `done()` stops once you reach p2.

One way involves that `BresIter` collects all visited points in the `pixels` vector. This lets you approach the line as a full **set** of points (instead of approaching it like an iteration loop). You can call `iterAll1` if you want to do it this way.

If you instead write your own sequential loop, similar to those in
`iterAll2`, you can achieve things like tracing along the line path,
until a certain condition is met. E.g. that you hit or find a certain
target, or collide with e.g. a wall blocking your shooting path.

We will use the latter approach to test line-of-sight between two
creatures. We make this utility class `04cmds/18CanSee.ts`:

```
export class CanSee {
  public static canSee(a:WPoint, b:WPoint,
    map:DMapIF, onlyEnvir:boolean):boolean
  {
    let i:BresIter  = BresIter.BresIter1(a, b);
    for (; !i.done();) {
      let p:WPoint = i.next();
      let c:MapCell = map.cell(p);
      if (c.opaque()) { return false; }
    }
    return true;
  }
  public static canSee2(a:Mob, b:Mob,
    map:DMapIF, onlyEnvir:boolean):boolean
  {
    return this.canSee(a.pos, b.pos, map, onlyEnvir);
  }
}
```

We can now use this in two places: We can change the AI, so it
only chases enemies it can see. And we can change the map
drawing function, so it only draws monsters that are visible to
the player.

We clone our `SleepAI.ts` to `Sleep2AI.ts`. The updated cloned
`Sleep2AI.ts` will contain this variant of `turn()`:

```
turn(me:Mob, enemy:Mob, game:GameIF):boolean {
  if (!Sleep2AI.isNear(me,enemy)) { return true; }

  let map = <DMapIF> game.curMap();
  let canSee = CanSee.canSee2(me,enemy,map,true);
```

```
    if (!canSee) { return true; }

  me.mood = game.rnd.oneIn(3)
    ? Mood.Wake : Mood.Asleep;
  return true;
}
```

Beware we must update `MoodAI.stockMood()` to use `Sleep2AI` instead of `SleepAI`.

The updated drawing mechanism, which only draws LoS visible monsters, will have its inner loop looking like this:

```
for (t.x=0, w.x=vp.x; t.x<tdim.x; ++t.x, ++w.x) {
  let c:MapCell =
    (map.legal(w) ? map.cell(w) : this.outside);
  let dist:number = w.sqDist(plypos);
  let far:boolean = (dist>farDist);

  let seeMob = !!c.mob && !far
      && CanSee.canSee(c.mob.pos,plypos,map,true);
  let g:Glyph = (seeMob ? c.mob!.g : c.glyph18());

  let i = GlyphMap1.inf(g);
  if (far) {
    bg=unlit; fg=(c.lit?farlit:unlit);
  } else { // near
    bg=i.bg; fg=i.fg;
    if (!c.lit) { c.lit = true; }
  }
  term.at(t.x, t.y, i.c, fg, bg);
}
```

The important bit with `seeMob` has this logic: **If** there is a mob, **and** we are near to that mob, **only** then will we calculate the `canSee` check (because doing so is expensive). In this way, even though the dungeon map might contain 200 monsters, we will only do this calculation for maybe 10 of those monsters which are inside a near-radius circle.

Because we now control drawing of mobs ourselves, we can no longer use the old `glyph()` method. We add a `glyph18()` method to `MapCell`, which only draws environments:

```
glyph18():Glyph { return this.env; }
```

`drawMapPly` must be changed to use our new `drawMap18()`.

```
//this.drawMap0(term,map,vp);
this.drawMap18(term,map,vp,plypos,g);
```

If you try to run `index18_bats.ts` again, you should now only see a nearby circle around the player drawn clearly. And inside that circle, only those mobs which are directly visible to the player (without wall obstacles in between), should be drawn. Outside the near circle, only earlier visited parts should be drawn, faintly blue.

19 Combat Difficulty Dynamics

(In which we consider various parameters of difficulty for monster encounters)

F 19.1: Battles can quickly spiral out of control

19.1   NEITHER TOO EASY NOR TOO HARD

This chapter is a discussion of general principles, intended to get you started thinking about things that affect the difficulty of your game. There is no code here, but the ideas influence the code in other chapters.

Until chapter 18, we always drew the entire accessible map on screen. But if we were actually inside a dungeon, we would only see the parts close to us, not obscured by walls. As this is 'just' a game, we could choose to ignore that. But precisely **because** it is a game, our original approach had drawbacks. Namely, that the player could tell exactly where everything is all the time. Which is unfortunate, because a prime currency in games and game design, is **information**, and **uncertainty** about information. Consider card games. A lot are about exploiting what you know, to deduce more of what you don't yet know ("we have already seen 3 queens played, and I hold the remaining queen in my hand"). Like crime mystery novels, in a way the game is over (or boring), once you have all the information. The game is more interesting when you know **some** parts, but sense there is further information to be had.

A primary challenge we currently set for the player, is to manage how, where and when he engages enemies. We have earlier hinted at balancing the game, such that the player can deal with a single enemy, but will have difficulties when facing more than one. However, encountering a given number of opponents is not a simple static property of the game (though it *could* be, in a different kind of game, where random encounters would be launched into a separate combat screen). Instead, because our game is played tactically in two dimensions, the number of active enemies is governed by a combination of several factors.

One factor is how monsters are **placed** in the dungeon - purely at random, deliberately clustered, or precisely measured, e.g. one monster per room.

One factor is the dungeon **layout** - is it open, or lots of narrow closed-off spaces?

One factor is how fast we can **heal**, in and out of combat. If battles are drawn out, and force us to flee and back up over longer distances, this increases the risk of picking up multiple enemies in a single fight - which might then possibly turn out to be our **last** fight.

Another factor is how far ahead we can scout and **spot enemies**, before we catch **their** attention - can we spot them, before they spot us? Yet a factor is at what distance they will **notice us**. A possible variation is to have monsters that vary in this regard. Moria, as an example, does this so you may watch out for kinds of monsters that are more likely to sense you.

You might think of the design of the **balance** of these effects as like trying to control the rate of a spreading fire, a contagious infection, or a critical event with radioactive material. Either the player can manage to put out the 'combat fires' before they escalate to include neighboring monsters. Or else the fighting will gradually escalate and spiral out of control, dragging ever more monsters into the conflict, until the player is overwhelmed. This way of thinking about the issue highlights how **your design** can fail in both directions: Clearly, once the 'fire' spreads beyond a certain point, the player may have no chance to subdue it. In the opposite direction, if we allow the player too strong control, there will be no risk, and cleaning the dungeon of enemies becomes a predictable boring chore of killing off monsters one by one, with no surprises.

This gives us hints on two aspects: The **distance** at which monsters are woken up and notice us, and the distance ahead we can spot them, are tied together. If we can spot monsters much farther off than where we risk waking them, there is no risk and surprise there. The other aspect is **how fast we heal**. If we are too enthusiastic with fast healing, we risk making it too easy for the player to only fight a single monster at a time.

The distance-related parameters give us some dials to turn, regarding gradually increasing the difficulty as the player progresses further into the game. We might create later harder monsters, which **notice** the player from further away. And we might reduce the **visibility** in the dungeon, on later levels. As an example, Moria starts out with fully lit rooms which light up as soon as you step into them. Later levels will have partially dark or foggy rooms which are more difficult to light fully.

Because of all this, we've chosen to reduce what the game draws, so only nearby parts or parts in view are drawn in full detail.

20 Monster Difficulty Progression

(In which we design a structure for our enemy monsters)

F 20.1: Auto-generated monsters will often resemble 1000 variations of the same thing

20.1   ENEMY PROGRESSION STRUCTURE, WHY

By now we have 3 enemy types - the dangerous **cats**, the harmless **ants**, and the competent and interesting **bats**. It still makes for a rather limited and finite game. Once the player has experimented a bit and figured out to which degree he can handle the enemies, there are no further hidden depths, evolution, development or surprises hidden there.

Building a game is an attempt to tell a story that will entertain and distract for some time, and hopefully not bore too soon. So we look for tools and tricks to keep the game interesting for longer. It could be by varying what the **player** can do, what his **enemies** can do, **what** he encounters, what he can **interact** with, or which **rules** are active.

One way is to have a chain - a **progression** - of ever more difficult enemies. The player can then strive for improvements to his technique, skill and toolset, with which he might defeat these progressively stronger enemies. So we will embark on equipping our game with such a chain of gradually more gruesome foes.

20.2   PLAN FOR THE PROGRESSION STRUCTURE

We will introduce enemies a,b,c,d,e,f,g etc., with the higher letters being more dangerous. Our initial effort here is quite generic: For each higher level, we will just give a monster 5 more hit points, and let them hit for 1 more point of damage. If we were to stop there, our "difficult" monsters would be rather boring and bland, and hardly worth the effort. But this is just meant to form a baseline. Eventually, we will also give them different behaviours and abilities, so they truly will feel different.

20.3 THE MONSTER PROGRESSION STRUCTURE

We'll set up some glyphs to represent our monsters. In
`07Glyph.ts`, insert the following sequence just after `Cat`:

```
Cat,       Dog,     Eye,        Frog,
Golem,     Harpy,   Imp,        Jackal,
Kobold,    Lich,    Mold,       Naga,
Orc,       Pirate,  Quasit,     Rat,
Snake,     Troll,   UmberHulk,  Vampire,
Worm,      Xorn,    Yeti,       Zombie,
```

To match this, insert these calls in `GlyphInf1.initGlyphs`, again
after the call for `Cat`:

```
add(bg,       '#bf8',      'c',Glyph.Cat);
add(bg,       '#bf8',      'd',Glyph.Dog);
..  (similar lines for all the mob types.)
add(bg,       '#bf8',      'y',Glyph.Yeti);
add(bg,       '#bf8',      'z',Glyph.Zombie);
```

(You may add similar for `GlyphInf0`, but you don't have to, unless
you plan to activate the 'older' graphics.)

20.4 BUILDING THE PROGRESSION MONSTERS

We will need a cloned builder `20Builder2i.ts` from
`18Builder2h.ts`, which will add mobs to levels in a new way, with
a method aptly named `addMapLevel_Mob`. For this, we change
`addMobsToLevel` and `makeMobs` (you can delete the code for
`makeAnts` and `makeBatsAndAnts`, which is then no longer used):

```
addMobsToLevel(map:DMapIF, rnd:Rnd) {
  switch (map.level) {
    case 0: this.makeCatRing(map,rnd); break;
    default:this.makeMobs(map,rnd,15); break;
  } // (now using makeMobs)
}
```

```
makeMobs(map:DMapIF, rnd:Rnd, rate:number) {
  let dim = map.dim;
  let p = new WPoint();
  for (p.y=1;p.y<dim.y-1;++p.y) {
    for (p.x=1;p.x<dim.x-1;++p.x) {
      if (!rnd.oneIn(rate)) { continue; }
      if (map.blocked(p)) { continue; }

      this.addMapLevel_Mob(p,map,rnd);
    } // (now using addMapLevel_Mob)
  }
}
```

We can make `addMapLevel_Mob` like this:

```
addMapLevel_Mob(pos:WPoint, map:DMapIF, rnd:Rnd) {
    this.addLevelMob(pos,map,rnd,map.level);
}
addLevelMob(p:WPoint, map:DMapIF,
            rnd:Rnd, baseLevel:number):Mob {
  let level = rnd.spiceUpLevel(baseLevel);
  if (level < 1) { level = 1; }
  // otherwise 0 would cause @..
  let g = this.level2glyph(level);
  return this.addNPC(g, p.x,p.y, map, level);
}
level2glyph(L:number):Glyph {
  let glyph_ix:number = L + Glyph.Ant - 1;
  let g = GlyphMap1.ix2glyph(glyph_ix);
  return g;
}
```

We must account for those `spiceUpLevel` and `ix2glyph` we used
here. We will add the `spiceUpLevel` method to class `Rnd` in
`07Rnd.ts`. As its name suggests, its purpose is to sometimes pick
levels a little higher:

```
spiceUpLevel(L: number):number {
  if (this.oneIn(3)) {
    let dir = this.oneIn(3) ? 1: -1;
```

```
    L = this.spice(L+dir, dir);
    if (L < 0) { L = 0; }
  } // (There are no negative levels.)
  return L;
}
spice(L: number, dir:number):number {
  return this.oneIn(4) ? this.spice(L+dir, dir) : L;
}
```

And `GlyphMap1` in `16GlyphInf1.ts` must get `ix2glyph`. It allows us to pick `Glyph` enums by their raw number index (and attempts to protect us if we trigger a bug by being too clever that way, i.e. by using a wrong number):

```
static max:number = Object.keys(Glyph).length / 2;
static ix2glyph(ix:number):Glyph {
  if (ix<0) { throw `ix ${ix} is less than 0!`; }
  if (ix>=this.max) { throw `ix ${ix} >= ${this.max}!`; }
  let g:Glyph = <Glyph> ix;
  return g;
}
```

20.5   SCALING THE MONSTER QUALITIES

We will adjust the monsters, so they get their hit points and weapon damage based on their level. We will modify `addNPC` in `20Builder2i.ts` to consider the level of the mob. It used to look like this:

```
addNPC(g:Glyph, x:number, y:number,
       map:DMapIF, level:number) {
  let mob = new Mob(g,x,y);
  map.addNPC(mob);
  return mob;
}
```

It must now be changed to call `setLevelStats()`, which we'll account for in a bit:

```
addNPC(g:Glyph, x:number, y:number,
       map:DMapIF, level:number) {
  let mob = new Mob(g,x,y);
  this.setLevelStats(mob,level); // ch20
  map.addNPC(mob);
  return mob;
}
```

We will give them hit points as 5 times their level, and monsters
will hit for an **average** of `level` damage. Implementing
setLevelStats in the following way takes care of their hit points:

```
setLevelStats(mob:Mob, mobLevel:number) {
    mob.level = mobLevel;
    mob.maxhp = mob.level * 5;
    mob.hp = mob.maxhp;
}
```

For this to work, we must add the level field to Mob:

```
    level:number = 0;
```

We must adjust HitCmd to apply the monster level in the damage
calculation:

```
  exc():boolean {
    let me = this.me.name, him = this.him.name;
    let rnd = this.g.rnd;
    let dmg:number = this.calcDmg(rnd, this.me);
  ..
  calcDmg(rnd:Rnd, me:Mob): number {
    let level = me.level;
    let lim = level+1;
    if (me.isPly) { lim = 3; }
    let dmg = rnd.rndC(0,lim);
    return dmg;
  }
```

20.6 AN UPDATED AI

We will also update our AI a bit. We want a 'standard monster AI' to use for random mobs, which will be a mixture of our newest 'bat mood features', and our earlier AI features.
In particular, it should not move as fast as the bat did. We make a new 20AISwitcher2.ts, which borrows the bat AI, but reduces its speed to 1 instead of 2.

```
export class AiSwitcher2 implements MobAiIF {
  constructor(public ai5_std:MobAiIF) {}
  ai2_cat:MobAiIF = new MobAI2_cat();
  ai3_ant:MobAiIF = new MobAI3_ant();
  ai4_bat:MobAiIF = MoodAI.stockMood(2);
  turn(me:Mob, enemy:Mob, game:GameIF):boolean {
    var ai:MobAiIF;
    switch (me.g) {
      case Glyph.Ant: ai=this.ai3_ant;break;
      case Glyph.Bat: ai=this.ai4_bat;break;
      case Glyph.Cat: ai=this.ai2_cat;break;
      default:        ai=this.ai5_std;break;
    }
    return ai.turn(me,enemy,game);
  }
}
```

Of course, 20Builder2i.makeAI() must return this new AiSwitcher2. (The 1 here is the slower speed.)

```
makeAI():MobAiIF|null {
  return new AiSwitcher2(MoodAI.stockMood(1));
}
```

We will also update makeMap. It used to prefer the TestMap, we will now make it prefer MapGen1:

```
makeMap(rnd:Rnd, level:number):DMapIF {
  let dim = WPoint.StockDims;
  var map:DMapIF;
  switch (level) {
```

```
    default: // (used to be testMap, now it's MapGen1.)
    case 1:  map = MapGen1.test(); break;
    case 0:  map = TestMap.test(dim, rnd, level); break;
  }
  return map;
}
```

20.7   Testing the Progression Monsters

To try it out and test it, we'll increase the player's hit points to 15:

```
makePly():Mob {
  let ply = new Mob(Glyph.Ply,20,12);
  ply.hp=ply.maxhp=15;
  return ply;
}
```

Then we can run the game and try to see how deep we can go, before the monster difficulty is too high for our 'base player'. To run, we'll add index20_prog.ts:

```
ScreenMaker2_Fixed.Gfirst( new Builder2i() );
```

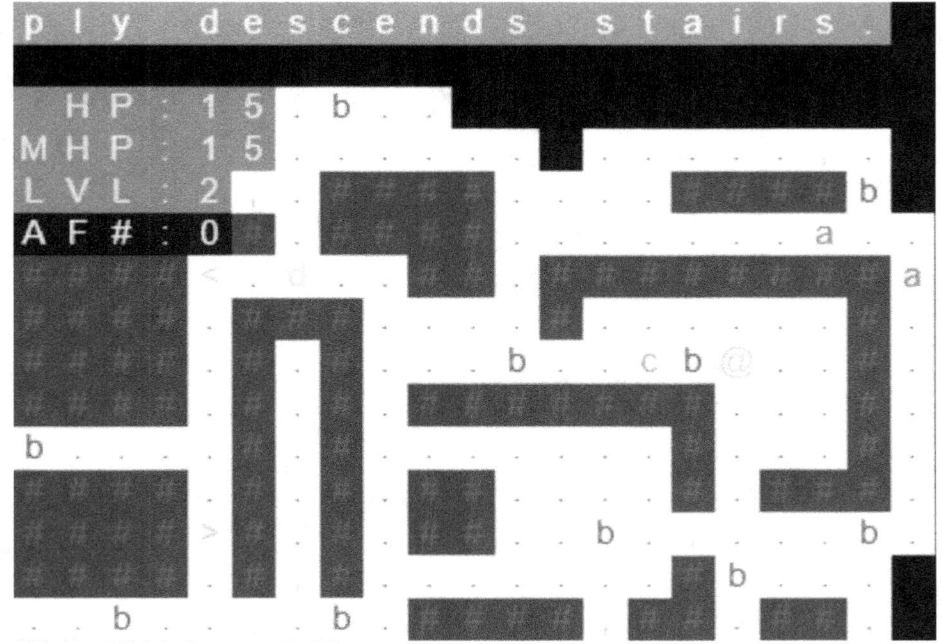

F 20.2: The whole alphabet is waiting for him in there, I promise

F 20.3: The stuff you find in dungeons, was dropped by less lucky adventurers, killed before you arrived

21 ITEMS IN THE DUNGEON

(In which we fill our dungeon with random items)

F 21.1: If they die, you can have their stuff

21.1   PLAN FOR ITEMS SUPPORT

With our progression of dangerous monsters, we have sort of left our player behind: The monsters grow ever stronger, but there is no way the **player** can grow stronger to keep up. We will thus look at ways to increase the player's power.

One approach we will take, is to offer *items* the player can apply. We will scatter sundry items around the dungeon, for the player to find, pick up, and use. Some items may be useless, some may be dangerous, and some might be useful in obvious or less obvious ways. Our first items will be weapons, to hit harder, and armour, to reduce the damage we take.

21.2   HOLDING ITEMS IN THE MODEL

What properties do we need to know about an item? As we are going to show them in the dungeon, we will need a **glyph**.

We intend to have items of different strength, so we will also note a **dungeon level** for each item, to decide its general power range.

In the near future, we intend to **wear** some of the items. To that end, we will mark our items with a **slot** enum, which says how you can wear the item. `02model/21Slot.ts` is:

```
export enum Slot {
  NotWorn   = 0, MainHand = 1,  OffHand   = 2, BothHands= 3,
  Head      = 4, Hands    = 5,  Back      = 6, Legs     = 7,
  Feet      = 8, Last     = 9
}
```

With those three properties, the `Obj` class for our game-model items will thus start out like this: `02model/21Obj.ts`

```
export class Obj {
  level:number=0;
  constructor(public g:Glyph, public slot:Slot) {}
}
```

We will add it to `07MapCell.ts`, like this: (changed parts)

```
obj: Obj|undefined;

  glyph21(): Glyph {
    return this.obj ? this.obj.g : this.env;
  }
```

This change to `glyph21()` makes it so any objects present are included when drawing the dungeon. (We must of course update `drawMap` to use `glyph21`).

We extend `DMap` and `DMapIF` with these methods, so we that may add objects:

```
.. (DMap)
addObj(o:Obj, p:WPoint) { this.cell(p).obj = o; }
.. (DMapIF)
addObj(o:Obj, p:WPoint):void;
```

This constitutes a basic tooling to handle objects. But we don't **have** any objects in the game yet.

21.3 Defining the Items

Our builders will have to scatter items throughout our dungeon-maps somehow. This raises questions of how to manage the properties of items. One approach might be to instantiate them directly as instances, sort of 'hard-coding' them. Another approach might involve holding a table of item descriptions and properties, to consult either when spawning objects, or when accessing the properties of an item ("It's called a longsword, it hits for 4 damage and weighs 2 pounds"). Our approach will mimic this latter recipe-approach. This way, we may consult those item "recipes" repeatedly, as we generate items to distribute around the dungeon.

We need to add some glyphs for items, e.g. these: (`Glyph`, `GlyphInf`)

```
    Door_Closed,
    Dagger,
    Shield,
    Cap,
    Gloves,
    Cape,
    Leggings,
    Boots
}
.. // (initGlyphs in 16GlyphInf1.ts)
    add(bg,      'blue',      '-',Glyph.Dagger);
    add(bg,      'red',       '(',Glyph.Shield);
    add(bg,      'purple',    '(',Glyph.Cap);
    add(bg,      'lime',      '(',Glyph.Gloves);
    add(bg,      'blue',      '(',Glyph.Cape);
    add(bg,      'cyan',      '(',Glyph.Leggings);
    add(bg,      'pink',      '(',Glyph.Boots);
```

For the recipes, we could do this: (`03build/21ObjTypes.ts`)

```
export interface ObjTypeIF {
  g:Glyph;
  s:Slot;
}


export class ObjTypes {
  static objtypes:ObjTypeIF[] = [
  {g: Glyph.Dagger,   s:Slot.MainHand},
  {g: Glyph.Shield,   s:Slot.OffHand },
  {g: Glyph.Cap,      s:Slot.Head },
  {g: Glyph.Gloves,   s:Slot.Hands},
  {g: Glyph.Cape,     s:Slot.Back },
```

```
    {g: Glyph.Leggings,s:Slot.Legs },
    {g: Glyph.Boots,    s:Slot.Feet }
    ]
}
```

At this early stage, `ObjTypeIF` is an extremely parsimonious effort.
It boils down to mentioning which of our glyphs represent items
- e.g. the dagger item and the shield item, and which slot they
relate to. However, we may eventually extend `ObjTypeIF` with
further properties, and by then it will be more useful, allowing us
to detail many facets of our items and what they can be used for.

To use `ObjTypes` to get stuff into our builder, we will extend it
with a few helpers. We would like it to have the following
methods:

- it should be able to add a random item to a given map, if
  we provide it with the point it should place it at - we call
  this method `addRndObjForLevel()`. This is the method our
  builder will use to place items. Our map already knows
  how to add-object-to-map, so we can implement
  `addRndObjForLevel`, if we make a function that can **create**
  random items (not *place* them).
- `rndLevelObj()` is that create-function: It will create a
  random item, for a given level - that is, of a given level
  strength. It will do three things. First, it will pick a random
  object-type-index. Second, it will look up the object
  template for that index. Lastly, it will create the actual
  object instance, based on that template.
- we use `getTmpl()` to look up the template for an index. In
  theory, we could just index the `objtypes` array directly, but
  we like to protect such a dynamic random lookup, to catch
  if we by accident attempt to look up a non-existing
  template, e.g. index -1
- `makeTemplateObj()` is the separate helper we use to create
  the templated object instance. It does one extra little thing:

> It will 'spice up' the suggested level, with a small chance to get higher levels.
>
> - lastly, we also make addObjTypeToMap(), which adds **specific kinds** of objects, instead of random items.

Thus, we extend ObjTypes with these 6 helpers:

```
static ixForGlyph(g:Glyph):number {
  return this.objtypes.findIndex(t => t.g == g);
}
// PLACES objects:
static addObjTypeToMap(p:WPoint, map:DMapIF, rnd:Rnd,
                       objType:Glyph, level:number):Obj
{
  let ix = this.ixForGlyph(objType);
  let tmpl:ObjTypeIF = ObjTypes.getTmpl(ix);
  let obj = this.makeTemplateObj(level,rnd,tmpl);
  map.addObj(obj,p);
  return obj;
}
static addRndObjForLevel(p:WPoint, map:DMapIF,
                         rnd:Rnd, level:number):Obj
{
  let obj = this.rndLevelObj(level,rnd);
  map.addObj(obj,p);
  return obj;
}
// MAKES objects:
static rndLevelObj(level:number, r:Rnd):Obj {
  let ix = r.rnd(ObjTypes.objtypes.length);
  let tmpl:ObjTypeIF = ObjTypes.getTmpl(ix);
  return this.makeTemplateObj(level,r,tmpl);
}
static makeTemplateObj(level:number, rnd:Rnd,
                       tmpl:ObjTypeIF):Obj {
  let objLevel = rnd.spiceUpLevel(level);
  let obj = new Obj(tmpl.g, tmpl.s);
  obj.level = objLevel;
  return obj;
```

```
    }
    static getTmpl(ix:number):ObjTypeIF {
      let len = ObjTypes.objtypes.length;
        if (ix < 0 || ix >= len) {
          throw `bad ix:${ix}, not ${len}`;
        }
        return ObjTypes.objtypes[ix];
    }
```

We clone `20Builder2i.ts` into `21Builder2j.ts`. We can then
extend our builder with this:

```
addItems(map: DMapIF, rnd:Rnd) {
  for (let p=new WPoint(); p.y<map.dim.y;++p.y) {
    for (p.x=0;p.x<map.dim.x; ++p.x) {
      if (map.blocked(p)){ continue; }
      if (rnd.oneIn(40)) {
        ObjTypes.addRndObjForLevel(
          p,map,rnd,map.level
        );
      }
    }
  }
}
```

..Which we will call in `makeLevel`, just before `addMobsToLevel`:

```
makeLevel(rnd:Rnd, level:number):DMapIF {
  let map = this.makeMap(rnd, level);
  this.addLevelStairs(map,level,rnd);
  this.addItems(map,rnd); // ch21
  this.addMobsToLevel(map,rnd);
  return map;
}
```

From here on, it's possible to run our items-attempt with
`index21_items.ts` as

```
ScreenMaker2_Fixed.Gfirst( new Builder2j() );
```

21.4　SENSING THE ITEMS

To aid the feeling that the objects are present in the dungeon, we'll add a describing flash message to our game screen. Whenever our player steps over an item, we will display a temporary message like `shield is here`.

First, we extend our `Obj` class to have a description property:

```
desc():string {
  let label = this.name();
  return `${label}${this.level}`;
}
name():string { return Glyph[this.g]; }
```

To implement the flash message mechanism, we modify `09MoveCmd.ts` to call `flashIfItem()` whenever it moves the **player**:

```
exc():boolean {
  let map = <DMapIF> this.game.curMap();
  let legal = !map.blocked(this.np);
  if (legal) {
    map.moveMob(this.mob, this.np);
    if (this.mob.isPly) {
      this.dealWithStairs(map);
      this.flashIfItem();
    }
  }
  return legal;
}
```

`flashIfItem` checks whether the new tile contains an object. If so, we emit the flash message:

```
flashIfItem() {
  let map:DMapIF = <DMapIF> this.g.curMap();
  let np = this.g.ply.pos;

  let o:Obj|undefined = map.cell(np).obj;
```

```
if (o) {
  let msg = `${o.desc()} here.`;
  this.g.flash(msg);
}
}
```

21.5 GAINING LOOT WHEN KILLING AN ENEMY

Whenever we defeat a monster, there could be a chance it would leave some loot behind. Thus, in `mobDies()` in `11HealthAdj.ts`, we could add these bits:

```
.. // at end of mobDies():
  this.mightDropLoot(m, map, game);
}
// and implement it with this:
static mightDropLoot(m:Mob,map:DMapIF,game:GameIF) {
  if (game.rnd.oneIn(2)) { return; }
  this.dropLoot(m.pos,map,game, m.level);
}
static dropLoot(pos:WPoint, map:DMapIF,
                game:GameIF, level:number
) {
  let lootCell = map.cell(pos);
  let canDrop = (lootCell.env == Glyph.Floor);
  var s:string;
  if (!canDrop) {
    s = `Something falls into an inaccessible place.`;
  } else {
    let rnd = game.rnd;
    let objLevel = level+1;
    let obj = ObjTypes.addRndObjForLevel(
      pos,map,rnd,objLevel
    );
    s = `Something rolls on the floor: ${obj.desc()}`;
  }
  game.msg(s);
```

```
}
```

Now, half the time we win in combat, some loot shows up.

This completes our efforts in this chapter. We have realized a kind of 'museum', where you can walk around and **observe** items, but you are not allowed to **interact** with them. Which may be reasonable for now, given that the items don't really have any qualities yet.

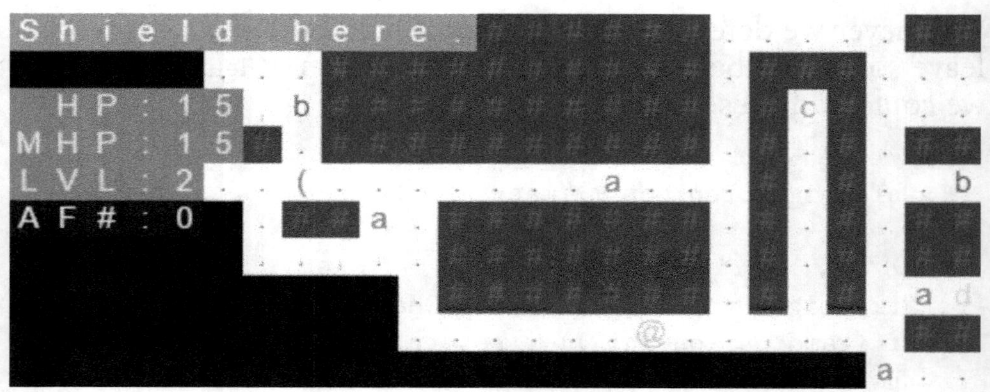

F 21.2: Where there is one thing, there are bound to be more

22   Player Bag Inventory

(In which we let the player interact with the items)

F 22.1: An early design for the Fit-All, favorite backpack of professional dungeoneers, known to hold a polearm with ease

22.1   Somewhere to Put Your Stuff

With the previous chapter we now have items scattered around our dungeon, and we can walk around and **observe** them, like a kind of perverse museum. We would like the player to be able to **interact** with the items somehow. There are many shapes such interaction could have in a game.

- A most **extreme** variant would be that an item is **used** up as soon as the player steps on it.

- Slightly less extreme, the player could have the **choice** of using an item whenever he stands on top of it (it can still only be used once).

- In a more flexible direction, we could allow the player to **hold** a single item and carry it around, for once-use or moving.

- In the typical **flexible** variant we are allowed to carry **multiple** items, and the carried items go in an intermediate item store before we possibly later equip them or once-use them. Such a player **bag** mechanism is traditionally called an **inventory**.

22.2   Plan

Here we will go for that last approach, the inventory model. We would like the player to be able to **pick up** items, **use** items, **view** his current list of items, and **drop** items again.

In our approach we will apply a pickup-item command and a drop-item command. We will extend our model with a player *bag* container, which the pickup and drop commands will operate on. Then we'll build an inventory screen that shows a list of currently carried items. From this screen we can choose which items to drop or use.

In a later chapter, we'll extend our game model with another container for **equipped** parts. It will function akin to the inventory bag, but it applies *slots*, which represents 'pegs' that you can equip stuff on, e.g. your main weapon hand, your head, neck or feet. We will use it to track which kind of weapon you are wielding, and what kind of armor you are wearing, to determine how much damage your attacks will do, and how much attacks against you are reduced by your worn armor.

22.3 IMPLEMENTATION

`02model/22Bag.ts` looks like this:

```
export class Bag {
    objs:Obj[] = [];
    len():number{return this.objs.length;}
    add(o:Obj){this.objs.push(o);}
    removeIx(ix:number) {
      this.objs.splice(ix,1);
    }
}
```

We will add it to `02model/GameIF.ts` :

```
export interface GameIF {
  ..

  bag:Bag|undefined;

  ..
```

.. and we then clone `17GameModel3.ts` into `02model/22GameModel4Bag.ts`:

```
  ..

export class Game4 implements GameIF {

  ..
```

```
  bag:Bag = new Bag();
  ..
```

(you can touch up Game3, Game2 etc. with this:)

```
  bag:Bag|undefined;
```

We will need a way for the player to pick up an item from the
dungeon floor. This entails removing it from the map cell, and
transferring it to his bag. We make `04cmds/22PickupCmd.ts`:

```
export class PickupCmd extends CmdBase {
  constructor(g:GameIF) { super(g.ply,g); }
    exc():boolean {
    let game = this.game;
    let map = <DMapIF> game.curMap();
    let ply = game.ply;
    let bag = <Bag>game.bag;
    let c = map.cell(ply.pos);
    let obj = c.obj;
    if (!obj) {
      game.flash('Nothing to get here.');
      return false;
    }
    c.obj = undefined; // Remove from floor.
    bag.add(obj); // Put into bag instead.
    let msg = `ply gets ${obj.desc()}. `;
    game.flash(msg);
    return true;
  }
}
```

To include the command, we add this case to `parseKeyCmd` in
`09ParsePly.ts`:

```
  ..
    case 'g':
      if (this.game.bag) {
        return new PickupCmd(this.game);
      }
      break;
```

To include our updated game model, `Game4` with the bag, we must clone our earlier builder `21builderj.ts`. We will also add a few helpers to it, to allow us to quickly test the inventory features. We will stuff a few items directly into the player bag when the game launches - `addItemToPlayerBag()`. This will allow us to immediately try out *viewing* the inventory, and to test dropping of items. We will also force a few items to spawn right next to the player, to aid in testing pickup - `addItemNextToPlayer()`.

`03build/22Builder2k.ts`:

```
  makeGame():GameIF {
    let rnd = new Rnd(42);
    let ply = this.makePly();
    let game = new Game4(rnd, ply, this);
    game.dung.level = 1;
    this.enterFirstLevel(game);
    game.ai = this.makeAI();
    this.initLevel_One(game);//ch22.
    return game;
  }

  initLevel_One(g: GameIF) {
    let L1 = g.dung.getLevel(1,g);
    this.addItemToPlayerBag( <Bag> g.bag);
    this.addItemNextToPlayer(g.ply,L1);
  }
  addItemNextToPlayer(ply: Mob, map: DMapIF) {
    let a = ply.pos;
    let p = new WPoint(a.x+1,a.y);
    map.addObj(new Obj(Glyph.Shield, Slot.OffHand), p);
    map.cell(p).env = Glyph.Floor;

    p = new WPoint(a.x,a.y+1);
    map.addObj(new Obj(Glyph.Shield, Slot.OffHand), p);
    map.cell(p).env = Glyph.Floor;
  }
```

```
addItemToPlayerBag(bag: Bag) {
  bag?.add(new Obj(Glyph.Dagger, Slot.MainHand) );
}
```

To try it out, we need a runner - `index22_inv.ts`:

```
ScreenMaker2_Fixed.Gfirst( new Builder2k() );
```

If you now run `index22_inv.ts`, you can try pressing 'G' either
when standing on an item, or when **not** standing on any item.
Hooray! We can now pick up items! Or .. at least make them
disappear. If only we could somehow **see** what items we are
carrying..?

22.4   LOOKING AT OUR BAG INVENTORY

To look at our inventory, we'll make an inventory menu screen.
(`06screen/22InvScreen.ts`)

```
export class InvScreen extends BaseScreen {
  name:string = 'inv';
  bag:Bag;
  constructor(game:GameIF, maker:MakerIF) {
    super(game,maker);
    this.bag = <Bag> game.bag;
  }
  pos2char(pos:number) {
    return String.fromCharCode(65+pos);
  }
  char2pos(c:string) {
    let pos=c.charCodeAt(0)-'a'.charCodeAt(0);
    if (pos<0 || pos>=this.bag.len()) {
        pos = -1;
    }
    return pos;
  }
```

```
draw(term:TermIF) {
  term.txt(0,0,'You carry','yellow','black');
  let pos=0;
  for (var o of this.bag.objs) {
    let c = this.pos2char(pos);
    term.txt(0,1+pos++, `${c} ${o.desc()}`,
             'yellow', 'black');
  }
}
onKey(e:JQuery.KeyDownEvent,
      stack:Stack):boolean
{
  let pos = this.char2pos(e.key);
  if (pos >= 0) {
    this.itemMenu(pos, stack);
  } else {
    stack.pop();
  }
  return true;
}
itemMenu(pos:number, stack:Stack) {
  //let item:Obj = this.bag.objs[pos];
  // (Will soon do something..)
}
}
```

To let the player activate the inventory screen by pressing 'I', we
add this to `parseKeyCmd` in `09ParsePly.ts`:

```
case 'i':
  if (this.game.bag) {
    s = new InvScreen(this.game,this.maker);
  }
  break;
```

With this, you can execute the runner again, to pick up some
items and press I to **look** at your inventory: (Figure 22.2)

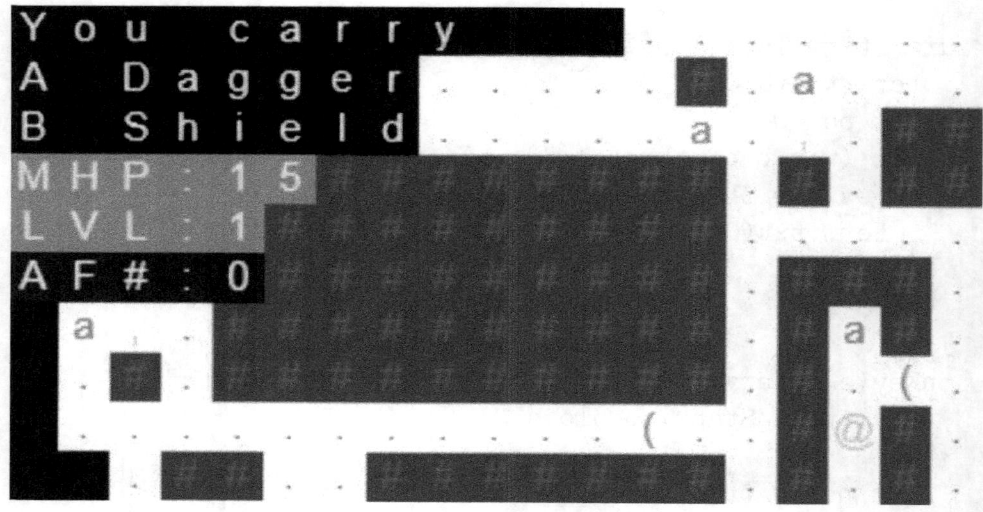

F 22.2: Behold all the two items we are carrying

22.5 DROPPING STUFF AGAIN

We must also let the player **drop** items. 04cmds/22DropCmd.ts
would be:

```
export class DropCmd extends CmdBase {
  constructor(public obj:Obj, public ix:number,
              g:GameIF) { super(g.ply,g); }
  exc(): boolean {
    let game = this.g;
    let map = <DMapIF>game.curMap();
    let ply = game.ply;
    let c = map.cell(ply.pos);
    if (c.hasObj()) {
      game.flash('No room to drop here.');
      return false;
    }
    c.obj = this.obj;
    let bag = <Bag>game.bag;
    bag.removeIx(this.ix);
    game.msg(`You drop ${c.obj.name}.`);
    return true;
```

```
    }
}
```

But we need somewhere to activate that drop-command. We
could just let it happen, whenever you select an item on the
inventory screen. But we have plans to do **more** with items than
just always drop them. So we need a way to specify **what** we
want to do with an item.

One approach could be to display the "what" choices when the
player picks an item, i.e. "what do you want to **do** with item X?".
We will call this choice-menu the `ItemScreen`. At first, it will only
have the option "drop", and of course "cancel" with e.g. the
`Escape` key.

So we update `InvScreen.itemMenu()` to call the `ItemScreen` like
this:

```
itemMenu(pos: number, stack: Stack) {
  let item:Obj = this.bag.objs[pos];
  stack.pop();
  stack.push(
    new ItemScreen(item,pos,this.game,this.make)
  );
}
```

and the `ItemScreen` will be this: (06screen/22ItemScreen.ts)

```
export class ItemScreen extends BaseScreen {
  name:string = 'item';
  constructor(public obj:Obj, public ix:number,
              game:GameIF, maker:MakerIF) {
    super(game,maker);
  }

  draw(term:TermIF) {
    // Remove prev menu:
    super.draw(term);
    let fg = 'lightblue', bg='#025';
```

```typescript
    let y=1;
    term.txt(0,y++,
      `Do what with ${this.obj.desc()} ?`,
        fg,bg);
    term.txt(0,y++,'u use',    fg,bg);
    term.txt(0,y++,'d drop',   fg,bg);
    term.txt(0,y++,'t throw',  fg,bg);
    term.txt(0,y++,'w wear',   fg,bg);
    DrawMap.renderMsg(term, this.game);
}


onKey(e:JQuery.KeyDownEvent,
      s:Stack):boolean
{
  console.log('key:', e.key);
  switch (e.key) {
    case 'd': this.dropItem(s); break;
    default: s.pop(); break;
  }
  return true;
}


dropItem(ss:Stack) {
  // This completes ply's turn,
  // so execute command and return.
  if (this.dropBagItem()) {
      this.pop_And_RunNPCLoop(ss);
  } // NPCs must do their turns now.
}


dropBagItem():boolean {
  let game = this.game;
  let map = <DMapIF> game.curMap();
  let ply = game.ply;
  let c = map.cell(ply.pos);
  if (c.hasObj()) {
    game.flash('No room to drop here.');
    return false;
```

```
    }
    c.obj = this.obj;
    let bag = <Bag> game.bag;
    bag.removeIx(this.ix);
    game.msg(`Ply drops ${c.obj.name()}. `);
    return true;
  }
}
```

To make that `ItemScreen` work, we must account for
`pop_And_RunNPCLoop()`. What is its purpose? It completes a turn!
Because the player's drop-command has now been completed
with `dropBagItem()`, we are done with the `ItemScreen`, which
must thus be popped off. And because the player's turn is done,
it is also time to run the `NPCLoop()`.

This is a generally useful function, so we will add it to
`BaseScreen`. There is no special magic in it - it is just `NPCLoop` in
combination with popping a completed sub-screen. But naming
it helps us remember to do the right combination.

So, to `06screen/09BaseScreen.ts`, add

```
pop_And_RunNPCLoop(s:Stack) {
  s.pop();
  this.npcTurns(s);
}
```

With this, we can now walk around, pick up stuff, and drop it
again. In other words, we have promoted ourselves from
museum guest to janitor..

F 22.3: You can't have everything. Where would you put it?

23 Equipping Items on Player

(In which we add a use for our items)

F 23.1: Our hero, clad in the gear his predecessors were slain in, little good it did them

23.1 SOME USE FOR ITEMS

In the previous chapter, we managed to get the player's grubby hands on the dungeon items. As a result the player is now a sort of janitor that can run around and organize and rearrange the items found in the dungeon. But we haven't really given him any way to **use** the items. (In theory, we **could** let him use the items this way - just by moving and dropping the items - if the items functioned as **traps** that would ensnare or damage the monsters, **lures** and **bait** that would attract the monsters, **obstacles** that would prohibit the monsters from passing, or **scarecrows** that would repel the monsters.)

23.2 INTENT & MOTIVATION

Now, we want the player to **equip** items. To **wield** weapons, and to **wear** armour. To achieve this, we will introduce a container akin to his bag, but organised differently. It will contain peg **slots** that indicate the location of worn items (e.g. hands, legs, feet, head). It will be the `Worn` map - a map of which items are currently worn. The slots are formed by the `Slot` enumeration we introduced earlier with the `Obj` class.

(Note: Maps, in computer lingo, are not spatial geographical maps. Instead, they are associations between a list of keys and a list of values those keys **map** to. For example mapping our **equipment slots** - arms, head, feet - to **worn items** - gloves, helm, boots.)

Whenever the player puts on or takes off a wearable item, it will be transferred between his bag and this equipment map. During combat, our code can then inspect the `Worn` map, to see with how much power his weapon will hit, or how effective his armour will be in reducing the damage he takes.

23.3 PLAN FOR IMPLEMENTING EQUIPMENT

To implement this, we must explain the worn `Slot` enum, and introduce the `Worn` map container in the game model.

We must have commands to **equip** an item and to **unequip** an item.

We must integrate the **equip** command with the bag inventory, and we will need a UI screen for the worn equipment, partly to support **unequipping**, partly to **show** the player what he is wearing at a given time.

We must adjust the `HitCmd` damage mechanisms, to involve **weapon damage** from any wielded weapon, and **damage reduction** by any worn armour.

23.4 WORN MODEL

This is the `Slot` enum earlier from chapter 21. We already used it there to tag our objects, to indicate whether and how they could be worn. We will now use this enum as peg keys in the `Worn` map. `03build/21Slot.ts`:

```
export enum Slot {
  NotWorn   = 0, MainHand = 1, OffHand  = 2, BothHands= 3,
  Head      = 4, Hands    = 5, Back     = 6, Legs     = 7,
  Feet      = 8, Last     = 9
}
```

You might notice something peculiar is going on with `BothHands` and `MainHand`, more on that later. `NotWorn` of course is for other kinds of items not supposed to be worn.

Then we need a class for the `Worn` map container model itself. `02model/23Worn.ts`:

```typescript
export class Worn {
  _objs: Map<Slot, Obj> = new Map();
  add(o:Obj) {
    this.legalObj(o);
    this._objs.set(o.slot, o);
  }
  remove(slot:Slot) {
    this.legalSlot(slot);
    this._objs.delete(slot);
  }
  has(slot:Slot):boolean {
    return this._objs.has(slot);
  }
  len():number{
    return this._objs.size;
  }
  get(slot:Slot):Obj|undefined {
    return this._objs.get(slot);
  }
  legalSlot(slot:Slot) {
    if (!this.has(slot)) {
      console.log(this._objs);
      throw `slot not worn: ${slot}`;
    }
  }
  legalObj(o:Obj) {
    let slot:Slot = o.slot;
    if (slot == Slot.NotWorn) {
      console.log(slot, o);
      throw
      `slot NotWorn cannot be worn. ${o.name()}`;
    }
    if (slot == undefined) {
      console.log(slot, o);
      throw `no slot on ${o.name()}`;
    }
  }
}
```

Let us look at what `Worn` offers:

- It has the expected methods to add and remove objects.
- It has methods to query whether we have a certain slot equipped, and to get any object equipped in a given slot.
- Finally, it has methods to check whether a given object or slot can be equipped. These are guards against wrong usage - that is why they throw exceptions.

Of note is, that `Worn` currently has no protection against equipping an item on top of another. Instead, the prior item would just **vanish**! A better design might be, that `add` (and `remove`) would instead be `tryAdd` (and `tryRemove`). It could then return `false`, if we try to equip something on top of something else. Similarly, `remove` might complain if we try to remove an item we are not carrying. We won't exactly do that, because we instead take care of those things in the **commands** we will make to operate on this model. But it's an idea to consider. Yet another idea would be that equipping automatically would swap out any earlier equipped items. But that is concerns for the commands, not the model.

As we did earlier with the inventory bag, we must integrate this new model part into our existing game model. Thus we integrate the `Worn` model in `GameIF` and `Game5`, cloned from `Game4`: (`02model/23GameModel5Worn.ts`)

```
// to GameIF:
  worn:Worn|undefined;
// to Game5, cloned from Game4:
  worn:Worn = new Worn();
// to fix up older Game4/GameN etc:
  worn:Worn = <Worn><unknown> undefined;
```

23.5   EQUIP & UNEQUIP COMMANDS

We must make the commands for equipping and unequipping.
They will take care of verifying proper arguments, and emit error
responses to the user, if he tries something funny. It is for this
user feedback, that we want to handle this in the commands and
not in the Worn model.

04cmds/23WearCmd.ts:

```
export class WearCmd extends CmdBase {
  worn:Worn;
  constructor(public obj:Obj, public ix:number,
              public g:GameIF) {
    super(g.ply,g);
    this.worn = <Worn> g.worn;
  }
  exc(): boolean {
    let game = this.g;
    let obj:Obj = this.obj;
    if (!this.wearable(obj)) {return false;}
    if (this.alreadyWorn(obj)) {return false;}
    if (this.handsFull(obj)) {return false;}
    game.bag!.removeIx(this.ix);
    this.worn.add(obj);
    game.msg(`You wear ${obj.name()}. `);
    return true;
  }
  wearable(obj:Obj):boolean {
    let canWear = (obj.slot != Slot.NotWorn);
    if (!canWear) {
      this.g.flash(`${obj.name()} is not wearable. `);
    }
    return canWear;
  }
  alreadyWorn(obj:Obj):boolean {
    let already = this.worn.has(obj.slot);
    if (already) {
      let label = Slot[obj.slot];
```

```
      this.g.flash(`${label} already worn.`);
    }
    return already;
  }
  handsFull(obj:Obj):boolean {
    if (!Worn.isWeapon(obj)) {return false;}
    let worn = this.worn;
    let inHand:Obj|undefined = worn.weapon();
    if (!inHand) { return false; }
    let overlap = this.overlaps(obj.slot, inHand!.slot);
    if (overlap) {
      let f=`unequip ${inHand!.name()} first.`;
      this.g.flash(f);
    }
    return overlap;
  }
  overlaps(slot:Slot, hand:Slot):boolean {
    return slot==Slot.BothHands
        || hand==Slot.BothHands
        || hand==slot;
  }
}
```

So the **Wear** command checks 3 prerequisites, and completes the
equip action if those are satisfied. If they are not, the user
instead gets a flash error. The checks concern

- whether the object can be equipped at all
- whether we are already wearing something in that slot. A
  better implementation might be to automatically swap out
  whatever was equipped before. Note this choice would
  affect whether swapping worn items counts as one or two
  turns.
- whether we are already wielding a weapon.

You might wonder why the weapon check is not already handled
by the second wearing-check? It actually might be. But
traditionally, weapons are often weird special cases, where you

can either wield a single two-handed weapon with both hands, or one weapon item (or a shield) in each hand. Therefore, it is not enough to just check a single weapon slot. There are various ways to implement two-handed weapons. One way is to have a separate `Slot.BothHands` slot, which may not be equipped at the same time as `Slot.MainHand` and `Slot.Offhand`.

The `EquipCmd` highlights a choice in coding style. It has been split into 4 functions - the main `exc` function, and 3 utility functions. If we didn't split it up, it would clock in as 30 lines of code. By splitting it up, it instead grows to 40 lines of code, which achieve no more work or features. So one might wonder, why are we wasting 40 lines when 30 lines would suffice? One answer is, that you might very well just write it as that single block of 30 lines. But this is what we gain from splitting it up: This way,

- `exc()` becomes a sort of 'menu overview', which gives a high-level view of what our **equip** command does - that it does a `wearable` check, an `alreadyWorn` check, and an `already-wielding-a-weapon` check, before it does the simple bag -> worn swap.
- the 3 check methods each isolate and concern a single feature and behaviour - you can read them in isolation, and verify exactly what they do and how they do it. If you want to remove or change them, there is one precise place this happens.
- (most importantly) the control flow becomes easy to follow - we can see, that each of the checks has the ability to abort the equipping action.
- the actual effect of the command, the item swap, stands out and is uncluttered and simple.
- if you want to extend and complicate the **equip** command, this existing structure hints you might do so with further isolated methods hooked into `exc()`.

To sum it up, this way of splitting it up makes the code much easier to work with, **if** we consider ourselves as "people whose situation it is to continuously modify this code". The focus on 30 lines instead of 40 only makes sense, if our view is "write the code once and be done with it" (then we might have the belief it would be faster to write "only" 30 lines of code).

Note: The goal is not to 'split up the code as much as possible'. If you really did that, the code would again become unreadable, scattered into innumerable fragments. Our aim with splitting it up is to express its composing features as clearly as possible. Particularly to ease modifying or extending those features, and to avoid separate features accidentally affecting each other.

23.5.1 UNEQUIP COMMAND

For the **Unequip** command, we act off a chosen slot. Our checks are somewhat simpler - we just need to check, that the slot refers to something actually equipped, which we can unequip.

`04cmds/23UnequipCmd.ts`:

```
export class UnequipCmd extends CmdBase {
  constructor(public slot:Slot,
              public g:GameIF) { super(g.ply,g); }
  exc(): boolean {
    let slot = this.slot;
    if (slot == Slot.NotWorn) { return false; }
    let game = this.g;
    let worn = <Worn> game.worn;
    if (!worn.has(slot)) {
      let label:string = Slot[slot];
      let s = `${label} not WORN (${slot})`;
      game.flash(s); return false;
    }
    let o:Obj|undefined = worn.get(slot);
    if (!o) { throw `no item ${slot}?`;}
    worn.remove(slot);
    game.bag!.add(o);
```

```
      game.msg(`ply removes ${o.desc()}`);
      return true;
   }
}
```

Though we now have the appropriate commands, there is not yet any way we can **use** them. We'll need some other code to be **executing** those commands.

23.6   EQUIP INTEGRATION

The obvious place to integrate the **Equip** command, is through the inventory screen somehow. We can't do it directly on that screen though. We had an earlier discussion when we implemented the drop-item command, where we concluded that we would want to do several possible things with items. And so we came up with the ItemScreen menu.

So in that 06screen/22ItemScreen.ts, we make these changes, to allow the user to activate the **equip** command by pressing the w key:

```
..
class ItemScreen extends BaseScreen {
  name:string = 'item';
  worn:boolean; // ch23
  constructor(public obj:Obj, public ix:number,
              game:GameIF, maker:MakerIF) {
    super(game,maker);
    this.worn = !!game.worn; // ch23
  }
  .. // in draw, after the drop menu-item:
    if (this.worn) {
      term.txt(0,y++,'w wear',  fg,bg);
    }
..
  onKey(e:JQuery.KeyDownEvent,
```

```
      s:ScreenStack):boolean {
  switch (e.key) {
  case 'w': this.wear(s); break;
.. // (rest of original onKey)
  // (the rest of onKey takes care of pop.)


  wear(ss:Stack):boolean {
    if (!this.worn) { return false; }
    let ok = new WearCmd(
      this.obj, this.ix, this.game
    ).turn();
    if (ok) {
      this.pop_And_RunNPCLoop(ss);
    }
    return ok;
  }
}
```

23.7 TESTING WORN-ITEMS FEATURES

We now have enough to start testing (some of) our equipment
features. To run it all, first clone `03build/22Builder2k.ts` into
`03build/23Builder2L.ts`. Update it to use `Game5` instead of `Game4`.
Then we need `index23_worn.ts`:

```
ScreenMaker2_Fixed.Gfirst( new Builder2L() );
```

With that, we have integrated our **Equip** command - we can
equip items when the game is running, If we were to run our
program now, then the item menu screen, triggered from the
inventory screen, would look like this:

We don't have any place to integrate our **Unequip** command yet
though.

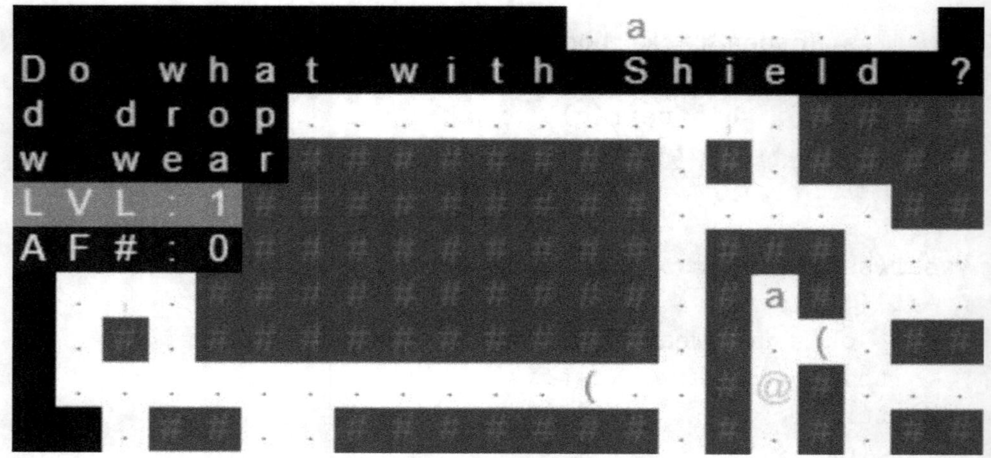

F 23.2: What do we say to Mr Shield?

23.8 WORN EQUIPMENT DISPLAY

Given that we can't yet do anything for our **Unequip** command,
let us instead focus on providing the user with a way to **see** what
he currently has equipped. We will make an equipment screen,
which we insist on calling the WornScreen. It will run through all
possible equipment slots, and draw a label for each of them.
Some of them will currently have an item equipped, some not.
The slots **with** equipment we'll paint in yellow, the **empty** ones
we'll paint in grey. The grey slots can then serve as inspiration
and ambition for the player - "if I ransack the dungeon, one day I
might be able to equip an item in slot X!" For the equipped
items, we'll of course show their names.

06screen/23WornScreen.ts

```
export class WornScreen extends BaseScreen {
    name:string = 'worn';
    worn:Worn;
    constructor(game:GameIF, maker:MakerIF) {
      super(game, maker);
      this.worn = <Worn> game.worn;
    }
```

```typescript
    slot2char(pos:Slot):string {
        return String.fromCharCode(
            65+(pos-Slot.MainHand)    );
    }
    char2slot(c:string):Slot {
      let i:number =
            (c.charCodeAt(0) - 'a'.charCodeAt(0))
            + Slot.MainHand;
      return i in Slot ? i as Slot : Slot.NotWorn;
    }
    draw(term:TermIF) {
      let y:number=1;
      term.txt(0,y++, 'You are wearing:',
              'yellow', 'black');
      for (let slot=Slot.MainHand;
            slot<Slot.Last;
            ++slot
      ) {
        let c:string = this.slot2char(slot);
        let label:string = Slot[slot];

        let wi:Obj|undefined = this.worn.get(slot);
        let worn:string = (wi ? wi.desc() : '');
        let fg = (wi ? 'yellow' : 'darkgray');
        term.txt(0,y++, `${c} ${worn} (${label})`,
                fg, 'black');
      }
      DrawMap.renderMsg(term, this.game);
    }
    onKey(e:JQuery.KeyDownEvent,
        stack:Stack):boolean
    {
      // ..handle unequip somehow..
      return true;
    }
}
```

With our new `WornScreen` ready, we must provide a way for the player to trigger his equipment inventory. We add the following part to his actions in `09ParsePly.ts`. Note that such *information actions* do not count as turns! You **could** make a game where inspecting information would count as turns, but it is not traditionally done.

```
case 'u':
   if (this.game.worn) {
     s = new  WornScreen(this.game,this.maker);
   }
   break;
```

If we run the game again, we can now **see** what we have equipped: *(See Figure 23.3)*

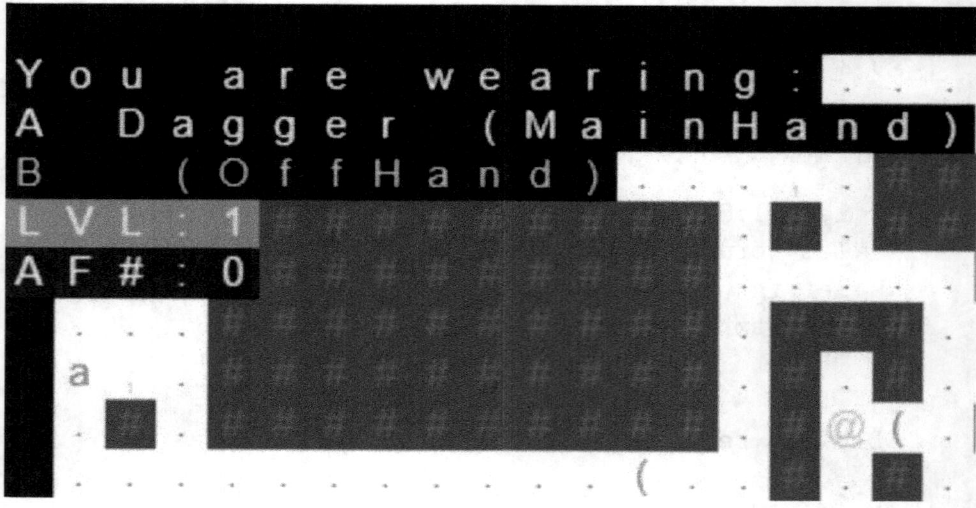

F 23.3: Good to know we aren't wearing it around our neck

23.9 UNEQUIPPING COMMAND INCLUDED

Now that we have an equipment screen, we also have a place for our **Unequip** command. We can integrate it into `23WornScreen.ts` like this:

```
onKey(e:JQuery.KeyDownEvent,
      stack:ScreenStack):boolean {
  let slot = this.char2slot(e.key);
  if (slot==Slot.NotWorn || this.unequip(slot)) {
    stack.pop();
  }
  return true;
}
unequip(slot:Slot):boolean {
  return new UnequipCmd(slot,this.game).turn();
}
```

Voila, we can now equip, view and unequip. But it is all just a fashion statement, since the worn items don't **do** anything yet.

23.10 COMBAT EFFECTS OF WORN EQUIPMENT

Our intention with providing the player with items to equip, was to give him a way to get stronger and more powerful. We must introduce some ways the worn items can affect the player's power.

We will do so by modifying the `HitCmd`, so that the `Worn` class somehow provides variable inputs to it. The worn weapons should control some sort of hitting damage power. And the worn armour should reduce damage taken to some degree.

First, let's extend the `Worn` class, with some calculations that pool together numbers from the worn items. We will calculate a kind of **Armour Class** (AC), and a number for weapon damage:
(`02model/23Worn.ts`)

```
// extra for class Worn:
AC():number {
    let AC:number = 0;
    for (let [,v] of this._objs) {
        AC += v.level;
    }
    return AC;
}
AC_reduce():number { // it's 10-20-30-40.
    let AC = this.AC();
    let reduce = 1.0/(AC*0.1 + 1.0);
    return reduce;
}
public static weapons:Slot[] =
    [ Slot.BothHands,
      Slot.MainHand,
      Slot.OffHand];
static isWeapon(o:Obj) {
    return o.slot in Worn.weapons;
}
weapon():Obj|undefined {
    for (let slot of Worn.weapons) {
        if (this.has(slot)) {
            return this.get(slot);
        }
    }
    return undefined;
}
weaponDmg():number {
    let weapon:Obj|undefined = this.weapon();
    if (weapon) { return weapon.level+1; }
    return 2; // unarmed, hands/fists.
}
```

Our weapon number is simply the level of the weapon, plus 1.
We make it so that weapons from level 0 has the damage number
1. The number is a roll range from zero to N, so the average
damage will be half that number. Note that as the code stands,

stronger weapons have a much better chance of hitting, because
zero-rolls will be rarer. And beware we add the one, so e.g. a
level 3 weapon will hit for 2: `0.5 * (3+1)`.

We then modify `HitCmd` to work like this:

```
export class HitCmd extends CmdBase {
  constructor(
    public me:Mob, public him:Mob, public g:GameIF
  ) { super(me,g); }
  exc():boolean {
    let me = this.me.name, him = this.him.name;
    let rnd = this.g.rnd;
    let dmg:number = this.calcDmg(rnd, this.me);
    if (this.him.isPly) {
      let orig=dmg;
      let factor = this.g.worn!.AC_reduce();
      dmg = Math.ceil(dmg*factor);
      console.log(`${orig}→${dmg} (${factor})`);
    }
    let rest = (this.him.hp - dmg);
    let s=dmg? `${me} hits ${him} for ${dmg}→${rest}`
            : `${me} misses ${him}`;
    if (this.me.isPly || this.him.isPly) {
      this.g.msg(s);
    }
    HealthAdj.adjust(this.him,-dmg,this.g,this.me);
    return true;
  }
  calcDmg(rnd:Rnd, me:Mob): number {
    return rnd.rndC(0,this.power(me));
  }
  power(me:Mob):number {
    return me.isPly ? this.ply_Power(me)
                    : this.NPC_Power(me);
  }
  NPC_Power(m:Mob):number{ return m.level+1; }
  unarmed():number { return 3; }
  ply_Power(ply:Mob):number {
```

```
    let g = this.g;
    if (g.worn) { return this.wornPower(g,g.worn); }
    return this.unarmed();
  }
  wornPower(g:GameIF,w:Worn):number {
    return w.weapon() ? w.weaponDmg() : this.unarmed();
  }
}
```

We want to give the player some hints about these mechanisms,
so we'll add these numbers to the dashboard. In `renderStats()`
in `07DrawMap.ts`, we adjust these bits:

```
.. // in renderStats()
  let ply = game.ply;
  let nEA = game.worn?.AC_reduce().toFixed(2);
  let nAC = game.worn?.AC();
  let nAP = game.worn?.weaponDmg();
  let  EA = ` EA:${nEA}`;
  let  AC = ` AC:${nAC}`;
  let  AP = ` AP:${nAP}`;
  ..
  term.txt(0,y++,  L, 'yellow', 'teal'); // ch13.
  term.txt(0,y++, EA, 'yellow', 'teal');
  term.txt(0,y++, AC, 'yellow', 'teal');
  term.txt(0,y++, AP, 'yellow', 'teal');
```

The labels are 'Attack Power', 'Armor Class', and 'Effective Armor'.

23.11   ARMOR MECHANICS BACKGROUND

23.11.1   TRADITIONAL D&D ISSUES

Our armour class design is not the traditional armour class from
fantasy games. There are a number of design schools for these.
A very traditional one is D20-based. In those, the enemy's attack
dice must hit above your armour class - the higher the armour

class, the smaller the chance to roll a higher number. In worst case, the defender would have maximum armour, and only a critical hit of 20 would be able to penetrate and do damage. The horrible thing about such a traditional armour class, is that the final points, e.g. from AC 17 to 20, would increase your defence ridiculously. E.g., going from 18 to 19 would reduce your damage to half, an increase of 100%!

23.11.2   ARMOR CLASS CREEP

Another problem concerns the player collecting armour-class directly. If the player would often find items of increasing power, where he could keep adding small integers to his armour class, the number would continue to grow and grow. 50, then 100, then 200, and so on. It would be difficult to both make the initial small armour class have any effect, and to also assign meaningful effect to those ever higher 100,200,.. numbers. One way to escape that, is to introduce a level of indirection, where the directly collected armour numbers are used to indirectly buy armour class numbers at diminishing returns. For example, the first point of AC would cost 1, the second would cost 2, the third would cost 3 and so on. This way, an armour class of 10 would cost 55 points. It doesn't solve all, but it would reduce the speed with which armour class would run amok.

```
1 2 3   4   5   6   7   8   9 10
1 3 6  10  15  21  28  36  45 55
```

23.11.3   ANOTHER APPROACH

Alas, the main flaw with this approach is, that we eventually would reduce damage taken to almost nothing. The flaw lies in that it **subtracts** damage. Because of this, we will take a different approach. Instead, our armour class will reduce damage by a **factor**. That is, we will divide the damage by a factor to make it smaller, instead of subtracting from it. This scales in a much better way, because even though we divide the damage, there will still be some left seeping through.

23.11.4   AIMING FOR BALANCE

We are also on another mission here. One of our overarching goals is to balance the game. We are concerned with how many hit points monsters have, how much damage they do, and how much damage creatures take. At the same time, we are aiming to let the player grow in power.

To balance this, we can pick some target numbers to aim for. We could decide, that we expect the player to eventually reach an armour class of 10 on level 1, of 20 on level 2, 30 on level 3 and so on. In symmetry, we could decide that monsters on level 1 will hit for 1 on average, for 2 on level 2, and hit for N on level N. If we keep the player's hit point pool unchanged, we can see that e.g. an armour class of 50 must be in balance with an average damage of 5. The obvious way to do this, is to let the armour reduce the damage by `(armourclass/10)` . That is, an armour class of 50 would reduce by a factor of 5, and an armour class of 30 would reduce by a factor of 3.

This is not a locked design. Currently it would depend on the player never getting more hit points. For power sense and utility, we may be interested in letting the player gain **some** extra hit points, and balance that into it somehow. For example, growing from 20 to 100 hit points. However, it may be easier to keep a sense of the numbers and their balance, by not letting hit points grow extreme, like from 20 to 10.000. In general, if you let numbers grow too high, you'll give yourself extra work making them readable for the player, e.g. by switching to scientific notation or k/m units.

But for now, let's stick to the basic design. With a target armour class of 10-20-30, we can allow the player to collect e.g. 10

different pieces of armour per level, each contributing with an average armour class of 1. It might also be 5 pieces of armour that give 2 AC each, or maybe each level just provides 5 expected AC instead of 10.

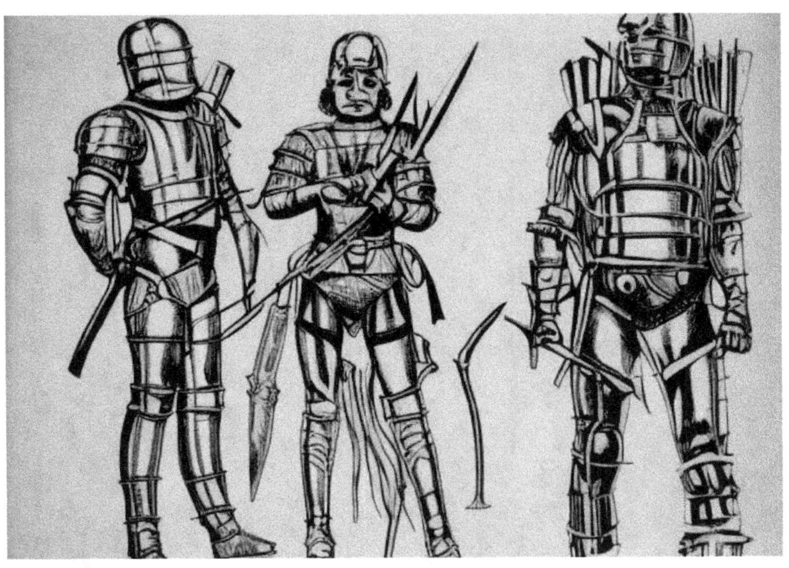

F 23.4: Fashion sense in the dungeon can be summed up as "If the owner is dead, I'm wearing it"

F 23.5: You too can be decked out in .. whatever that is

24   Spells, Buffs I

(In which we add temporary duration status effect spells)

F 24.1: Any sufficiently advanced magic is indistinguishable from shiny trinkets

24.1　Monsters Different Through Spells

Earlier we made a progression of gradually more difficult monsters, in essence by just increasing their hit points, and the damage they hit for. We hinted we would later add more variety to them. That time has now come. There are infinite ways to give them variety, mainly by varying their behaviour. Our approach here will be to add spells and magical effects to the game, and allow the mobs to cast these spells. At some later point, we will also give the player access to the spells.

24.2　Intent

The initial spells will be similar kinds of limited-duration state changes, which will differ in their effects. This type of spell is sometimes called a buff, a debuff, a damage-over-time (DoT), a status effect, or a duration effect. We will use the term **buffs** for all such effects, even though technically debuffs connote negative effects, whereas buffs imply positive effects.

The kinds of spells we have seen so far (really, commands or actions) have been **one-time effects**. Our combat attack was such a one-time effect - just imagine it was named "magic-blast" instead of "weapon hit".

A buff is distinguished by instead being a **lasting effect**. Normally it has a limited duration - e.g. for the next 15 turns, or a 10% chance to wear off each turn. But it might even be **permanent**, maybe a disease or a cursed weapon, which persists until you find an antidote. Buffs represent a, most often temporary, **change of state**.

As buffs are often negative effects, limitless durations are unpleasant, short-lived durations are preferable, and ways to clear or remove debuffs are welcome.

To give a taste of what debuffs are about, have a look at this enum collection of buff effects. `02model\24BuffEnum.ts` will contain the `Buff` enum.

```
export enum Buff {
Confuse=0,  Afraid=1,       Root=2,     Blind=3, Paralyze=4,
   Slow=5,  Freeze=6,  Petrify=7,       Burn=8,     Poison=9,
  Shock=10,  Charm=11,    Sleep=12,      Stun=13,    Bleed=14,
Silence=15, Disarm=16,Levitate=17
}
```

In this chapter we focus on getting the basic buff mechanism in place. So we will not address all of these straight away, but first build the foundations that will allow them to work.

24.3 PLAN

- We will need mechanisms in the monster AIs that will attempt to cast spells.

- We will need a `BuffCmd` to **cast** buffs.

- As buffs are distinguished by enduring across multiple turns, we will have a structure to track each single active buff (`BuffIF`).

- We will need a place to **store** those buff trackers. This will be in the mobs themselves - we will outfit each mob with a container holding its active buffs (`ActiveBuffs`).

- We must do the actual **lifecycle tracking** of the active buffs. We will do so, as we process the turn for each mob, at the **end** of his turn. We may have to message-notify the player about important buff effects ('you are hurt by the poison for 7 damage').

- We will want a kind of HUD panel to visibly highlight current buffs on the player.

- In the next chapter, we then implement the actual **effects** for the buffs.

To recap: The NPCs will cast spells - a `BuffCmd`. The `BuffCmd` will add a `BuffIF` to the target's `ActiveBuffs`. The normal *turns processing* will do updates on the `ActiveBuffs`. Any buffs active on the player will be visible in the HUD, and various subsystems of the game will independently react, whenever a creature is affected by a given `Buff`, e.g. making the creature stumble or take damage from poison.

24.4   MAKING AIs USE SPELLS

We start with the AI. Let's try to make our mobs cast spells. "Our mobs", in this regard, is really the `WakeAI` running our moody bats from chapter 18. So we clone `18WakeAI.ts` into `05ai/24SpellAI.ts`.

24.4.1   SpellAI

We then modify `turn()` and the constructor. The change to `turn()` is, that the mob will try `maybeCastSpell` when doing its turn. The `SpellAI` constructor gets a `spellRate` saying how often the monster casts a spell. Of course, we don't yet know what `maybeCastSpell` will do. So far, `SpellAI` will look like this:

```
export class SpellAI implements MobAiIF {
  constructor(public speed:number,
                public spellRate:number) {}
  aiDir:MobAiIF = new MobAI2_cat();
  aiRnd:MobAiIF = new MobAI3_ant();
  turn(me:Mob, enemy:Mob, game:GameIF):boolean {
    if (this.maybeCastSpell(me,enemy,game)) {
      return true;
    }
    let r = game.rnd;
```

```
  for (let i=0;i<this.speed;++i) {
    var ai = r.oneIn(2) ? this.aiDir : this.aiRnd;
    ai.turn(me,enemy,game);
  }
  let far = !SleepAI.isNear(me,enemy);
  if (far) {
    me.mood =
      r.oneIn(3) ? Mood.Asleep : Mood.Wake;
  }
  return true;
  }
}
```

To get this AI into the game, we add this line to `MoodAI`:

```
static stockMood24(speed:number, spellRate:number):MobAiIF {
  return new MoodAI(new SleepAI(),
                    new SpellAI(speed,spellRate));
}
```

So we clone `O3build/23Builder2L.ts` into
`O3build/24Builder2m.ts`, and change `makeAI()` to

```
makeAI():MobAiIF|null {
  return new AiSwitcher2(MoodAI.stockMood24(1,8));
}
```

..which in turn requires a launcher `index24_spells.ts`:

```
ScreenMaker2_Fixed.Gfirst(new Builder2m());
```

But what should `maybeCastSpell` do? Well, we must decide

- **if** we want to cast a spell,
- if so, **pick** a spell-type (buff),
- then **execute** a spell command.

The mob AI should **decide** to use a spell, possibly every random
3rd move, possibly more or less often depending on how close
the player is. It should then **pick** a random buff-type from the
Buff enum by some strategy, e.g. the mob's own level, or

in-range-of mob's own level. Finally, we'll **execute** a `BuffCmd`
(which we don't have yet), with the chosen buff enum value:

```
.. // (for SpellAI)
maybeCastSpell(me:Mob, enemy:Mob, game:GameIF):boolean {
  let r = game.rnd;
  if (!r.oneIn(this.spellRate)) { return false; }
  let buff = this.pickBuff(me, r);
  return this.cast(buff,me,enemy,game);
}
```

`pickBuff` should probably use the me-monster's level or
properties, or the `Rnd`, to pick a spell type. But to get started, we
can cheat with this **very** basic buff-picker:

```
pickBuff(me:Mob, r:Rnd):Buff { return Buff.Confuse; }
```

24.4.2 VISIBILITY

There is an issue with how monster spell-casting currently
would work: Any awake monster anywhere on the level, can
currently cast spells to attack the player. There might be insanely
all-powerful monsters somewhere in the universe, but this level
of adversity was not what we had in mind for our player here. A
more reasonable level would be, that monsters can only attack
you if they can **see** you. We will therefore include our earlier
`CanSee` check from the better-bats chapter. With this, the first
lines of `maybeCastSpell` become this:

```
maybeCastSpell(me: Mob, enemy: Mob, game:GameIF):boolean {
  let map = <DMapIF> game.curMap();
  if (!CanSee.canSee2(me,enemy,map,true)) { return false; }
  let r = game.rnd;
  ..
```

24.4.3   Buff Cast Command

Then we need that `cast()` method for the spell - it could be this:

```
cast(buff:number, me:Mob,
     enemy:Mob, game:GameIF):boolean {
  let spell = new BuffCmd(buff,enemy,game,me);
  return spell.npcTurn();
}
```

24.5   The Buff Command

This leads us to implement `BuffCmd`. It should put the buff on the target mob, so we can track which buffs are currently on it. It will call its own method `addBuffToMob`, which we again don't have yet.

24.5.1   Book-Keeping for Buff Tracking

To get going, we will need a structure to hold data to track an active buff. It should know

- **which** buff type it is,

- **how long** the buff will still be active for,

- any dynamic **effect** involved in the buff (e.g. poison or bleed damage).

Thus we make `02model\24BuffIF.ts` which contains these bits: (the `TickIF` is for dynamic effects)

```
export interface TickIF {
  tick(time:number):void;
}
export interface BuffIF {
  buff:Buff;
  time:number;
```

```
  effect:TickIF|undefined;
}
```

24.5.2   The Actual Command

With this, we can make `04cmds/24BuffCmd.ts`:

```
export class BuffCmd extends CmdBase {
  constructor(public buff:Buff,
              public tgt:Mob,
              game:GameIF, me:Mob){ super(me,g); }
  exc():boolean {
    let effect:TickIF|undefined = undefined;
    switch (this.buff) {
      //case Buff.Poison: effect=new PoisonTick(m,g); break;
    }
    let active:BuffIF = {
      buff:this.buff, time:8,  effect:effect
    };
    this.addBuffToMob(active,this.g,this.tgt);
    return true;
  }
}
```

(Beware that `PoisonTick` above here is not yet accounted for.
We'll get to it in a bit.)

24.6   Storing Buffs on Mob

`addBuffToMob()` should add the `BuffIF` to the target mob
somehow. We need a kind of 'active buff container' on the Mob
class, to track its active buffs.

We will make a class `ActiveBuffs`, which will be a container of
`BuffIF`'s, and have some sort of `add` method. We will then put an
`ActiveBuffs` member on each `Mob`. Behold,
`02model/24ActiveBuffs.ts`:

```
export class ActiveBuffs {
  _map: Map<Buff, BuffIF> = new Map();
  add(b: BuffIF, game: GameIF, mob: Mob) {
    this._map.set(b.buff, b);
  }
  // (Maybe only show these in a later section..)
  del(b: BuffIF, game: GameIF, mob: Mob) {
    this._map.delete(b.buff);
    if (mob.isPly) {
      game.msg(`${Buff[b.buff]} wears off.`);
    }
  }
  is(buff: Buff): boolean {
    return this._map.has(buff);
  }
  get(buff: Buff): BuffIF|undefined {
    return this._map.get(buff);
  }
  cleanse(buff:Buff, game:GameIF, mob:Mob) {
    let b = mob.buffs.get(buff);
    if (b) { this.del(b,game,mob); }
  }
  ticks(mob:Mob, game:GameIF) {
    for (let b of this._map.values()) {
      --b.time;
      if (b.effect) { b.effect.tick(b.time); }
      if (b.time<=0) { this.del(b,game,mob); }
    }
  }
}
```

We insert such an `ActiveBuffs` property into the class `Mob`, in `02model\09Mob.ts`:

```
  buffs:ActiveBuffs = new ActiveBuffs();
```

All this allows us to now implement `BuffCmd.addBuffToMob()`:

```
addBuffToMob(active:BuffIF,
             game:GameIF, mob:Mob) {
  if (mob.isPly || this.me.isPly) {
    let who = mob.name;
    let what:string = Buff[active.buff];
    let by = this.me.name;
    game.msg(`${who} is ${what} by ${by}`);
  }
  mob.buffs.add(active,game,mob);
}
```

24.7 Mob Buffs Lifecycle

Getting the active buffs onto the mobs is only half the story. We have to manage their **life cycle**, so they don't remain on the mobs for longer than they should. Specifically, they should only remain there for `BuffIF.time` number of turns. To aid us with this, we give the `ActiveBuffs` class a `ticks()` method, which for each active buff will decrement its buff count-down (`time`), and remove the buff when it's done. Notably, it will also execute any associated tick-effect of the buff.

```
ticks(mob:Mob, game:GameIF) {
  for (let b of this._map.values()) {
    --b.time;
    if (b.effect) { b.effect.tick(b.time); }
    if (b.time<=0) { this.del(b,game,mob); }
  }
}
```

So, who is going to call that `ticks()` method? We must do it in the `npcTurns()` loop. We will have to do it separately for the player and for the NPCs. The best place to do it is **after** a turn (the same way we handle auto-heal). This way, any effects it causes will be displayed along with the other stuff that happens, as part of the turn the player just did.

Imagine if we instead executed the buff-ticks just **before** the player should input his turn: That would mean that while you were pondering what action to take next, it would be with the threat "..but **actually**, *something may already have happened to you which you haven't yet been told about !*" (e.g. that you are now poisoned). Clearly we want to apply the buff ticks in a manner which allows us to report any effects to the player, before we pass the initiative back to him.

To incorporate `ticks()`, we modify `09BaseScreen.ts` with the following bits:

```
tickBuffs(m: Mob) {
  if (!m.buffs) { return; }
  m.buffs.ticks(m,this.game);
}
finishTurn(m: Mob) {
  this.tickBuffs(m);
}
npcTurn(m:Mob, ply:Mob) {
  let ai = this.game.ai;
  if (ai) { ai.turn(m,ply,this.game); }
  this.finishTurn(m);
}
finishPlyTurn(q:TurnQ) {
  let ply = q.curMob();
  if (!ply.isPly) { throw `${ply.name} not ply?'`; }
  this.finishTurn(ply);
  if (this.game.autoHeal) {
    this.game.autoHeal.turn(ply, this.game);
  }
}
```

24.8 Buffs on Dashboard

We also need a way to let the player follow what is going on. For the monsters, we won't tell him every single thing that happens with debuffs, only whenever a debuff is applied to a monster ("the orc is confused").

For the player's buffs, we will give him more details. We want a HUD status panel telling the player which debuffs currently affect him, and their remaining count-down timers. E.g., status labels like '(5) confused'.

To achieve this, we extend class `DrawMap` with the method `renderBuffs`, which we call at the end of `renderStats`:

```
  static renderBuffs(term:TermIF,
                     buffs:ActiveBuffs,
                     y:number):number {
    let bmap:Map<Buff,BuffIF> = buffs._map;
    let bg = '#502';
    let fg_danger = '#ff3300';
    for (let [buff,buffIF] of bmap) {
      let label:string = Buff[buff];
      let r:string = this.remain(buffIF);
      let sbuff:string = `${r} ${label}`;
      term.txt(0,y++,sbuff, fg_danger, bg);
    }
    let AFF = `AF#:${bmap.size}`;
    term.txt(0,y++,AFF,'yellow', bg);
    return y;
  }


  static remain(b:BuffIF): string {
    return `${b.time}`;
  }

// the end of renderStats() becomes:
```

```
    term.txt(0,y++,   L, 'yellow', 'teal');
    let buffs:ActiveBuffs = ply.buffs;
    y = this.renderBuffs(term, buffs, y);
  }
```

With this, we should see a list of current afflictions at the
bottom of the dashboard. Our enemy monsters can now cast
debuffs on us, and these will show up - and count down - in our
game display.

24.9 Effects of Confusion

However, being afflicted with our single Confuse debuff will not
yet do anything. So we need to implement a behaviour for being
confused. Stay tuned for chapter 25!

25 Spells, Buffs II

*(In which we make our debuffs **do** something)*

F 25.1: The stench from a powerful area-of-effect debuff can be overwhelming, and is the probable cause of its effect

25.1 Spell Effects

The previous chapter gave us the basic supports to handle debuffs. They get applied, and appear in our UI, but don't actually **do** anything. We never added any behaviour for them. It's time we flesh out the actual **effects** which the names of our debuffs enum hinted at. Let's walk through the details that go into the spells. They fall into various categories.

25.1.1 Damage Over Time

Poisoned means you'll **lose hit points** from poison damage at regular intervals, so-called **ticks**. (*"Poison hurts you for n damage." "You feel sick."*)

Bleeding is akin to poisoning. It may require countering to not have worsening consequences. You probably cannot weather sustained bleeding. (*"You bleed for n damage."*)

Burning is another damage effect similar to poisoning and bleeding. (*"You burn for n damage".*)

25.1.2 Blocked Movement or Action

Rooted means your feet **cannot move** away from the tile you are currently standing on. However you can still reach and hit neighbours. (*"You(r feet) are rooted (in place)".*) Is it possible to fight against rooting to break it early?

Levitation is akin to being rooted. You may have trouble **moving** or hitting stuff, but you can probably cast spells and use your backpack items. (*"You are floating." "You hover." "You float." "You levitate."*)

Paralyzed means you are **unable to move** or **act**. It is a dangerous effect, tantamount to instant death. Its details must be carefully crafted, to allow the player any chance of escaping. (*"You are* *paralyzed." "You feel paralyzed."*) It could be e.g. a 66% chance to lose your turn.

Charmed means you will be **friendly** instead of hostile towards an enemy, maybe even if he keeps hitting you? (*"But he is so cute.."*) Would behave much like **fear**.

Afraid (Fear) above all means, that you can't launch **attacks** against one or more enemies, though you are free to **flee**. For variation, it might include risk of unintended movement away from the feared subject. (*"You are (too) afraid!"*)

Silenced stops the player from making **sound**. It is mainly a spell-casting block against wizards. It doesn't affect warriors using simple weapons. Similarly, wizards can still use magic that doesn't require sound. They can drink potions and zap wands, but not read spell scrolls or books. What you want it to block is a design choice. *Your* rules might say zapping a wand requires speaking a spell. (*"You are silenced."*) Note that we are not going to implement silence here, but it is a genre staple.

Disarmed is the opposite of silence - a warrior will be unable to properly **wield** his weapon for a bit - he may have numb hands or fingers, or a stunned arm. Whereas a wizard might not be affected. (*"You hit with your bare hands." "bare-handed."*) You will cause unarmed-damage.

25.1.3 IMPAIRED MOVEMENT OR ACTION

Confused means half your attempts at moving will be in **random directions**. Probably likewise your attempts at hitting. (*"You act/feel/are confused."*)

Slowed causes the player to move at **half speed**. One way to implement it is to toss a coin for whether attempts to move or attack become wait-turns instead. (*"You are slow." "You move slowly." "You act slowly." "You feel slow." "You are slowed."*)

Stunned or bashed (by a shield): A mix of some of the other effects (e.g. slow or confuse or fear), causing the player to temporarily react in a delayed, slowed, stunned or restricted way. (*"You are stunned!" "You are out of balance." "You lose your balance."*) Probably of short duration. Maybe stun is a single-turn can't-hit-back?

Frozen may be a mix of several effects. The player might take frost damage. The player might be slowed. More interestingly, the effect may require the player to keep moving, to either avoid worsening effects (freezing-stiffening), or to clear the effect again. (*"You freeze." "You are cold." "You feel cold."*)

25.1.4 OTHER KINDS OF BUFFS

Blinded means you **cannot see** monsters, and you can only see walls you have seen earlier, or are feeling by standing next to them. (*"You are blind(-ed)!"*)

Petrified is similar to frozen - it might worsen to a **fatal** stiffening, if not countered somehow. (*"You petrify!"*)

25.2 IMPLEMENTING Buff Effects

We will now visit each of the buff values, and implement relevant effects for their behaviour. E.g. being afraid, being confused, being blind etc.

```
// Order:
Confuse=0,  Afraid=1,      Root=2,     Blind=3, Paralyze=4,
   Slow=5, Freeze=6, Petrify=7,     Burn=8,     Poison=9,
  Shock=10,  Charm=11,    Sleep=12,    Stun=13,    Bleed=14,
Silence=15, Disarm=16,Levitate=17,
}
```

25.3 Impaired Mechanism

A certain subset of our effects involve being impaired. They have in common, that they may affect many or all commands. Does this mean we'll need repetitive effects-code across all the commands?

Luckily no. We run our commands with a level of indirection - instead of calling `exc()` directly, we call the method `turn()` in `CmdBase`, which then in turn calls `exc()` (pun duly noted). This lets us inject extra code in the `turn()` method, whereby we can include code common for **all** our commands.

We will let `turn()` call an `able()` check. If `able()` fails, the command will not succeed (but might still use up a turn!). The `Able` response looks like this: (04cmds/25Able.ts)

```
export interface Able {
  able:boolean; // false when blocked.
  turn:boolean; // Wasted a turn.
}
```

The impairment effects come in two kinds: One kind is an immediate block, which upfront says 'you cannot do this action currently' - it won't waste a turn (`able == false`). The other kind is a proper impairment - you can **attempt** the action, but are likely to fumble it, and waste your turn doing so (`turn == true`).

The various impairment effects impact different things - some impair movement, some impair attacking. To this end, we will pass an `Act` enum to `able()`, specifying the kind of action we are attempting. This way, `able()` will work both for `Move` actions and for `Hit` actions. (04cmds/25Act.ts)

```
export enum Act {
  Move, // requires you are unrestrained
  Hit,  // requires courage and reach, 'unrestrained'
  Act   // requires control of yourself
}       // - not confused/bound/paralyzed/sleeping.
```

The changes described above amount to this, when we add them
to `09CmdBase.ts`:

```typescript
export abstract class CmdBase implements CmdIF {
  m:Mob|undefined = undefined;
  g:GameIF|undefined = undefined;

  // (default is other than Hit and Move:)
  act:Act = Act.Act;

  able(m:Mob, g:GameIF,act:Act):Able {
    let cant = {able:false,turn:false};
    let foil = {able:false,turn:true};
    let able = {able:true, turn:false};
    //..(do various checks..)
    return able; // nothing blocked us.
  }

  public turn():boolean {
    let r = this.able(
      <Mob>this.m,<GameIF>this.g,this.act
    );
    if (!r.able) { return r.turn; }
    return this.exc();
  }
  .. // rest of CmdBase.
```

25.3.1 MAKING TURNS INTERRUPTIBLE

We laid the foundations, that now allow us to implement turn
failure, long ago. Ever since we introduced commands and the
`CmdIF` in chapter 9, we've taken great care to wrap all our calls to
exc, dividing them into turn-calls and raw composing-calls. We
now reach the purpose of doing so.

(`CmdIF` with its three exc wrappers:)

```typescript
export interface CmdIF {
  exc():boolean;
```

```
setDir(dir: WPoint): CmdIF;

turn():boolean;
raw():boolean;
npcTurn():boolean;
..
```

As we try to fit in the `able()` checks to allow commands to fail,
we reveal that we execute in different situations. Sometimes we
execute to complete a creature **turn**. Other times, we execute to
compose bigger commands of smaller commands.

It is only the `turn` calls we want to be interruptible - the `raw` calls
should be left alone. We only want `able()` checks on 'turn'
executions, not on composing executions. So when we call `turn`
or `npcTurn`, we want able checks. And when we call `raw`, we are
just composing.

For example, in `09MoveCmd.ts`, we use `raw()` for the `StairCmd`:

```
new StairCmd(dir,this.g).raw();
```

Across all our Mob AI's, we use `npcTurn()`. It resolves to `turn()`,
so mobs too can be debuffed to fail. And in `09GameScreen.ts`,
`plyTurn` itself uses `turn()` - this goes for all screens executing
player turns:

```
private plyTurn(s:StackIF, c:string,
        e:JQuery.KeyDownEvent|null):boolean {
  let parser = new ParsePly(this.game, this.make);
  let cmd = parser.parseKeyCodeAsTurn(c,s,e);
  return cmd ? cmd.turn() : false;
}
```

25.3.2 AFRAID

Handling the **afraid** buff, is simply a check for whether the attacker is too **afraid** to do a given action. If he is afraid, his attempts to hit will not succeed. We can implement `afraid()` as a boolean function in `09CmdBase.ts` like this:

```
afraid(me:Mob, g:GameIF):boolean {
  let afraid = me.is(Buff.Afraid);
  if (afraid && me.isPly) {
    g.flash('Ply is afraid!');
  } // you are too afraid to hit.
  return afraid;
}
```

When it is the player himself, we warn him with a flash message, that he is 'too afraid'. The check should apply to physical hit attacks, so we will add it to `able()` like so:

```
able(m:Mob, g:GameIF,act:Act):Able {
  let cant = {able:false,turn:false};
  let foil = {able:false,turn:true};
  let able = {able:true, turn:false};
  let hit = (act == Act.Hit);
  let mov = (act == Act.Move);
  let HOM = (hit || mov);
  if (hit && this.afraid(m,g))  { return cant; }
  return able; // nothing blocked us.
}
```

For this to work, we must ensure that `HitCmd` is a `Hit` act, so we adjust `11hitCmd.ts` this way:

```
export class HitCmd extends CmdBase {
  act:Act = Act.Hit;
  ..
```

We will do `charmed`, `rooted` and `levitating` next, because of their similarity to `afraid`.

25.3.3 CHARMED

Charm is akin to **afraid**, just with the different message *"It's too cute!"* Also, if the charmer hits you, the status is cleared, and you can once again hit him ("the charm wears off").

To `09CmdBase.ts`, we add this:

```
charmed(me:Mob, g:GameIF):boolean {
  let charmed = me.is(Buff.Charm);
  if (charmed && me.isPly) {
    g.flash("It's too cute!");
  } // you are too charmed to attack it.
  return charmed;
}
```

And we add a `charmed()` call to `able()`:

```
if (hit && this.afraid(m,g))  { return cant; }
if (hit && this.charmed(m,g)) { return cant; }
```

We must make hits clear charm. We add the following bits at the end of `HitCmd.exc()`:

```
..  // end of exc:
  this.clearCharm(g);
  return true;
}

clearCharm(g:GameIF) {
  let h = this.him;
  if (!h.is(Buff.Charm)) { return; }
  h.buffs.cleanse(Buff.Charm,this.game,h);
}
..
```

25.3.3.1   IDEAS FOR VARIATIONS OF CHARMED

Could we make `charmed` more different from `afraid` ? Maybe `afraid` is general, and `charmed` is relative to specific creatures? Maybe related to who hits first? Maybe tie it to stealing from our bag? Maybe the status is cleared, whenever the affected mob is **hit**? But only by the charmer..? If so, we would have to keep track of **who** charmed? (in effect, of "**who** is being charming"). Maybe the buff should be reversed, so it is instead the charming creature who has an `is_charming` buff?

25.3.4   ROOTED

Being **rooted** should do the opposite of `afraid`, i.e. allow hitting but not **moving**. So instead of `HitCmd`, we add this to `09MoveCmd.ts`:

```
export class MoveCmd extends CmdBase {
  act:Act = Act.Move;
..
```

Then `rooted()` in `09CmdBase.ts` as:

```
  rooted(me:Mob, g:GameIF):boolean {
    let rooted = me.is(Buff.Root);
    if (rooted && me.isPly) {
      g.flash('Ply is rooted!');
    }
    return rooted;
  }
```

Which we append in `able()` with

```
  if (mov && this.rooted(m,g))  { return cant; }
```

Based on playtesting, we can tell a few things about root: It is definitely annoying. And our choice of cardinal movement directions instead of 8-way makes it even worse - we cannot even try to reach or counter-attack diagonally. Root is a prime candidate for having shorter duration than the other effects.

25.3.5 LEVITATING

Levitate means you can neither hit with a weapon, nor move. But you can still use spells and items in your bag. It is similar to rooted and afraid, but affects both attacks and movement. `09CmdBase.ts` now gets:

```
levitate(me:Mob, g:GameIF):boolean {
  let levitate = me.is(Buff.Levitate);
  if (levitate && me.isPly) {
    g.flash("Ply levitates!");
  } // you cannot reach/get down.
  return levitate;
}
```

Which we add in `able()` like this - HOM is true with both hit and move.

```
if (HOM && this.levitate(m,g)){ return cant; }
```

Playtesting and common sense tells us, that levitate is even worse than root. Unless you have missile weapons, it is almost a death sentence.

25.3.6 BLINDED

Blind requires changing how we **draw**. Monsters should no longer be drawn while we are blind. For dramatic effect, we could consider drawing the nearby parts of the dungeon in subdued colors too, like we do with distant parts.

In `DrawMap.drawMap18()`, we add this snippet at the top:

```
static drawMap18(term:TermIF, map:DMapIF,
                vp:WPoint, plypos:WPoint,g:GameIF) {
  let buffs = g.ply.buffs;
  let blind = buffs && buffs.is(Buff.Blind);
```

Then, in its inner loop, we change to this:

```
for (t.x=0, w.x=vp.x; t.x<tdim.x; ++t.x, ++w.x) {
  let c:MapCell =
    (map.legal(w) ? map.cell(w) : this.outside);
  let dist:number = w.sqDist(plypos);
  let far:boolean = (dist>farDist) && !blind; // ch25
  let seeMob = c.mob && !far && (!blind || c.mob.isPly)
    && CanSee.canSee(c.mob.pos,plypos,map,true);
  ..
```

This achieves a number of things: - if we are blind, we behave as if everything is 'far away', and thus drawn as something we can't currently see, drawn from memory. - seeMob will depend on blind, unless it's the player himself. Even when blind, we wish to draw the player's sprite.

Note: It is often tradition in roguelikes, that being blind also changes log event descriptions to "you hit it", "it hits you".

25.3.7 PARALYZED

Paralyzed means that the player almost can't act. To avoid it being an instant death sentence, we must allow the player to regain some initiative.

One aggressive style for paralysis would be, that the player's turn is skipped upfront (based on chance), and reduced to a *(more)* prompt: "You are paralyzed!" intermixed with enemy action messages.

A less brutal style would let the player attempt actions, with success-rates depending on the chosen action, with some 'simpler' kinds of actions having a higher chance of succeeding.

We will go with this second style: Instead of actions being totally blocked, you will have a percentage chance of being able to do something. E.g. a 33% or 25% chance of managing a (single) action.

We will also let the player *inspect* his state (those are not turns/actions per se). This makes little sense from a 'paralysis perspective', but good sense from a gameplay perspective: If you are in high danger, you should have good means to 'consider your options'. So we can decide that non-turns, like checking the message log and looking in your inventory, are still allowed.

A major factor is what kind of duration we give to paralysis. We might give paralysis a high chance to **wear off**, maybe 15% each turn. We could go further, and give certain actions a high chance to reduce or remove your paralysis, e.g. let successful movement either remove or shorten your remaining duration.

Note that all our `able()` checks until now have precisely been `able` checks, not `foil` checks. This changes with paralysis, which will be our first `foil` check. Here, it is important that we place the `foil` checks **after** `able` checks, because a `foil` check may waste a turn!

25.3.7.1 PARALYSIS IMPLEMENTATION ATTEMPT

We will assign escape-weights to the different kinds of actions. Movement will have a higher chance (33%) of breaking paralysis and shorten it. Attacking will have a lower chance (25%) of breaking it. Other actions will have an even lower chance (20%). When you don't succeed, the debuff counter just decrements by one. When you succeed, you get your action, **and** 1-2 extra is subtracted from the remaining time.

We will first add `pct()` to `07Rnd.ts`:

```
pct(rate:number):boolean { return this.rnd(100) < rate; }
```

Then in `09CmdBase.ts` we implement `paralyzed()`:

```
  paralyzed(me:Mob, g:GameIF):boolean {
    if (!me.is(Buff.Paralyze)) { return false; }
    let rate=0;
    switch (this.act) {
      case Act.Move: rate=33;break;
```

```
    case Act.Hit:   rate=25;break;
    case Act.Act:   rate=20;break;
  }
  let paralyzed = !g.rnd.pct(rate);
  if (paralyzed) {
    if (me.isPly) { g.flash('ply paralyzed!'); }
  } else { // allowed an action.
    let buff = me.buffs.get(Buff.Paralyze);
    buff!.time -= g.rnd.rndC(1,2);
  }
  return paralyzed;
}
```

Which we call unconditionally at the **end** of `able()`, like this:

```
if (HOM && this.levitate(m,g)){ return cant; }
if (this.paralyzed(m,g)) { return foil; }
```

Interestingly and unexpectedly, playtesting suggests it is less annoying than root.

25.3.8 SLEEPING

Sleep means we only get attempts to act, when we take damage. Given that we only wake then, mobs will move around us quickly. Sleep is similar to paralysis, but worse, as there is no random chance to wake. Another difference is that taking damage wakes you up. As outlined, sleep would often endure straight till it times out, given that only damage interrupts it.

So how can we achieve this effect? One way to implement 'damage wakes you up', is to piggy-back on the auto-heal mechanism. To wake up on damage, we modify `17AutoHeal.ts`:

```
public static combatReset(mob:Mob, game:GameIF) {
  this.clearSleep(mob,game);
  let ah = game.autoHeal;
```

```
static clearSleep(m:Mob,g:GameIF) {
  if (!m.is(Buff.Sleep)) { return; }
  m.buffs.cleanse(Buff.Sleep,g,m);
  if (m.isPly) { g.msg('ply wakes up!'); }
}
```

The `asleep()` check in `CmdBase` is

```
asleep(me:Mob, g:GameIF):boolean {
  if (!me.is(Buff.Sleep)) { return false; }
  if (me.isPly) { g.flash('ply sleeps!'); }
  return true;
}
```

Like paralysis, we must call it unconditionally at the **end** of
`able()`:

```
if (this.asleep(m,g)) { return foil; }
```

25.3.9 SLOWED

If you are **slowed**, at random half of your attempts to move or hit
will instead be delays. We add the `slow()` check method to
`09CmdBase.ts`:

```
slow(me:Mob, g:GameIF):boolean {
  if (!me.is(Buff.Slow)) { return false; }
  if (g.rnd.oneIn(2)) { return false; }
  if (me.isPly) { g.flash('ply slows!'); }
  return true;
}
```

Beware the `able()` check for `slow` must also be one of the later
checks, as it is a `foil` check. We must first do all those checks,
which do **not** risk consuming a turn.

```
if (this.slow(m,g)) { return foil; }
```

25.3.10 POISONED

If you are **poisoned**, burning, or bleeding, you will periodically take damage. We handle this with `TickIF` on your buff. `PoisonTick.ts` is such an example of `TickIF`:

```
export class PoisonTick implements TickIF {
  tick(time:number):void {
    if (time % 2) {return;}
    let dmg = 1;
    if (this.mob.isPly) {
      this.game.msg(`the poison hurts:${dmg}`);
    }
    HealthAdj.dmg(this.mob,dmg,this.game,null);
  }
  constructor(public mob:Mob,
              public game:GameIF) {}
}
```

In the previous chapter, the `PoisonTick` lines in `BuffCmd.exc()` were commented out. You can now enable it, to look like this:

```
  ..
  exc():boolean {
    let m = this.tgt, g = this.game;
    let effect:TickIF|undefined = undefined;
    switch (this.buff) {
      case Buff.Poison: effect = new PoisonTick(m,g); break;
    }
  ..
```

25.3.11 BURNING

We implement **burning** akin to poisoned, just with a `BurnTick` instead of a `PoisonTick`. It does a bit more damage. As such, it has no technical difference from poisoning. It could be made different by risk of damaging or destroying flammable items worn or carried.

```
export class BurnTick implements TickIF {
  tick(time:number):void {
    if (time % 2) { return; }
    let g = this.game;
    let dmg = g.rnd.rndC(2,4);
    if (this.mob.isPly) {
      g.msg(`ply burns! ${dmg}`);
    }
    HealthAdj.dmg(this.mob,dmg,g,null);
  }
  constructor(public mob:Mob, public game: GameIF) {}
}
```

In `24BuffCmd.ts` in `exc()`, add this after the case for `Buff.Poison`:

```
case Buff.Burn: effect = new BurnTick(m,g); break;
```

25.3.12 FROZEN

Freeze is a combination of slow and damage-over-time. So you will move slower, and you may take damage. We fashion it so that the more often you move, the less it damages you. Possibly you don't take any damage if you keep moving.

To implement it, we will maintain a 'move age' on mobs, which counts when they last moved. This way, we can penalize mobs for not moving often enough. So, to `Mob`, we add this:

```
sinceMove:number=0;
```

Then to `MoveCmd.exc()`, we add this:

```
    if (legal) {
      this.mob.sinceMove = 0;
      map.moveMob(this.me,np);
```

And finally, to `BaseScreen.finishTurn()`, we add this:

```
++m.sinceMove;
```

Now we can implement the `FreezeTick` that does damage:

```
export class FreezeTick implements TickIF {
  tick(time:number):void {
    if (time % 2) { return; }
    if (this.mob.sinceMove < 2) {return;}
    let g = this.game;
    let r = g.rnd;
    let dmg = r.rndC(0,2);
    if (this.mob.isPly) {
      g.msg(`ply feels cold! ${dmg}`);
    }
    HealthAdj.dmg(this.mob,dmg,g,null);
  }
  constructor(public mob:Mob, public game: GameIF) {}
}
```

We must enable it in `24BuffCmd.ts`:

```
case Buff.Freeze: effect = new FreezeTick(m,g); break;
```

Then, in `09CmdBase.ts`, we add its obstructing effect:

```
freeze(me:Mob, g:GameIF, move:boolean):boolean {
  if (!me.is(Buff.Freeze)) { return false; }
  if (g.rnd.oneIn(2)) { return false; }
  if (me.isPly) { g.flash('ply is frozen!'); }
  return true;
}
```

..which we call at the end of `able()`:

```
if (this.freeze(m,g,mov)) { return foil; }
```

Thought: Maybe freezing should also cause random shattering of frost-susceptible items like potions and drinks?

25.3.13 Bleeding

Bleeding differs from e.g. poisoning, by punishing movement. You will take small damage from bleeding if you move rarely, and more damage if you move.

We add a case for `Buff.Bleed` in `BuffCmd.exc()`:

```
case Buff.Bleed: effect = new BleedTick(m,g); break;
```

With `25BleedTick.ts` being

```
export class BleedTick implements TickIF {
  tick(time:number):void {
    if (time % 2) { return; }
    let move = this.mob.sinceMove;
    let r = this.game.rnd; ;
    let dmg = (move > 2) ? 1 : r.rndC(2,5);
    if (this.mob.isPly) {
      this.game.msg(`ply bleeds! ${dmg}`);
    }
    HealthAdj.dmg(this.mob, dmg, this.game, null);
  }
  constructor(public mob:Mob, public game: GameIF) {}
}
```

25.3.14 Petrified

Petrify is a lot like freeze. The main difference is that petrify is **fatal** if you don't move, because petrify damage continues to grow.

```
export class PetrifyTick implements TickIF {
  tick(time:number):void {
    if (time % 2) { return; }
    let last = this.mob.sinceMove;
    if (last < 2) {return;}
    let r = this.game.rnd;
    let dmg = r.rndC(last,last*2);
```

```
  if (this.mob.isPly) {
    this.game.msg(`ply petrifies! ${dmg}`);
  }
  HealthAdj.dmg(this.mob, dmg, this.game, null);
 }
 constructor(public mob:Mob, public game: GameIF) {}
}
```

25.3.15 STUN

Stuns, above all, are short. Preferably only 2-4 turns. They are
physical. Ideally, you should only be stunned by someone
immediately next to you, physically attacking you.

Stuns require a countering "balance" thing to regain your
balance and clear your stun; e.g. if you back away from the guy
who bashed you, you regain your balance in one turn.

Stun happens in a direction. You are pushed off balance. You
have a chance to regain your balance. You do this by moving a
step back in the direction you were pushed. If you manage to do
so, your stun debuff is cleared. Otherwise, it remains as a 2-3
turn confusion-slow.

The net effect is that enemies which stun can be managed by
this precise backwards-dance. And conversely, if you are stunned
without free space to maneuver, it will be dangerous.

To implement it, we could proceed as follows: - When the Stun
debuff is constructed, we check the relative positions of the
attacker and the target, to determine the direction of the stun. -
From the stun direction and the target's current position, we also
determine the 'save position', i.e. the position target must move
to, in order to shake off the stun. - As the stun's TickIF reaches
first tick, it checks whether target has reached his 'save' position.
If so, the stun is cleared ('your head clears'). If not, he gets the
full stun effect ('you feel dizzy'). As this chapter already contains

plenty, we'll leave out the implementation of stun for now, but I
may revise with its implementation later.

25.3.16 DISARMED

Disarm means physical attacks with our wielded weapon instead
become bare-hand attacks, given that we are not really wielding
our weapon then. Thus we change `wornPower()` in `HitCmd.ts` to
this:

```
wornPower(g:GameIF,w:Worn): number {
  let disarm = g.ply.is(Buff.Disarm);
  if (w.weapon()) {
    if (disarm) {
      g.msg('ply hits bare-handed.');
    } else {
      return w.weaponDmg();
    }
  }
  return this.unarmed();
}
```

25.3.17 SHOCKED

Shocked is a static electricity effect. It causes your physical
attacks to do extra damage, but both to your adversary and to
yourself. It's based more on game mechanics than on realism.

We add it as these changes to `HitCmd`: The parts of `HitCmd.exc()`
that used to **apply** the damage, we've moved into the method
`doDmg()`. Instead, the main `exc()` method now determines the
relevant damage, both the normal damage and any reverse
static-shock damage, and then calls `doDmg()` to apply that
damage, in both directions when necessary.

```
exc():boolean {
  let g=this.game;
```

```
    let m=this.me;
    let r = g.rnd;

    let dmg:number = this.calcDmg(r,m);
    let back:number=0;
    if (m.is(Buff.Shock) && r.oneIn(2)) {
      dmg = this.shockDmg(dmg);
      back = r.rndC(2,3);
    }

    let me = m.name, him = this.him.name;
    this.doDmg(dmg,this.him,m,g,me,him);
    if (back>0) {
      this.doDmg(back,m,m,g,'SHOCK',me);
    }

    this.clearCharm(g);
    return true;
  }
  shockDmg(dmg:number): number {
    return Math.floor(dmg*3/2);
  }
  doDmg(dmg:number, tgt:Mob, atk:Mob, g:GameIF,
        me:string, him:string) {
    if (tgt.isPly) {
      let orig=dmg;
      let factor = this.g.worn!.AC_reduce();
      dmg = Math.ceil(dmg*factor);
      console.log(`${orig}→${dmg} (${factor})`);
    }
    let rest = (tgt.hp - dmg);
    let s=dmg? `${me} hits ${him} for ${dmg}→${rest}`
            : `${me} misses ${him}`;
    if (atk.isPly || tgt.isPly) {
      g.msg(s);
    }
    if (dmg) {
      HealthAdj.adjust(tgt,-dmg,g,atk);
```

```
    }
  }
```

25.3.18 CONFUSED

We have postponed discussing the `confuse` effect, because it is a bit special. It cannot be handled by the original `CmdBase.able()` - if we tried, it would become.. confusing.

The basic problem is that under confusion, the `MoveBump` command can't itself know if it is a `Move` command or a `Hit` command - it only learns this, when it figures out if there is an enemy in the space we randomly move towards. This is caused by the `confuse` effect, which may alter the direction - and thus change a hit to a move, or a move to a hit.

We solve this in two ways: We let the move command and the hit command each manage their own `able` checks. And we put the `confuse` effect inside the `MoveBump` command.

We also give the `MoveBump` command its own harmless version of the `able()` method. This way, it will postpone the able check to be handled by Move and Hit instead.

```
able(m:Mob,  g:GameIF,act:Act):Able {
   return { able:true,  turn:false }
} // (For MoveBumpCmd, each sub-cmd checks instead.)
```

Being **confused** will randomly alter the direction of moving and hitting. So we must change how `MoveBumpCmd` behaves. We modify `MoveBumpCmd` to include the `confused` call, at the start of `exc`, like this:

```
exc():boolean {
   let g=this.g;
   let m=this.me;
   this.confused(g,this.dir);
```

We implement the `confused` method, which does a chance effect, in `09CmdBase.ts`:

```
confused(g:GameIF, dir:WPoint):boolean {
  if (!this.me.is(Buff.Confuse)) { return false; }
  let r = g.rnd;
  if (r.oneIn(2)) { return false; }
  if (this.me.isPly) {
    g.msg('Ply is confused!');
  }
  let cd = r.rndDir2();
  dir.x = cd.x; dir.y = cd.y;
  return true;
}
```

With all our buffs done, it's time we let `24SpellAI.ts` pick different buffs for the different mobs, instead of always picking Confuse:

```
pickBuff(me:Mob, r:Rnd):Buff {
  // Levitate is last buff:
  let range:number = (Buff.Levitate)+1;
  // Clip levels to buff-range:
  let buffIx:number = me.level % range;
  // Pick the Buff at <buffIx> offset:
  let buff:Buff = Buff.Confuse + buffIx;
  console.log(`${me.name} buff: ${buff}`);
  return buff;
}
```

25.3.19 SUMMARY OF THIS CHAPTER'S CHANGES

`able()`, in its full form, ends up looking like this:

```
able(m:Mob, g:GameIF,act:Act):Able {
  let hit = (act == Act.Hit);
  let mov = (act == Act.Move);
  let HOM = (hit || mov);
  let cant = {able:false,turn:false};
  let foil = {able:false,turn:true};
```

```
    let able = {able:true, turn:false};
    //this.confused(m,g);// Confuse MUST be a MBC thing
    if (hit && this.afraid(m,g))  { return cant; }
    if (hit && this.charmed(m,g)) { return cant; }
    if (mov && this.rooted(m,g))  { return cant; }
    if (HOM && this.levitate(m,g)){ return cant; }
    if (this.paralyzed(m,g))      { return foil; }
    if (this.sleep(m,g))          { return foil; }
    if (this.slow(m,g))           { return foil; }
    if (this.freeze(m,g,mov))     { return foil; }
    if (this.petrify(m,g,mov))    { return foil; }
    return able; // nothing blocked us.
}
```

25.3.20 CLOSING THOUGHTS

In this chapter, we have gone a bit overboard with debuffs, mainly to explore the subject. In practice, in your games, it will be important to balance and adjust debuffs. When they work best, debuffs alter the active game rules we play by, subtly or in not-so-subtle ways. But when debuffs involve loss-of-control, it is all too easy to make the game literally unplayable. You may consider giving the player tools and counters to deal with the debuffs. Whatever you do, buffs and debuffs have the power to immensely shape - or distort or wreak havoc on - the feeling of playing your game.

26 Digging

(In which we let the player remove walls he doesn't like)

F 26.1: In the serious adventurer's backpack, you also find lots of heavy mining equipment

26.1　Mr Gorbachev, Tear Down This Wall

Sometimes, the tunnels, rooms and walls don't turn out perfectly. Sometimes, a room is not reachable. Other times, we'd just like to take a shortcut, instead of taking the long way round. To address this, we could add support for **digging**.

26.2　Digging Cost

What does digging entail? Well, if the player could just remove any wall, at any time, at no cost, it would be as if the walls weren't really walls to begin with. That is, they wouldn't really pose an obstacle. So it seems, that digging away a rock wall should have some sort of **cost**.

We could let it cost 10 digging-turns. Or we could assign each wall a **random** digging-cost between 5 and 15 digging-turns. Yet a simpler variant could be to assign it a digging-**chance**. Such that if you roll below a random chance of e.g. 15%, the wall is removed. This means it would sometimes remove with a single digging action, but on average take 7 digging actions to remove (it is not as simple as adding up the 15 percents). There is a tiny chance it would take 100 actions or more! (about 1 in 11½ million). Made like this, we would not want to dig away walls at random or during combat, but if we really really want to remove a wall, we can.

26.3 INTERFACE DESIGN

To dig, the user needs some way to **activate** digging. A number of ways could be suggested:

- you might hold down a **modifier** key (e.g. shift or control) as you move, to specify digging.
- you might activate a digging-**mode** ('modal'), causing you to dig as you move, until you turn it off.
- you might have a **separate** set of keys just for digging in various directions (silly).
- **tool** - it might be an act of wielding - as long as you wield a pick-axe or shovel instead of a weapon, it's digging time.
- **automatic** - it might just be what happens, when you walk into walls. Similar to bump-to-attack, we'd then have bump-to-dig.

We will go with the first variant, holding down a modifier key while moving.

04cmds/26DigCmd.ts:

```
export class DigCmd extends CmdBase {
  constructor(
    public dir:WPoint, public me:Mob,
    public g:GameIF
  ) { super(me,g); }
  exc(): boolean {
    let game = this.g;
    let ply = game.ply;
    let map = <DMapIF> game.curMap();
    let np = ply.pos.plus(this.dir);
    let cell = map.cell(np);
    let e = cell.env;
    if (e != Glyph.Wall && e != Glyph.Rock) {
      game.flash('No rock to dig in.');
      return false;
    }
```

```
    let rnd = game.rnd;
    let dug = rnd.oneIn(10);
    if (dug) {
      cell.env = Glyph.Floor;
      game.msg('ply broke the rock.');
    } else {
      game.flash('ply digs..');
    }
    return true;
  }
}
```

To provide this to the player, we must change `parseKeyCmd()` in class `ParsePly`. At the bottom, where we used to call `moveBumpCmd`, we rewrite that part to now be this:

```
parseKeyCmd(
    c:string, ss:StackIF,
    e:JQuery.KeyDownEvent|null
): CmdIF|null {
  let shift = e?.shiftKey;
..

.. (all existing code here)..
..

  if (!dir.empty()) {
    return (shift
              ? this.digDir(dir)
              : this.moveBumpCmd(dir) );
  }
  return null;
}
digDir(dir:WPoint):CmdIF {
  return new DigCmd(dir, this.ply, this.game);
}
```

The change is, that instead of just calling `moveBumpCmd`, we switch to `digDir`, whenever the shift key is pressed.

With this, the player should be able to (attempt to) dig into walls, by holding down shift as he attempts to move into them.

This is the most basic form of mining and rock removal. A very popular complication is to introduce veins of different strength rock types, and precious minerals inside those veins - metals and gems. For that to make sense, you would typically also want some selection of shops, crafting, trade and merchants, to have some **use** for those minerals.

We can test it with the same runner we used for chapter 25.

27 Ranged Missile Spells

(In which creatures get to shoot missiles)

F 27.1: You may tell a mage his fireball skills are weak, but he might not appreciate it

27.1 MOTIVATION

Our creatures can fight with weapons in melee range. They can also cast an assortment of duration debuffs. But we don't yet have any way to fire missiles at range. Ranged combat adds variety and opportunities, and often simply has a nice feel to it. We want to be able to point in a direction or at a target, and blast away at stuff.

27.2 BALANCE AND LIMITS

If we could point anywhere and keep firing at everything, it would unbalance the game, not least relative to other abilities. We need ways to constrain a ranged ability. One traditional limit regards which directions are possible - maybe you can only fire in the 4 cardinal directions, or in 8 directions. Another limit is some kind of cost - maybe shooting has a cooldown of 21 turns. Maybe it eats your mana. Maybe you can only shoot the number of charges your wand holds. Maybe you can only shoot out to a limited distance? Maybe the strength of the hit depends on how far you shoot - a long range shot could either be stronger (accelerating) or weaker (losing momentum).

27.3 POSSIBILITIES

Our initial goal is a specific kind of bullet shooting. Once we have such a mechanism up and running, we can reuse the same principle for totally different things:

- shooting arrows and crossbow bolts
- **throwing** ordinary items
- **launching** a summoned monster or helper creature
- launching **ourselves** across the room

- pushing an **enemy** away from us
- ejecting a **stream of lava**, ice, electricity, gas, fire, dragon's breath, or water
- **disintegrating** rock
- magnetically **pulling** things closer

27.4 PLAN

Our initial spell will be the so-called **magic missile**. It might be reused as fire-bolt, frost-bolt and lightning-bolt. It will fire in a specific NSEW direction. In principle, we could make it just fire and then immediately hit, reporting what it hit. However, for the humane experience, we'll instead implement it as an animated bullet-moving-one-cell-at-a-time.

27.5 APPROACH & MECHANISM

There are no laws dictating how a missile spell has to function. But we have some ideas about how ours should work. We intend it to do a sort of crude animation. We will introduce and display a projectile in the map. We will make this projectile do a moving animation across the screen. We will alternate between drawing a bullet character on the screen, then erasing it again before drawing it in its next position. Once the bullet either hits something or is otherwise exhausted, we'll dispose of it.

We'll need to make the animation neither too fast nor too slow. A complete bullet trajectory should not take more than 1 second. Let's assume we on average shoot 10 tiles. This suggests each animation step should take around 100 ms. For now, we'll go with such a fixed animation interval. But consider that you could instead work with an accelerating bullet speed. This way, short-range shots could still have a smooth slow speed, without unduly dragging out far-range shots proportionally. That is, a shot four times as far doesn't have to last four times as long.

We haven't done animation before now. All our game turns have been done as single-take updates, with the screen only redrawn once. To achieve animation in the way we now intend, we need to split up our turns into some kind of multi-step affair. We will introduce a new helper screen, to handle our animations. This new screen will be provided with a kind of 'stepper iterator'. The screen will continuously prompt the stepper for a next step and draw the changes, until the stepper reports that it is done.

27.6 DESIGN

The screen will be called StepScreen. We will hook it up to a periodic interval timer, which fires e.g. every 100 ms. At every timer pulse, the stepper is prompted to update the game state. Once the stepper says it's done, the step screen pops back off again, and we are back to the normal game screen. Note that the StepScreen will not react to user keyboard input - it **only** reacts to timer events. (There is a caveat here: We could support some kind of break/escape, to allow the player to get out of erroneous infinite loops, but that is a fight for another day).

So what is the stepper then? Well, it's very much like our existing game commands. The difference is that the stepper can be polled repeatedly, and will report once it has completed. We will design a general StepIF stepper interface, and implement some kind of 'bullet step'.

Consider, that even though we'll initially use the animation step screen for a bullet animation, it has no limits as such - it might as well be used for a nuclear fireball flooding spell that expands in all directions.

Our bullet step, whichever way it ends up working, will have roughly three phases. An initial phase that **launches** the bullet from the appropriate starting position in an appropriate direction. Then a live **travel** phase, where the bullet continues to travel through the landscape, one character cell at a time. Finally, an **impact** phase, where the bullet encounters either a victim or a wall, which causes it to explode, do damage, and stop.

The rules for the bullet are up to you. Instead of stopping, the bullet might instead bounce and ricochet off some surfaces, so that the player might even hit himself if he shoots carelessly.

27.7 A Bullet Spell

In our first efforts with these spells, we'll outfit the player with a simple missile spell. This gives us an easy way to test it. Later, we will probably revoke that spell from the player again - it is too powerful and unrestrained. We will instead give him other spells, which will be suitably restrained in some way, so he can't just blast up the entire dungeon willy-nilly.

The player will press a key to activate the spell. But which way should the missile then fire? We'll have to prompt the player for a direction first. Luckily we already have the `DirCmdScreen` back from our door-opening days, so we can simply pass our bullet spell to that screen. So to `ParsePly`, we'll add this switch case and these methods:

```
case 'm': s = this.bulletCmd(ss); break;

  bulletCmd(ss:StackIF):SScreenIF {
    return this.dir(
      new BulletCmd(this.ply,this.game,ss,this.maker)
    );
  }
  // (dir was already with doorCmd)
  dir(cmd:CmdIF) {
```

```
    return new CmdDirScreen(cmd,this.game,this.maker);
  }
```

Our spell will be the `BulletCmd`. It should activate a `StepScreen` with a 'bullet stepper', and that stepper must be initialized with the player's current position, and the direction that the `Dir` screen chose. Thus `04cmds/27BulletCmd.ts` will be this:

```
export class BulletCmd extends CmdBase {
  dir:WPoint = new WPoint();
  constructor(public me:Mob, public g:GameIF,
              public ss:StackIF, public maker:MakerIF)
  {super(me,g);}
  setDir(dir:WPoint):CmdIF{this.dir=dir; return this;}
  exc():boolean {
    let g=this.g;
    let m=this.me;
    let dmg = 4;
    let school = School.Magic;
    let sprite = Glyph.Bullet;
    let effect = null; // no step-effect.
    let next = new BlastStep(dmg,school,m,g);
    let step:StepIF =
      new DirStep(effect,next,sprite,m.pos.copy(),g);
    step.setDir(this.dir);
    this.ss.push(new StepScreen(g,this.maker,step));
    return false;
  }
}
```

`Glyph.Bullet` doesn't exist, let's add it:

```
// in 07Glyph.ts:
  Bullet,
// in 16GlyphInf1.ts, initGlyphs():
  add(bg,      'blue',    '*',Glyph.Bullet);
  // If you are brave, you can use unicode icons here:
  // https://unicode-table.com/en/sets/star-symbols/
```

We will need to account for the `StepScreen` and those stepper parts. For steppers - the 'step commands', we define this interface:

`04cmds/27StepIF.ts`

```typescript
export interface StepIF {
  // steps return their 'next step'
  excS():StepIF|null;
  setPos(pos:WPoint):void;
  setDir(dir:WPoint):void;
  setTarget(tgt:Mob):void;
  setTime(time:number):void;
}
```

`04cmds/27TimedStep.ts`

```typescript
export class TimedStep implements StepIF {
  time:number=0;
  excS():StepIF|null       {throw 'base excs'; }
  setPos(pos:WPoint):void{throw 'base setPos';}
  setDir(dir:WPoint):void{throw 'base setDir';}
  setTarget(tgt:Mob):void{throw 'base setTarget';}
  setTime(time:number):void { this.time = time; }
}
```

The `StepScreen`, which works with `StepIF`'s, is this:
`06screen/27StepScreen.ts`

```typescript
export class StepScreen extends BaseScreen {
  name:string = 'step';
  constructor(game:GameIF, maker:MakerIF,
              public step:StepIF|null) {
    super(game,maker);
  }
  onKey(e:JQuery.KeyDownEvent, stack:Stack):boolean {
    return false;
  } // keys dont do anything during anim.
  draw(term:TermIF) { super.draw(term); }
  onTime(s:Stack):boolean {
    if (this.step == null) {
        throw 'step is null';
```

```
        }
      this.step = this.step.excS();
      if (this.step) { return true; }
      this.pop_And_RunNPCLoop(s);
      return true;
    }
}
```

We will need a sprite mechanism, for the animations the
steppers do. `MapCell` will get this extra sprite field, and we'll get
an updated `glyph()` method:

```
  public sprite:Glyph|undefined;
  glyph27():Glyph {
    if (this.sprite) { return this.sprite; }
    return (this.obj ? this.obj.g : this.env);
  }
```

We must then update `DrawMap.drawMap18()`, with this changed
part:

```
  let g:Glyph = (seeMob ? c.mob!.g : c.glyph27());
  if (c.sprite) { far = false; }
  let i:GlyphInf1 = GlyphMap1.inf(g);
```

The idea here being, that we ignore the reduced-far-drawing
mechanism, whenever there is a sprite to draw. This is a design
choice - you might as well decide that sprites shouldn't be drawn
outside the visibility range.

Now we can make the actual bullet step, using the sprite
mechanism:

```
export class DirStep extends TimedStep {
  map:DMapIF;
  dir:WPoint|null = null;
  setDir(dir:WPoint):void { this.dir = dir; }
  constructor(
    public effect:StepIF|null,
    public next:StepIF|null,
```

```ts
    public sprite:Glyph,
    public pos:WPoint, public game:GameIF
  ) {
    super();
    this.map = <DMapIF> game.curMap();
  }
  excS():StepIF|null {
    let p = this.pos;
    let map = this.map;
    map.cell(p).sprite = undefined;
    if (this.dir == null) {
      throw 'DirStep.dir is null';
    }
    p.addTo(this.dir);
    // ie abort, don't carry on.
    if (!map.legal(p)) { return null; }
    let cell = map.cell(p);
    let done = cell.blocked();
    if (!done) {
      cell.sprite = this.sprite;
      if (this.effect) {
          this.effect.setPos(p);
          this.effect.excS();
      }
    } else { // transfer args.
      if (this.next) {
        this.next.setPos(p);
      }
    }
    return done ? this.next : this;
  }
}
```

We also need the `BlastStep`, to do damage if the bullet hits:

`04cmds/27BlastStep.ts`

```ts
export class BlastStep extends TimedStep {
  target:Mob|null = null;
```

```
  pos:WPoint|null = null;
  setTarget(tgt:Mob):void { this.target = tgt; }
  setPos(pos:WPoint):void { this.pos = pos.copy(); }
  school():School { return this._school; }
  constructor(
    public amount:number,
    public _school:School,
    public actor:Mob,
    public game:GameIF
  ) { super(); }
  excS():StepIF|null {
    let tgt = this.target;
    if (!tgt) { tgt = this.tgtFromPos(); }
    if (tgt) { // should track attacker and defender both.
      let school = School[this._school];
      let hp = tgt.hp;
      this.game.msg(
        `${tgt.name}${hp} is hurt ${this.amount} ${school}.`
      );
      HealthAdj.dmg(tgt,this.amount,this.game,this.actor);
    } else {
      console.log(' blastStep did not hit any mob.');
    }
    return null; // this is a final step.
  }
  tgtFromPos():Mob|null {
    if (this.pos) {
      let map = <DMapIF> this.game.curMap();
      let cell = map.cell(this.pos);
      if (cell.mob) { return cell.mob; }
    }
    return null;
  }
}
export enum School{Fire,Frost,Magic,Earth,Lightning}
```

27.8 Timing Mechanism

For our animation mechanism to function, we must extend our existing framework with a timer aspect. First, we make the `04EventMgr.ts` class respond to timing:

```
.. // inside constructor, call
   this.initTimer();
..

  initTimer() {
    let interval_ms = 100;
    setInterval(this.onTimer.bind(this), interval_ms);
  }
  onTimer() {
    let change:boolean = this.screen.onTime();
    if (change) { this.screen.draw(this.term); }
  }
```

For this, `04RawScreenIF.ts` must be extended with `onTime()`.

```
onTime():boolean;
```

Thus, `05ScreenStack.ts` must get:

```
onTime():boolean {
    let change = false;
    let s = this.cur();
    if (s) { change = s.onTime(this); }
    return change;
  }
```

This ties into this extension in `05SScreenIF.ts`.

```
onTime(stack: StackIF): boolean;
```

This requires us to have empty placeholder `onTime`'s in our screens, particularly `09BaseScreen.ts`:

```
onTime(stack:Stack):boolean{return false;}
```

We'll need to do the following shim fixups:

```
onTime():boolean{return false;} // RawTestScreen
onTime():boolean{return false;} // StackTestScreen
onTime():boolean{return false;} // MapScreen
onTime():boolean{return false;} // DummyScreen
onTime():boolean{return false;} // OverScreen0
```

With all these parts, `EventMgr` will receive `onTimer()` events, and
forward them to `Stack.onTime()`. It will then forward them to
`StepScreen.onTime(s)`. That is the connection that brings our
animation mechanism to life.

Now that we have all the pieces, let's add a keyboard command to
`parseKeyCmd()` in `09ParsePly.ts`, so the player can access the
command:

```
    case 'm': s = this.bulletCmd(ss); break;
..
  bulletCmd(ss:StackIF):SScreenIF {
    return this.dir(
      new BulletCmd(this.ply,this.game,ss, this.maker)
    );
  }
  dir(cmd: CmdIF) {
    return new CmdDirScreen(cmd,this.game,this.maker);
  }
```

28 Item Spells for Player

(In which we let the player access spells through item use)

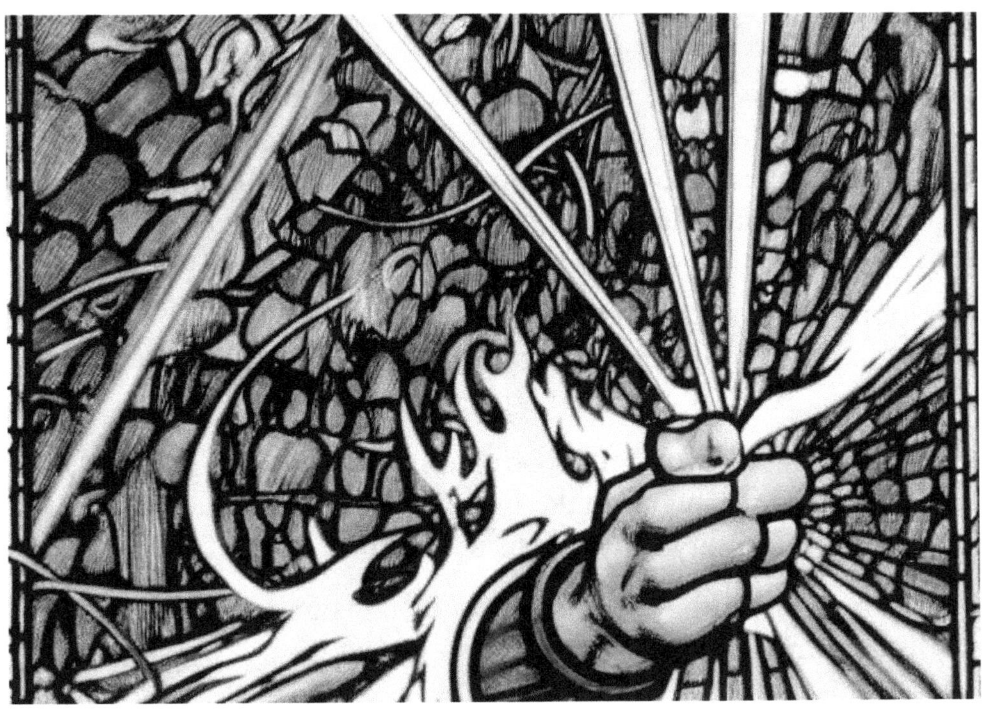

F 28.1: A powerful spell, emanating from the player's hand?

28.1 Player Power Through Items

28.1.1 If Enemies Have Spells, So Should Player

By now, we have given our enemies access to spells. But we have no mechanism that lets the **player** use them. Let's figure out a way for the player to cast spells.

We already have some spells - a number of debuffs, and a missile spell. We'll want a few utility spells too. We pick a heal command and a teleport command.

28.2 Constraining Player's Spell Use

We must decide how the player's access to spells should work. Without limits to how the player can use spells, the game would be difficult to balance - the player would be a walking nuclear bomb. So we must design some **limiting** mechanics or constraints.

One popular constraint is some kind of limited mana pool. Casting spells would cost mana, and once you run out of mana, you must wait until your mana pool replenishes.

Another possible constraint is timed cooldowns. Spells of different strengths would take more or less time to cool down (or to charge up), before you can use them again.

There are any number of possible mechanisms by which we might constrain access to spells.

28.3   OUR CHOICE OF COST: ITEMS

Here, we will control it with one-time-use items found in the dungeon. This way, you can only use spells for which you have found an item. Once you use the item, and the spell, that item is consumed and disappears - you might think of it like eating it.

This means you'll have as many spell 'shots', as you have found items for. There are ways you could vary this. Instead of items having a single charge, you might have items with multiple charges in them (typically wands), and maybe even the possibility of recharging them somehow. You could also let the item degrade and wear out with a chance mechanism, instead of a simple counter.

Or you might have a cooldown-and-recharge mechanism, that requires a rest period before the item is ready for use again. However we go about it, the aim is to put sensible limits on the rate of spell usage, so the player can't go fully nuclear on his environment.

28.4   POTION & SCROLL ITEMS

If we are to use items for spells, at the very least we'll need the items themselves. Ideas for first items could be a healing potion, and a teleport scroll. Let us start with those.

We can do so, by defining a `Scroll` glyph, by defining an `ObjType` for the `Scroll`, and by extending our builder's `addItemToPlyBag()` with such a scroll object. Now we have a scroll. Ditto for potion.

To `Glyph` and to `initGlyphs()` in `GlyphInf1`, we add this:

```
// 07Glyph.ts:
  Potion,
  Scroll
// 16GlyphInf1.ts:
```

```
add(bg,      'blue',    '!',Glyph.Potion);
add(bg,      'yellow',  '?',Glyph.Scroll);
```

Then to the `objtypes` array in `21ObjTypes.ts`, we add this:

```
{g: Glyph.Potion,  s:Slot.NotWorn},
{g: Glyph.Scroll,  s:Slot.NotWorn},
```

Already, this has added potions and scrolls to our dungeon! To help ourselves a bit, we'll also stuff a few in the player's bag. So, we clone `24Builder2m.ts` to `28Builder2n.ts`, and add these lines to method `addItemToPlayerBag()`:

```
bag?.add(new Obj(Glyph.Potion, Slot.NotWorn) );
bag?.add(new Obj(Glyph.Scroll, Slot.NotWorn) );
```

We will of course need a runner, `index28_useItems.ts`:

```
ScreenMaker2_Fixed.Gfirst(new Builder2n());
```

And voilà, we have potions and scrolls.. But given that we can't **wear** them, we need to do more.

28.5 A Menu to Use Items

To get further, we must extend the `22ItemScreen.ts` menu with a new choice - **use** item. We can display that menu label, and react with a case on keypress:

```
// 22ItemScreen.ts, in draw():
   term.txt(0,y++,'u use',    fg,bg);
// in onKey():
      case 'u': this.useItem(s); break;
// ..
  useItem(ss:Stack):void {
    let g = this.game;
    let finder =
      new FindObjSpell(this.obj,this.ix,g,ss,this.make);
    let spell:CmdIF|null = <CmdIF> finder.find();
```

```
  if (spell == null) { return; }
  ss.pop();
  if (spell) {
    if (spell.turn()) {
      this.npcTurns(ss);
    }
  }
}
```

This then requires us to add `04cmds/28FindObjSpell.ts`: (which so far does nothing)

```
export class FindObjSpell {
  constructor(public obj:Obj, public ix:number,
              public g:GameIF, public ss:Stack,
              public maker:MakerIF) {}

  find(): CmdIF|null {return null;}
}
```

28.6 IMPLEMENTING ITEM SPELL USE

At this point, we then require an actual implementation of `find()` for `FindObjSpell`. It must handle two things: It must procure the spell action. And it must allow us to destroy the consumed bag item. This surfaces a couple of problems:

- we haven't picked out which spell should happen.
- in case of multiple available spell-types, we haven't designed how our code can indicate which spell to call.
- consuming an item should only happen on completed spell cast.

For the second problem, we'll eventually just use an enum and something akin to a switch-statement, to map some enum values to commands.

The overall structure of `FindObjSpell` will look like this:

```
export class FindObjSpell  {
  constructor(public obj:Obj, public ix:number,
              public g:GameIF, public ss:Stack,
              public maker:MakerIF) {}


  usable(obj:Obj):boolean {
    let canUse = (obj.slot == Slot.NotWorn);
    if (!canUse) {
      this.g.flash(
        `${obj.name()} is not usable: ${obj.slot}`
      );
    }
    return canUse;
  }


  find(): CmdIF|null {
    let obj:Obj = this.obj;
    if (!this.usable(obj)) {return null;}

    let g = this.g;
    let me = g.ply;
    var cmd:CmdIF|undefined;
    // ??..
    return cmd;
  }
}
```

So, what spells should happen, and how do we select them? Our first spells will be TELEPORT & HEAL. For now, we'll simply switch based on the item type - the potion will be a heal potion, and the scroll will be a teleport scroll. Thus, `// ??` becomes this:

```
// instead of ?? we put:
  switch (obj.g) {
  case Glyph.Potion:
    cmd = new HealCmd(obj.level+4,me,g); break;
  case Glyph.Scroll:
```

```
      cmd = new PortCmd(6,me,g); break;
    default:
      return null;
    }
```

We'll then need those two spells. `04cmds/28HealCmd.ts` is

```
export class HealCmd extends CmdBase {
  constructor(
      public r:number,
      public me:Mob, public g:GameIF
  ) { super(me,g); }
  exc(): boolean {
    let g = this.g;
    let R = g.rnd;
    let r = this.r;
    let a = Math.ceil( r*0.5);
    let b = Math.floor(r*1.5);
    let hp = R.rnd(a,b);
    HealthAdj.heal(this.me, hp);
    let msg = `${this.me.name} feels better (${hp})`;
    g.msg(msg);
    return true;
  }
}
```

`04cmds/28PortCmd.ts` is:

```
export class PortCmd extends CmdBase {
  constructor(
      public r:number, public me:Mob, public g:GameIF
  ) { super(me,g); }
  exc(): boolean {
    let g = this.g;
    let map = <DMapIF> g.curMap();
    let p = this.pick(this.me.pos, this.r, map);
    if (!p) { return false; }
    map.moveMob(this.me,p);
    g.msg(`${this.me.name} shimmers`);
    return true;
```

```
  }
  pick(c:WPoint,r:number,map:DMapIF):WPoint|null {
    let R = this.g.rnd;
    let p = new WPoint();
    for (let ix=15; ix>0; ) {
      let dx=R.rnd(-r,r), dy = R.rnd(-r,r);
      p.x = c.x + dx;
      p.y = c.y + dy;
      if (!map.legal(p)) { continue; }
      --ix;
      if (map.cell(p).blocked()){continue;}
      return p;
    }
    return null;
  }
}
```

If you try to use the runner now, you can actually find **usable**
items in the dungeon, and you can **use them** for their spells (try
the ones in your starter inventory). Note we don't yet consume
the items on use, so you can right now reuse them indefinitely.

28.7 Add Zap Wand for Zap Spell

Phew, that was easy! ..Or was it? Let's try to add a wand which
zaps magic missiles:

```
// 07Glyph.ts:
  Wand
// 16GlyphInf1.ts:
  add(bg,       'red',       '-',Glyph.Wand);
```

But our simple `case` statements in `FindObjSpell.find()` can't
really handle this wand. The problem is that the zap spell
requires the user to specify a direction first - the direction he
wants to shoot in.

So we really need to activate the `DirCmdScreen` instead first. And we'll need some kind of command to pass to it. Naively, that would simply be the `BulletCmd` itself. But there is a tiny significant problem there: Because we are using an item, we also need to **consume** the item, if the spell is executed. But we don't want to consume the spell item before we complete triggering the spell.

One way we could achieve that, would be to wrap the `BulletCmd` in some kind of `UseDirItem` command. That is, the `DirCmdScreen` would pick up a direction and pass it to `UseDirItem`, and `UseDirItem` would again forward the direction on to an inner `BulletCmd`. But that is a cumbersome design - we would end up needing a host of such UseXXXItem helpers.

Instead, we will recognise we have a general issue here, of paying the 'cost' upon executing a given command. Because of this, we will expand the interface of `CmdIF`, to hold a possible cost. If the cost field contains a non-empty cost, we'll execute that cost as part of `turn()`.

`04cmds/28CostIF.ts`:

```
export interface CostIF {
  pay(): boolean;
}
```

Then these parts to `09CmdIF.ts`:

```
  cost:CostIF|undefined;
  setCost(cost:CostIF|undefined):void;
```

And these implementation parts to `09CmdBase.ts`:

```
  cost:CostIF|undefined;
  setCost(cost:CostIF|undefined) { this.cost = cost;}

  pay():boolean {
    if (!this.cost) { return true; }
    return this.cost.pay();
```

```
    }
  public turn():boolean {
    .. // at the end of turn():
    if (!this.pay()) { return true; }
    return this.exc();
  }
  ..
```

The intent here is: When we do a turn(), we call CmdBase.pay. If the command has no cost, pay is automatically satisfied. If instead the command has a cost, we call pay() on that cost. If pay() fails, it still counts as using a turn, but we don't get the desired effect.

This allows us to pay risky costs, for example zapping an empty wand, or insisting on attempting a spell when we are low on mana. Such things carry the risk of the wand exploding, disintegrating or backfiring, or our hero fainting from low mana.

(Note you might need a further complication here - some well-behaved games would ask the player to confirm yes/no if he would go through with a risky choice.)

Now with our cost structure in place, we can make a CostIF instance that consumes a used item: 28ItemCost.ts

```
export class ItemCost implements CostIF {
  constructor(public g:GameIF, public obj:Obj,
              public objIx:number){}
  pay(): boolean {
    this.g.msg(`You use ${this.obj.name()}. `);
    this.g.bag!.removeIx(this.objIx);
    return true;
  }
}
```

We can then update FindObjSpell.find to be this:

```
  find(): CmdIF|SScreenIF|null {
    let obj:Obj = this.obj;
```

```
if (!this.usable(obj)) {return null;}
let g = this.g;
let me = g.ply;
var s:SScreenIF|undefined;
var cmd:CmdIF|undefined;
switch (obj.g) {
case Glyph.Potion:
  cmd = new HealCmd(obj.level+4,me,g); break;
case Glyph.Scroll:
  cmd = new PortCmd(6,me,g); break;
case Glyph.Wand:
  cmd = new BulletCmd(g.ply,g,this.ss,this.maker);
  s = new CmdDirScreen(cmd,g,this.maker);
  break;
default: return null;
}
cmd.setCost(new ItemCost(g,this.obj,this.ix));
return s ? s : cmd;
}
```

That is, we allow it to return screens instead of commands. And
all the item commands now come with a cost, in the form of
consuming the used item.

In `22ItemScreen.ts`, `useItem()` must now be updated to this:

```
useItem(ss:Stack):void {
  let g = this.game;
  let finder =
    new FindObjSpell(this.obj,this.ix,g,ss,this.make);
  let spell:CmdIF|SScreenIF|null = finder.find();
  if (spell == null) { return; }
  ss.pop();
  if (spell instanceof CmdBase) {
    if (spell.turn()) { this.npcTurns(ss); }
  } else { // (it's a screen)
    ss.push(<SScreenIF> spell);
  }
}
}
```

The idea here is, that when `find()` returns a command, we execute it as a turn, and run `npcTurns`. But if `find()` returns a screen, we just push that screen. The new screen must then take care of what will happen - maybe it will lead to a turn, maybe the user just cancels again.

With this, we can both execute simple direct spells like the potion heal, as well as complicated spells, like the missile-wand (that require further user input).

28.8   SPELL CHARGES

We could easily extend this system to handle charges > 1, so that an item is only consumed, once you have used all its charges.

We could make it, so most items have 1 charge, and thus are consumed when you use them. Then we could make the wand have multiple charges. In `21Obj.ts` we could add

```
charges:number=1;
```

Then we could make a new cost, `28ChargedItemCost.ts`:

```
export class ChargedItemCost0 implements CostIF {
  constructor(public g:GameIF, public obj:Obj,
              public objIx:number){}
  pay(): boolean {
    let o = this.obj;
    if (o.charges<=0) { return false; }
    this.g.msg(`You use ${this.obj.name()}.`);
    --o.charges;
    if (o.charges>0) { return true; }
    this.g.bag!.removeIx(this.objIx);
    return true;
  }
}
```

Only once zero charges are left, do we destroy the item.

We guard against using anything already exhausted of charges. That case could instead offer a risky choice of '*are you sure you will try to use the empty wand?*', with risks of explosions and backfiring.

It is a questionable or inelegant approach to use the same code paths for single-use items and charge-items. It would be better to separate the two cases, as they possibly have as many differences as they have things in common. Single-use items should just be used up with no fanfare. They have no 'zero charges, are you sure?' exploding case. They cannot be recharged or charged up.

Charge-use items probably shouldn't emit a message on ordinary use. Their last use should warn that they are now empty. And when using their last charge, they should not disappear, but just become e.g. empty wands. **If** they should disappear, it should more correctly happen as a high risk when trying to fire them from their emptied state.

However, to handle such a split-up, we must be able to distinguish between single-use and charged items. It could either be done explicitly, or by simply leaving `charges` empty on single-use items. A simple such version would be

```typescript
export class ChargedItemCost1 implements CostIF {
  constructor(public g:GameIF, public obj:Obj,
              public objIx:number){}
  pay(): boolean {
    let o = this.obj;
    if (o.charges<=0) {
      this.g.msg(`You use ${this.obj.name()}`);
    } else {
      --o.charges;
      if (o.charges>0) { return true; }
      this.g.msg(`${this.obj.name()} used up`);
    }
    this.g.bag!.removeIx(this.objIx);
    return true;
```

```
    }
}
```

This then requires `charges` to default to zero, for ordinary items. We must do something to make wands charged. We can do so by adding this case to `makeTemplateObj()` in `21ObjTypes.ts`:

```
obj.level = objLevel;
if (obj.g == Glyph.Wand) {obj.charges = rnd.rnd(1,level);}
```

We must of course update the two usages of `ItemCost` to be `ChargedItemCost1`, in `FindObjSpell` and in `UseCmd`.

29 GENERIC SPELL INTERFACE

(In which we make a uniform mechanism to activate all spells through)

F 29.1: Are all those utility spells triggered by magical potions?

29.1   INTENT

We originally wanted the player and his enemies to have the same abilities, and to play by the same rules. We have been straying in that regard lately. The player has no access to debuffs, and the monsters can't teleport, heal, or shoot.

We also hinted we lack a way to **refer** to any given spell. We circumvented this in the previous chapter by switching on the object type, and then manually creating our spell commands one by one.

We will now address these things by making a kind of spell factory, and an enum naming all our spells.

29.2   SPELL ENUMERATION

Behold the enum `04cmds/29Spell.ts`:

```
export enum Spell {
Heal,        // U
D_Charm,     //B
D_Slow,      //S
D_Afraid,    //B
Missile,     // U
D_Poison,    // D
D_Confuse,   //S
D_Silence,   //B
Cleanse,     // U
D_Stun,      //S
D_Burn,      // D
D_Blind,     //B
Multiply,    // U
D_Freeze,    //S
D_Root,      //B
D_Shock,     // D
Port,        // U
```

```
D_Paralyze,//S
D_Sleep,    //B
D_Petrify, //S
Summon,     // U
D_Bleed,    // D
D_Levitate,//B
D_Disarm,   //B
None,
}
```

We have not given much thought to the power **ordering** of our spells until now. We intend the dungeon and its monsters to get more difficult as we delve deeper. It follows, that the early spells should be weaker, and the later spells more powerful. I have sorted the `Spell` enumeration above in an approximate order of power. I have also tried to mix and shuffle the different kinds of effects, so we don't get e.g. three slowing effects in a row.

We want the player to find more powerful items deeper in the dungeon. So the later spells should only appear on items found further down.

29.3 PLAN

To make our enum work, we'll make a factory class with a method that switches on all its possible values, and constructs commands for each them.

Is that all we need? Well, no.. Earlier, the zap spell required us to employ the `CmdDirScreen`. We face something similar here.

For the monsters, we need code to decide how they should use the spell. If they use the zap spell, it must target their aim in a reasonable manner. We may hope they will sometimes shoot their friends with so-called friendly fire. If they cast heal, maybe they could heal allies instead of just healing themselves?

How should the player cast debuffs? It could work in many ways, e.g. targeting nearest enemy, or allowing you to choose a target. We will simply make them missile spells, so that you shoot a debuff like a projectile.

We must also design how our item spells should be distributed. Earlier we had a separate item for each spell. But with 24 or more spells, that becomes tedious. Instead we'll put a spell field on the `Obj` class.

For now, armour and weapons should not have spells on them. Though there is an idea in having magic armour which confers magic abilities, we don't want to do so simply by putting any spell value directly on a helmet.

As in the item effects chapter, it makes sense for potions, scrolls and wands to have spell effects. Naïvely, we could combine all of them with all spells. Alternatively and traditionally, potions, scrolls and wands have effects divided between them:

- Wands would mostly be aimed projectile spells. They might hold our debuffs.
- Potions would affect the drinker, and the drinker's body in particular.
- Scrolls would be any sort of 'other' magic effect.

For now, we will go with 'any spell for any item', but the above ideas have merit.

29.4 PLAYER SPELL ACCESS

We'll first complete the player's spell arsenal. To help with this, we will give the player a spell menu screen, so we can test our spells: 29SpellScreen.ts

```
export class SpellScreen extends BaseScreen {
  name:string = 'spell';
```

```
constructor(game:GameIF,maker:MakerIF){super(game,maker);}
pos2char(pos:number) {
  return String.fromCharCode(65+pos);
}
char2pos(c:string) {
  let pos=c.charCodeAt(0)-'a'.charCodeAt(0); return pos;
}
draw(term:TermIF) {
  super.draw(term);
  term.txt(0,1,'Spells:','yellow','black');
  let top=1;
  let y=top,x=0;
  for (let s:Spell=0; s<Spell.None; ++s) {
    let c = this.pos2char(s);
    let L = Spell[s];
    term.txt(x,1+y++, `${c} ${L}`, 'yellow', 'black');
    if (y>12) { y=top;x +=14; }
  }
}
onKey(e:JQuery.KeyDownEvent,s:Stack):boolean  {
  this.game.log.clearQueue();
  s.pop();
  let pos = this.char2pos(e.key); this.itemMenu(pos,s);
  return true;
}
itemMenu(pos:number, ss:Stack):void {
  let s:Spell = pos;
  let label = Spell[s];
  if (!label) {return;}
  this.doSpell(s,ss);
}
doSpell(s:Spell, ss:Stack) {
  let finder = new SpellFinder(this.game,ss,this.make);
  let cost:CostIF|undefined = undefined;
  let spell:CmdIF|SScreenIF|null = finder.find(s,cost);
  if (spell == null) { return; }
  if (spell instanceof CmdBase) {
    if (spell.turn()) { this.npcTurns(ss); }
```

```
      } else { // (it's a screen)
        ss.push(<SScreenIF> spell);
      }
    }
}
```

We will let the screen replace the earlier bullet command in
`parseKeyCmd`, in `09ParsePly.ts`. So when you press M, you now
get a whole menu of spells.

```
//case 'm': s = this.bulletCmd(ss); break;
case 'm': s = new SpellScreen(this.game,this.maker); break;
```

29.5   SPELLFINDER FOR THE SCREEN

Then we must implement that `SpellFinder`, which the screen
used. This entails providing the player's missing spell
commands, notably his debuff spells, which will take the form of
missiles. Because of how we originally made the missile
command, it's a simple matter of plugging in a configurable blast
step, which applies a debuff instead of damage. In the code
below, this is handled by `PayloadCmd`.

`04cmds/29SpellFinder.ts`, similar to our earlier `FindObjSpell`:

```
export class SpellFinder {
 constructor(public g:GameIF, public ss:Stack,
             public maker:MakerIF) {}
 find(spell:Spell,
      cost:CostIF|undefined): CmdIF|SScreenIF|null {
   let g = this.g;
   let me = g.ply;
   let level = 1;
   var s:SScreenIF|undefined;
   var cmd:CmdIF;
```

```
  let b = this.buff;
  switch (spell) {
  case Spell.Heal:      cmd = new HealCmd(level,me,g); break;
  case Spell.D_Charm:    ({s,cmd}=b(Buff.Charm,   me));break;
  case Spell.D_Slow:     ({s,cmd}=b(Buff.Slow,    me));break;
  case Spell.D_Afraid:   ({s,cmd}=b(Buff.Afraid,  me));break;
  case Spell.Missile:
    s = this.dir(
      cmd = new BulletCmd(g.ply,g,this.ss,this.maker)
    );
    break;
  case Spell.D_Poison: ({s,cmd}=b(Buff.Poison, me));break;
  case Spell.D_Confuse:({s,cmd}=b(Buff.Confuse,me));break;
  case Spell.D_Silence:({s,cmd}=b(Buff.Silence,me));break;
  case Spell.Cleanse: cmd = new CleanseAllCmd(me,g); break;
  case Spell.D_Stun:     ({s,cmd}=b(Buff.Stun,   me));break;
  case Spell.D_Burn:     ({s,cmd}=b(Buff.Burn,   me));break;
  case Spell.D_Blind:    ({s,cmd}=b(Buff.Blind,  me));break;
  case Spell.Multiply:cmd = new MultiplyCmd(me,g); break;
  case Spell.D_Freeze:  ({s,cmd}=b(Buff.Freeze, me));break;
  case Spell.D_Root:     ({s,cmd}=b(Buff.Root,   me));break;
  case Spell.D_Shock:    ({s,cmd}=b(Buff.Shock,  me));break;
  case Spell.Port:    cmd = new PortCmd(6,me,g);break;
  case Spell.D_Paralyze:({s,cmd}=b(Buff.Paralyze,me));break;
  case Spell.D_Sleep:   ({s,cmd}=b(Buff.Sleep,  me));break;
  case Spell.D_Petrify:({s,cmd}=b(Buff.Petrify,me));break;
  case Spell.Summon: cmd = new SummonCmd(me,g);break;
  case Spell.D_Bleed:    ({s,cmd}=b(Buff.Bleed,  me));break;
  case Spell.D_Levitate:({s,cmd}=b(Buff.Levitate,me));break;
  case Spell.D_Disarm: ({s,cmd}=b(Buff.Disarm, me));break;
  default: return null;
  }
  cmd.setCost(cost);
  return s ? s : cmd;
}
buff(buff:Buff,me:Mob): CmdOrScreen {
  let buffCmd = new BuffCmd(buff,me,this.g,me);
  let {cmd,s} =  this.payload(buffCmd, me);
```

```
    return {cmd:cmd,s:s};
  }
  payload(inner:CmdIF,me:Mob):CmdOrScreen {
    let cmd:CmdIF = new PayloadCmd(
      me,this.g,this.ss,this.maker,inner
    );
    let dirScreen:SScreenIF = this.dir(cmd);
    return {cmd:cmd,s:dirScreen};
  }
  dir(cmd:CmdIF):SScreenIF {
    return new CmdDirScreen(cmd,this.g,this.maker);
  }
}
```

29.6 THE NEW SPELL COMMANDS

We saw a couple of new spells in there, so let's implement them:
04cmds\29MultiplyCmd.ts

```
export class MultiplyCmd extends CmdBase {
  constructor(
      public me:Mob, public g:GameIF
  ) { super(me,g); }
  exc(): boolean {
    let g = this.g;
    let map = <DMapIF> g.curMap();
    let p = this.find(map,g.rnd);
    if (p == null) { return true; }

    this.spawnMob(p,map,g);
    return true;
  }
  spawnMob(p:WPoint,map:DMapIF,g:GameIF) {
    let m = this.me;
    let b = <BuildIF3> g.build;
    b.addNPC(m.g,p.x,p.y,map,m.level);
    g.msg(`${m.name} breeds`);
```

```
  }
  find(map:DMapIF,r:Rnd):WPoint|null {
    let pos = this.me.pos;
    let c:WPoint[] = [];
    let a=new WPoint();
    for (a.y=-1;a.y<=1;++a.y) {
      for (a.x=-1;a.x<=1;++a.x) {
        let b = pos.plus(a);
        if (!map.blocked(b)) {c.push(b);}
      }
    }
    return this.pick(c,r);
  }
  pick(c:WPoint[], r:Rnd):WPoint|null {
    if (c.length == 0) { return null;}
    let ix = r.rnd(c.length);
    return c[ix];
  }
}
```

And, built on top of this, `04cmds\29SummonCmd.ts`

```
export class SummonCmd extends MultiplyCmd {
  spawnMob(p:WPoint,map:DMapIF,g:GameIF) {
    let m = this.me;
    let b = <BuildIF3> g.build;
    let s = b.addMapLevel_Mob(p,map,g.rnd);
    g.msg(`${m.name} summons ${s.name}`);
  }
}
```

These spells are really intended for the enemies to use, but as we
are making a unified spell interface, we make them generally
available.

`Multiply` makes monsters breed. That is, the monster clones
itself. And then those clones **also** clone themselves!

`Summon` instead summons similar-level monsters. If those
summoned monsters don't themselves summon or breed, it may

be less dangerous than multiply. But as the summoned monsters might be higher level, it may be otherwise dangerous. And as it summons similar-level monsters, it could indeed also summon its own (summoning) type. We might consider guarding against that, so it explicitly wouldn't summon its own type.

The player can cast summon (if he really wants to..) In fact, he can even cast **multiply**, but we probably shouldn't let him do that..

29.7 REUSABLE PAYLOAD MISSILE SPELL

We must account for `PayloadCmd`:

```
export class PayloadCmd extends CmdBase {
  dir:WPoint = new WPoint();
  constructor(public me:Mob, public g:GameIF,
              public ss:StackIF, public maker:MakerIF,
              public payload:CmdIF)
  {super(me,g);}
  setDir(dir:WPoint):CmdIF{this.dir=dir; return this;}
  exc():boolean {
    let g=this.g;
    let m=this.me;
    let sprite = Glyph.Bullet;
    let effect = null; // no step-effect.
    let next = new PayloadStep(m,g, this.payload);
    let step:StepIF =
      new DirStep(effect,next,sprite,m.pos.copy(),g);
    step.setDir(this.dir);
    this.ss.push(new StepScreen(g,this.maker,step));
    return false;
  }
}
```

It accepts an inner payload which it will execute if it hits. That part is done by the `PayloadStep`. It is just a slightly modified version of `BlastStep`:

```typescript
export class PayloadStep extends TimedStep {
  target:Mob|null = null;
  pos:WPoint|null = null;
  setTarget(tgt:Mob):void { this.target = tgt; }
  setPos(pos:WPoint):void { this.pos = pos.copy(); }
  constructor(
    public actor:Mob,
    public game:GameIF,
    public payload:CmdIF
  ) { super(); }
  excS():StepIF|null {
    let tgt = this.target;
    if (!tgt) { tgt = this.tgtFromPos(); }
    if (tgt) {
      this.payload.setTarget(tgt);
      this.payload.raw();
    } else {
      console.log(' payloadStep did not hit any mob.');
    }
    return null; // this is a final step.
  }
  tgtFromPos():Mob|null {
    if (this.pos) {
      let map = <DMapIF> this.game.curMap();
      let cell = map.cell(this.pos);
      if (cell.mob) { return cell.mob; }
    }
    return null;
  }
}
```

Thus, `PayloadCmd` simply lets us provide e.g. a `BuffCmd` to be executed when the missile hits.

We must adjust `09CmdIF.ts` to accomodate `setTarget`:

```typescript
  tgt:Mob|undefined; // ch29
```

```
  setTarget(tgt:Mob):void; // ch29
```

And we implement this in `CmdBase`:

```
  tgt:Mob|undefined; // ch29
  ..
  setTarget(tgt:Mob):void { this.tgt = tgt; } // ch29
```

With `SpellScreen` and `SpellFinder` in place, we have taken care
of the player. He can now execute any spell, at least for testing
purposes.

29.8   ITEM SPELLS, VERSION 2

Once we have made sure they all work, it's time to integrate the
spells with our items. It is not all our items that spells make
sense for - at least for now, our armour shouldn't trigger spells.
Instead, we'll mainly hook them up to potions, scrolls and wands.

We will not distinguish greatly between the different item kinds.
But we should maybe make wands rarer, since they are most
useful and powerful.

We will tie the spells to levels, so spell N is most likely to appear
at level N. Note that right now, weak spells will not appear on
deep levels. This could alternatively be changed, so dungeon
level N would contain items from any level between 0 and N.

We can start by adding the attribute to `Obj`:

```
..
constructor(public g:Glyph,
            public slot:Slot,
            public spell:Spell=Spell.None)
        {}
..
```

Then, in `makeTemplateObj` in `ObjTypes`, we add this:

```
  switch (obj.g) {
    case Glyph.Potion:
    case Glyph.Scroll:
    case Glyph.Wand:
      this.setItemSpell(obj,rnd);
  }
  return obj;
}
static setItemSpell(o:Obj,r:Rnd) {
  let L = r.spiceUpLevel(o.level);
  o.spell = this.spellForLevel(L);
}
static MaxSpell:number = Spell.None;
static spellForLevel(L:number):Spell {
  let s:Spell = L % this.MaxSpell;
  return s;
}
```

We must then change `FindObjSpell` to respect this new setting
in `find()`, so we'll rename the old `find` to `find28`, and make a
new `find29` that follows `Obj.spell`:

```
find29(): CmdIF|SScreenIF|null {
  let g=this.g;
  let obj:Obj = this.obj;
  if (!this.usable29(obj,g)) {return null;}
  let finder = new SpellFinder(g,this.ss,this.maker);
  let cost = new ChargedItemCost1(g,this.obj,this.ix);
  return finder.find(obj.spell,cost);
}
usable29(obj:Obj,g:GameIF):boolean {
  let canUse = (obj.spell != Spell.None);
  if (!canUse) {
    g.flash(`${obj.name()} is not usable: ${obj.slot}`);
  }
  return canUse;
}
```

29.9 RARE WANDS

We can make wands rarer, by changing `21ObjTypes.ts` like so:

```typescript
  static getRndTemplate(r:Rnd):ObjTypeIF {
    let ix = r.rnd(ObjTypes.objtypes.length);
    let tmpl:ObjTypeIF = ObjTypes.getTmpl(ix);
    return tmpl;
  }
  static rareWands(level:number,r:Rnd):Obj {
    for(;;) {
      let t = this.getRndTemplate(r);
      if (t.g == Glyph.Wand) {
        if (!r.pct(level*3)) { continue; }
      }
      return this.makeTemplateObj(level,r,t);
    }
  }
  static rndLevelObj(level:number, r:Rnd):Obj {
    return this.rareWands(level,r);
  }
```

It works this way: We pick random templates the same way we used to. But whenever the template picked is a wand, we do an extra probability percentage check. If that check fails, we loop back and try to pick another template.

On the low starter levels, we'll only have a chance of a few percent to get a wand. But as we approach the deep levels around 30, wands should appear as often as other items (i.e. around 90%).

We've hooked the `rareWands` method into the existing `rndLevelObj` method, so anybody using the latter will now get the services of our new method.

29.10 DISTINGUISHING ITEM QUALITIES

We could consider disguising the various spells behind physical attributes, like colors. This is normally used for scrambling in **Identification Systems**, but we might choose to instead keep the colors the same each time - we could do so, either by fixing the random number seed we use for scrambling them, or by just not scrambling them at all.

Now, about those colors.. The basic idea is to have a color for each kind of spell. So let's make ourselves an array of colors. Behold, 24 colors for 24 spells - `03build/29Colors.ts`:

```
export class Colors {
  static c:string[][] = [
  ['amber','amber'],
  ['','cinnober'],
  ['','crimson'],
  ['','vermillion'],
  ['','scarlet'],
  ['','indigo'],
  ['','teal'],
  ['','turquoise'],
  ['','azure'],
  ['','verdigris'],
  ['','violet'],
  ['','tangerine'],
  ['','lime'],
  ['','cerulean'],
  ['','beige'],
  ['','puce'],
  ['','tan'],
  ['','tawny'],
  ['','emerald'],
  ['','chartreuse'],
  ['','mauve'],
  ['','ruby'],
  ['','coral'],
```

```
    ['','taffy'],
  ];// 24 spells need 24 colors.
}
```

The reason each color has two items, is in case we want a color
name that HTML doesn't know about. Then we could put the
html color #AA99FF in the first item, and the display label in the
second. For now, we've only used names HTML knows about.

Inside the innermost loop of DrawMap.drawMap18(), we add this
bit:

```
if (far) {
  bg=unlit; fg=(c.lit?farlit:unlit);
} else { // near
  bg=i.bg; fg=i.fg;
  if (c.obj && c.obj.spell != Spell.None) { // ch29
    fg = Colors.c[c.obj.spell][1];
  }
  if (!c.lit) { c.lit = true; }
}
..
```

It says, that if the cell has an item, and that item has a spell, we
will color with that instead. We can do even better - in
Obj.desc(), we can do this:

```
desc():string {
  let label = this.name();
  if (this.spell != Spell.None) { // ch29
    let quality = Colors.c[this.spell][1];
    return `${quality} ${label}`;
  }
  return `${label}${this.level}`;
}
```

So when we look at a spell item, it will say things like crimson
potion here. If you don't like using colors for this, you can
instead use the proper spell name, with this line instead:

```
let quality = Spell[this.spell];
```

29.11 UPDATING THE ITEMS IN BUILDER

As we added the spell property to `Obj`, we added it as a third argument to the constructor. To be fair, we should introduce an updated builder to match this. We clone `28Builder2n.ts` to `29Builder2o.ts`, and make `index29_enumspell.ts`:

```
ScreenMaker2_Fixed.Gfirst(new Builder2o());
```

Then we can fix `29Builder2o.ts`, so all its new `Obj..` include the spell, i.e.

```
bag?.add(new Obj(Glyph.Scroll,Slot.NotWorn,Spell.Port));
```

We don't have to update it everywhere else though, since we wrote the constructor with a default.

29.12 ENEMY SPELL ACCESS

With `FindSpell`, we've taken care of the player. But we must also make it so the monsters can use all spells. That will be the class `NPCSpellFinder`.

Though it will work in a similar way to `FindSpell`, it must calculate and pick sensible arguments for the monster spells, instead of pushing input screens for them. However, the NPCs might still push screens, namely if they try to cast missile spells. For most spells, we can simply instantiate their commands, similarly to how `FindObjSpell` and `SpellFinder` did it. Behold, `04cmds/29NPCSpellFinder.ts`:

```
export class NPCSpellFinder {
  ply:Mob;
  constructor(public g:GameIF, public ss:Stack,
```

```
            public maker:MakerIF)
{ this.ply = g.ply; }
  find(me:Mob,spell:Spell,cost:CostIF|undefined):
  CmdIF|SScreenIF|null
{
  let g = this.g;
  let level = 1;
  var s:SScreenIF|undefined;
  var cmd:CmdIF;
  let b=this.buff;
  switch (spell) {
  case Spell.Heal:      cmd = new HealCmd(level,me,g); break;
  case Spell.D_Charm:   cmd=b(me,Buff.Charm    ); break;
  case Spell.D_Slow:    cmd=b(me,Buff.Slow     ); break;
  case Spell.D_Afraid:  cmd=b(me,Buff.Afraid   ); break;
  case Spell.Missile:
    cmd=this.aim(new BulletCmd(me,g,this.ss,this.maker));
    break;
  case Spell.D_Poison:  cmd=b(me,Buff.Poison   ); break;
  case Spell.D_Confuse: cmd=b(me,Buff.Confuse  ); break;
  case Spell.D_Silence: cmd=b(me,Buff.Silence  ); break;
  case Spell.Cleanse:   cmd = new CleanseAllCmd(me,g); break;
  case Spell.D_Stun:    cmd=b(me,Buff.Stun     ); break;
  case Spell.D_Burn:    cmd=b(me,Buff.Burn     ); break;
  case Spell.D_Blind:   cmd=b(me,Buff.Blind    ); break;
  case Spell.Multiply:  cmd = new MultiplyCmd(me,g); break;
  case Spell.D_Freeze:  cmd=b(me,Buff.Freeze   ); break;
  case Spell.D_Root:    cmd=b(me,Buff.Root     ); break;
  case Spell.D_Shock:   cmd=b(me,Buff.Shock    ); break;
  case Spell.Port:      cmd = new PortCmd(6,me,g); break;
  case Spell.D_Paralyze:cmd=b(me,Buff.Paralyze ); break;
  case Spell.D_Sleep:   cmd=b(me,Buff.Sleep    ); break;
  case Spell.D_Petrify: cmd=b(me,Buff.Petrify  ); break;
  case Spell.Summon:    cmd = new SummonCmd(me,g); break;
  case Spell.D_Bleed:   cmd=b(me,Buff.Bleed    ); break;
  case Spell.D_Levitate:cmd=b(me,Buff.Levitate ); break;
  case Spell.D_Disarm:  cmd=b(me,Buff.Disarm   ); break;
  default: return null;
```

```
    }
    cmd.setCost(cost);
    return s ? s : cmd;
  }
  buff(me:Mob,buff:Buff): CmdIF {
    return new BuffCmd(buff,this.ply,this.g,me);
  }
}
```

You may recognise this code as mostly identical to the player's
`SpellFinder`. The danger in having two is, that we have to update
them symmetrically. If we were to combine them, we'd only need
to maintain a single copy. Here I opted to keep them separate, to
keep the code cases simpler. You have been warned.

29.13 SHOOTING AI

Now that `NPCSpellFinder` offers us a bigger selection of spells
for the NPCs, it's time to make an updated spell AI. We clone the
old spell AI `24SpellAI.ts`, and modify it to pick from the new
`Spell` enum, instead of just the debuffs.

We will handle the NPC missile spell separately. A bit like the
player, NPCs can only shoot diagonally and in straight lines.
With the basic NPC spell, they would almost never shoot.
Because of this 'shot of opportunity' mechanism, NPCs should
track if they can shoot, and decide directly.

Our AI must therefore check if the monster is lined up with the
player. If it is, and if the monster uses a missile spell, it should
fire on the player N% of the time. Other spells will use the
normal spell rate we have used so far.

From the player's perspective, he could act based on the rate at
which NPCs will shoot. That is, if they are inclined to take every

opportunity shot, it would be unwise for him to give them that opportunity.

So that NPC monsters can trigger animated spells, we must extend the AI `turn()` interface with the screen stack and the maker. It unfortunately requires updating `turn()` in all these files:

```
05ai/14AiSwitcher.ts
05ai/18MoodAI.ts
05ai/18WakeAI.ts
05ai/20AISwitcher2.ts
05ai/24SpellAI.ts
06screen/09BaseScreen.ts
```

The signature change for `turn` is thus:

```
export interface MobAiIF {
  //turn(me:Mob, enemy:Mob, game:GameIF):boolean;
  turn(me:Mob, enemy:Mob, game:GameIF,
      ss:StackIF, maker:MakerIF):boolean;
}
```

In `BaseScreen`, `npcTurns` must pass `StackIF` to `npcTurn`.

Our new AI will look something like this: `05ai\29ShootAI.ts`

```
export class ShootAI implements MobAiIF {
  constructor(public speed:number,
              public spellRate:number) {}
  aiDir:MobAiIF = new MobAI2_cat();
  aiRnd:MobAiIF = new MobAI3_ant();
  turn(me:Mob, enemy:Mob, g:GameIF,
      ss:StackIF, maker:MakerIF):boolean {
    let r = g.rnd;
    let far = SleepAI.isNear(me,enemy);
    if (far) {
      me.mood =
        r.oneIn(3) ? Mood.Asleep : Mood.Wake;
      if (me.mood == Mood.Asleep) {
        return true;
```

```
      } // if mob now sleeps, don't do more.
    }
    if (this.didShoot(me,r,g,enemy,ss,maker)) {
      return true;
    }
    if (this.maybeCastSpell(me,enemy,g,ss,maker)) {
      return true;
    }
    for (let i=0;i<this.speed;++i) {
      var ai = r.oneIn(2) ? this.aiDir : this.aiRnd;
      ai.turn(me,enemy,g,ss,maker);
    }
    return true;
  }
  maybeCastSpell(me:Mob, enemy:Mob, game:GameIF,
                 ss:StackIF, maker:MakerIF):boolean
  {
    let map = <DMapIF> game.curMap();
    if (!CanSee.canSee2(me,enemy,map,true)) {return false;}

    let r = game.rnd;
    if (!r.oneIn(this.spellRate)) { return false; }
    //let buff = this.pickBuff(me, r);
    //return this.castBuff(buff,me,enemy,game);
    let spell = this.pickSpell(me, r);
    return this.castSpell(spell,me,enemy,game,ss,maker);
  }
  pickSpell(me:Mob, r:Rnd):Spell {
    // 'None' is last buff:
    let range:number = (Spell.None)+1;
    // Clip levels to spell-range:
    let spellIx:number = me.level % range;
    // Pick the Spell at <SpellIx> offset:
    let spell:Spell = <Spell> spellIx;
    console.log(`${me.name} spell: ${spell}`);
    return spell;
  }
  castSpell(spell:Spell, me:Mob,
```

```
        enemy:Mob, game:GameIF,
        ss:StackIF, maker:MakerIF):boolean
  {
      // We probably should pass enemy to spell-finder:
      // (so we can attack someone other than the player.)
      let finder = new NPCSpellFinder(game,ss,maker);
      let noCost:CostIF|undefined = undefined;
      let CoS = finder.find(me,spell,noCost);
      if (CoS instanceof CmdBase) {
          return CoS.npcTurn();
      }
      return true;
  }
  didShoot(me:Mob,r:Rnd,g:GameIF,him:Mob,
            ss:StackIF,maker:MakerIF):boolean {
    if (!this.aim(me.pos,him.pos)) { return false; }
    let spell = this.pickSpell(me,r);
    if (!this.isMissileSpell(spell)) {return false; }
    if (!r.oneIn(this.spellRate)) { return false; }
    let map = <DMapIF> g.curMap();
    if (!CanSee.canSee2(me,him,map,true)) { return false; }
    return this.shoot(spell,me,him,g,ss,maker);
  }
  aim(m:WPoint,e:WPoint) {
    let d = m.minus(e);
    if (d.x==0 || d.y==0) { return true; } // on axis.
    let ax = Math.abs(d.x), ay = Math.abs(d.y);
    return (ax==ay);// diagonal.
  } // check 8 dirs.
  isMissileSpell(s:Spell) { return s == Spell.Missile; }

  shoot(spell:Spell,me:Mob,enemy:Mob,g:GameIF,
        ss:StackIF,maker:MakerIF): boolean {
    this.castSpell(spell,me,enemy,g,ss,maker);
    return true;
  }
}
```

`didShoot` is the most complex part of that change. Its `aim()` rule is a quick check whether the two monsters are on a straight or diagonal line. If they are not, we immediately exit `didShoot`. We start with this, because it's false for most monsters, and thus an easy way to avoid doing further work.

Next we check the monster's spell type, because this also is both a quick thing to check, and false most of the time. Again, if it's not a missile spell, we can leave `didShoot`.

Next, we check the monster's chance to shoot - again a fast check. If it's not in the mood, no need to check further.

Lastly, we reach the expensive `CanSee` check, which we have thus managed to avoid most of the time. If we can't see the enemy, again we exit.

If we reach the end, we know both that we **can** shoot and that we **want to** shoot, so.. we shoot. This is the bit where we need to mess with screens.

We are going to animate the NPC shot, so we will push a stepper screen - the same that animates them when the player shoots. Once his shot has finished playing out, we need to get back to the game loop.

That is, we need to continue running the `npcTurns` loop. On the face of it, that doesn't seem so tricky. When the player was shooting, we would finish up **his** turn by running `npcTurns`. The same should happen at the end of the NPC's shooting animation.

But as that `npcTurns` call is executing, what happens if **another** NPC then starts shooting? Let's think that through. Will the stepping screen still be on the stack or not? Will something take care of popping it? If we pop the current stepping screen before we run `npcTurns` , it should work as intended.

There is one change we are required to make, though. In `finishPlyTurn`, we used to verify we had indeed reached the

player. That no longer holds, since we can now arrive here from
an NPC missile. So we must change it to this:

```
finishPlyTurn(q:TurnQ) {
  let ply = q.curMob();
  if (!ply.isPly) {return;} //throw `${ply.name}not ply?'`;
  this.finishTurn(ply);
  if (this.game.autoHeal) {
    this.game.autoHeal.turn(ply, this.game);
  }
}
```

We can make `NPCSpellFinder` handle the missile firing part with
this code:

```
..// a switch case:
   case Spell.Missile:
     cmd = this.aim(
       new BulletCmd(me,g,this.ss,this.maker)
     ); break;

 ..

  aim(cmd: BulletCmd): CmdIF {
    let dir = cmd.me.pos.dir(this.ply.pos);
    return cmd.setDir(dir);
  }
```

The `aim` method figures out the direction between the monster
and the player, which then becomes the movement direction for
the shot. Hopefully, the monster will only shoot when it is
aligned with the player in one of the 8 major directions. If a bug
causes it to shoot anyway, it will do a badly aimed shot that will
miss!

Note that `shoot` is really just `castSpell`, but we like to use proper
names, so our code tells the story of **why** we do things.

To bring `ShootAI` into the game, we add this to `MoodAI`:

```
   static stockMood29(speed:number,
                      spellRate:number):MobAiIF {
     return new MoodAI(new SleepAI(),
```

```
                     new ShootAI(speed,spellRate));
  }
```

Which we can use in the new builder (`29Builder2o.ts`):

```
makeAI():MobAiIF|null {
    return new AiSwitcher2(MoodAI.stockMood29(1,8));
}
```

If we now try to run the game again, the enemies should run amok with their totally new spell casting engine. Some of them should teleport, some should multiply or summon, and some should shoot.

We did not make monsters heal each other, but it's still a good idea.

30 An End, How to Win

(In which we add a win goal to the game)

F 30.1: Dungeon denizens vary in size

30.1   A Way to Win

The game we have built has no end. You can keep traveling downwards to deeper levels. At some point, you'll exhaust the monsters we have defined, and the game then starts to spawn **living dungeon furniture** that attacks you. Once you reach level 42, you will trigger a minor error if you attempt to descend deeper - some code complains that `48 is not strictly less than 48` (that is, it tries to use a glyph that doesn't even exist).

We face an inevitable truth of human designs - they either end with a finite limit, or repeat endlessly. (This is not strictly true: You might achieve some fractal random variation that keeps introducing branching levels of randomness, but still, you could then argue such a pattern constitutes a kind of repeating.)

30.2   A Means to an End - Design

We can choose to design a kind of end or goal for our game. In a flash of divine inspiration, we decide our end monster will be a powerful **dragon**. It is obvious the dragon is powerful, because we will represent it with a big capital **D**. It will probably be **red**. We could even consider making it in bold font.

Killing a big monster is a popular win criteria in many games. Another favorite is **finding** a special artifact ('the holy grail', 'the amulet of Yendor'), and possibly delivering said item to a special place. The archetypical example is bringing the yendor amulet back to the starting town level. We will be less discerning - as long as you manage to kill the dragon, you'll be presented with a winning congratulations banner.

30.2.1   SPECIAL IN WHAT WAY

We must think up some ways the dragon could be special. We could give it some dragon attacks. It should breathe fire, or some other kind of dragon breath. It might also do other trademark dragon attacks - tail lashes or bashes, possibly some clawing, something with talons and fangs. It might do some kind of mental dragon magic, confusion, paralysis or intimidation. The dragon might be fast. It might teleport itself or the player. If we are really ambitious, maybe it can move through walls, or destroy walls?

We could complicate winning a bit by outfitting the game with special dragon-defeating items to find, which would help the player. It is then up to our conscience, if it should even be possible to win without them.

If we add such special items, beware our dungeon has level memory. Each level is only generated once, and (almost) no extra monsters are spawned. It is possible to run out of dungeon, and so to run out of monsters - then there is nothing more to kill for a chance of loot. So if we introduce required items, we must ensure they are actually available. If we have item destruction, we should be careful whether they could be destroyed.

30.2.2   LOCATION LOCATION LOCATION

For the dragon himself, we'll need to place him. Instead of placing him in an exactly known location, we could instead assign a range of possible levels for him, and pick his actual position when we start a given game. To spice this up a bit, we could add a further rule: If you flee the level after encountering the dragon, we could reshuffle his placement. This way, fleeing the dragon would not be a safe choice - you would lose track of where the dragon now is, and you may even risk the dragon showing up on the level you just fled to! (unless you fled outside his range).

Given that we have monsters from A to Z (26), we have 26 levels. We could then place the dragon between L27 and L30. For those deepest levels, we may populate them with a selection of the worst monsters.

30.2.3   HOUSE CLEANING

We must clean up the monster creation code. It should no longer try to make monsters out of dungeon furniture. The culprit is the method `level2glyph()` in `Builder`, which is all too happy to provide us with any kind of glyph. Its upgrade we'll call `level2mobGlyph`. It will refuse to provide anything but glyphs that are really mobs. To work together with this, we will also re-examine which **levels** we pair the mob glyphs with: Instead of just clipping it to a ceiling, we'll try to target a range of levels - we want to avoid ending up with only a single monster type on the deepest level. Note, that even though we put a ceiling on the mob **glyphs**, we can still assign them ever higher **levels** to make them even more dangerous.

30.2.4   TURTLES ALL THE WAY DOWN

We will ponder whether we want endless deep levels or not. We have already decided that the dragon lives between 27 and 30. So if you venture to level 31, the dragon won't follow you or appear there (unless we decide to change that). A reason **for** endless levels, is to offer the player more resources to fight the dragon. This is also an argument **against** - namely that the challenge should be to defeat the dragon with 'only what you are given', across the first 30 levels.

30.2.5 INTERIOR DECORATION

On the one hand, the dragon should be a "surprise on a level", and so not reveal itself. On the other hand, maybe it would be nice to have a special level environment for the dragon? Also, if we could dim the lights somehow.. The big red D would look much better against a darker color than pure white.

30.2.6 HOW TO TRAIN YOUR DRAGON

What are the obvious areas in which the dragon could be strong or dangerous..

- It would have many hit points?
- It might heal itself?
- It might drain the player to heal itself?
- It might drain power from any nearby mobs?
- It might control nearby mobs to fight for it?
- It might have strong armour?
- It might be great at evading?
- It might have resistances?
- It might be fast?
- It might teleport around?
- It might alternate between being visible and invisible?
- It might teleport the player, away or nearer?
- It might use the environment for danger, e.g. collapsing nearby walls on the player, or hurling rocks?
- It might do a great deal of damage? Powerful attacks?
- It might reflect damage back, so it hurts you back as you hurt it?
- It might have access to all the spells?
- It might develop immunity if you use the same attacks twice in a row?
- It might be high level - level 31!
- It might often teleport away if it feels you are too close.

- It might love to teleport away (chance) if it senses you are lined up for a shot.
- It might have a sort of environment-destroying ability, e.g. dragon breath. It both gives a cool dragon effect, and causes you trouble.
- It might summon stuff?

30.3 PLAN

An order we can do it in:

- We can clean up our existing monster spawning code.
- We will let it use a reasonable mix of last 4 monsters.
- We can create the dragon glyph, and make it `red` (this is **extremely** important).
- We can add the `dragonLevel` property to the dungeon, and let the builder assign a random value from a range (27-30).
- We can make the builder use `addDragon()`, when it tries to set up the map for `dragonLevel`.
- We can put an `addDragon()` method in our builder - he'll be level 31.
- We can modify `initGlyphs()`, so the lights are darkened whenever we switch to the `dragonLevel`.
- We can give the dragon its own aggressive copy of `ShootAI`, with a couple of Han Solo modifications.
- We can cook up some dragon abilities - at the very least, some dragon breath.
- We can implement a dragon breath spell.
- We can make a 'you win!' screen to show when defeating the dragon.
- We can temporarily spawn the player and the dragon near each other, so we have a reasonable way to try it out, to tweak it and balance it.
- We **could** create a special level for it - a dragon's lair, if you will. *(later)*

• We can balance it all a bit.

30.4 IMPLEMENTATION

First, we clone our earlier builder to `30Builder2p.ts`.

We'll fix `addLevelMob()`, so it spawns high-level mobs instead of furniture. We change `30Builder2p.ts` like so:

```
.. // in addLevelMob:
  //let g = this.level2glyph(level);
  let g = this.level2mobGlyph(level,r); // ch30
..

 level2mobGlyph(L:number,r:Rnd):Glyph {
   let g = this.level2glyph(L);
   if (g <= Glyph.Sheep) { return g; }
   // instead return a mix of the last 4 levels:
   let ix = r.rndC(0,3);
   g = <Glyph> (Glyph.Sheep-ix);
   return Glyph.Sheep;
 }
```

We'll create a dragon glyph, and also some fire glyphs, for our dragon breath:

```
.. // 07Glyph.ts:
Sheep,
Dragon, // ch30
..

Bullet,// ch27
Fire1, // ch30
Fire2, // ch30
Fire3, // ch30

.. // 16GlyphInf1.ts:
add(bg,      '#294',     'S',Glyph.Sheep);
add(bg,      'red',      'D',Glyph.Dragon);
..
```

```
add(bg,         'orange','%',Glyph.Fire1);  // ch30
add('yellow','orange','%',Glyph.Fire2);  // ch30
add('orange','red',    '%',Glyph.Fire3);  // ch30
// or U+1F525 ..
```

30.4.1   GETTING THE DRAGON INTO THE DUNGEON

To know where to place the dragon, we want to extend our
dungeon with a `dragonLevel` number, and let it track a special
dragon level. However, this would break our old code, which
doesn't deal in dragon levels. So we will make an updated `Dung`
class, and an updated `Game6` class to hold it. We clone `13Dung.ts`
into `30Dung.ts`, and call the new class `Dung30`.

We clone `23GameModel5Worn.ts` into `30GameModel6Win.ts`, and
change it to use `Dung30`:

```
dung:Dung = new Dung30();  // ch30
```

`30Dung.ts` gets

```
export class Dung30 {
..
  dragonLevel:number = -1;  // ch30
..
```

And our builder assigns it a value:

```
initDragonLevel(g:GameIF) {
    let dung = <Dung30> g.dung;
    let r = g.rnd;
    let minDragon = 27;
    let maxDragon = 30;
    dung.dragonLevel = r.rndC(minDragon,maxDragon);
}
..
  makeGame():GameIF {
    ..
    let game = new Game5(rnd,ply,this);
    this.initDragonLevel(game);
```

We must generate a dragon level when we reach that number, so
we update the builder interface:

```
export interface BuildIF4 extends BuildIF3 {
  makeDragonLevels(rnd:Rnd, level:number,
                        dragonLevel:number):DMapIF;
}
```

We change 30Dung.ts to use that new interface:

```
getLevel(L:number, g:GameIF): DMapIF {

  let b = <BuildIF4> g.build;
  let map = b.makeDragonLevels(g.rnd,L,this.dragonLevel);
```

We modify our builder to match BuildIF4:

```
export class Builder2p implements BuildIF4 {

  makeLevel(rnd:Rnd,level:number):DMapIF {
    return this.makeDragonLevels(rnd,level,-1);
  }
  makeDragonLevels(rnd:Rnd, level:number,
                    dragonLevel:number):DMapIF {
    let hasDragon = (level == dragonLevel);
    let map = this.makeDragonMaps(rnd,level,dragonLevel);
    this.addLevelStairs(map,level,rnd); // ch13
    this.addItems(map,rnd); // ch21
    this.addMobsToLevel(map,rnd);
    if (hasDragon) {this.addDragon(map,rnd);}
    return map;
  }
```

The idea is that makeDragonLevels is the updated makeLevel, and
thus makeLevel will just forward to it. The same thing happens
to makeMap:

```
makeMap(rnd:Rnd, level:number):DMapIF {
  return this.makeDragonMaps(rnd,level,-1);
}
makeDragonMaps(rnd:Rnd, level:number,
               dragonLevel:number):DMapIF {
  let dim = WPoint.StockDims;
  var map:DMapIF;
  switch (level) {
    default:
    case 1:  map = MapGen1.test(level); break;
    case 0:  map = TestMap.test(dim, rnd, level); break;
    case dragonLevel: map=TestMap.test(dim,rnd,level);break;
  } // (here we could make a special dragon level)
  return map;
}
```

To make these changes work, we must also make `addDragon`:

```
addDragon(map: DMapIF, rnd: Rnd) {
  let p = <WPoint> FreeSpace.find(Glyph.Floor,map,rnd);
  this.addNPC(Glyph.Dragon,p.x,p.y,map,31);
}
```

30.4.2　Dimming the Lights

We change `16GlyphInf1.ts` like this:

```
static initGlyphs(hasDragon:boolean):number {
  this.glyphs = [];
  let bg = 1 ? '#fff' : 'black';
  if (hasDragon) { bg = '#201540'; }
```

With that, it can switch between dark background and light background (normal). We then change `30Dung.ts` to use it like this:

```
plySwitchLevel(newLevel:number, np:WPoint, g:GameIF) {
    ..
    this.dragonStyle();
}
dragonStyle() {
  let hasDragon = (this.level == this.dragonLevel);
  GlyphMap1.initGlyphs(hasDragon);
}
```

..

So the last line of `plySwitchLevel` will dim the lights when we
visit the dragon.

30.4.3 AN AGGRESSIVE DRAGON AI

We can clone `29ShootAI.ts` to `30DragonAI.ts`.

We can lift it into `20AISwitcher2.ts`, with

```
export class AiSwitcher2 implements MobAiIF {
..     // ch30: is fast, casts spells often.
  ai6_dragon:MobAiIF = new DragonAI(2,2);
.. // in turn:
  case Glyph.Dragon:ai=this.ai6_dragon;break;
```

..

Our first changes to `DragonAI`'s turn are these:

```
  port(rad: number,me:Mob,g:GameIF): boolean {
    return new PortCmd(rad,me,g).npcTurn();
  }
  static isNear(limit:number, me:Mob, enemy:Mob):boolean {
    let dist = me.pos.dist(enemy.pos);
    return dist < limit;
  }
..
  turn(me:Mob, enemy:Mob, g:GameIF,
      ss:StackIF, maker:MakerIF):boolean {
    let r = g.rnd;
    if (DragonAI.isNear(2,me,enemy)) {
```

```
    if (r.oneIn(3)) { return this.port(5,me,g); }
  } // if ply is near, often port away.
..// rest of turn
```

So, we get our own teleport command. And our own `isNear`
check, which takes a distance argument. We use them to often
get away, if the player is standing next to us. This should make it
hard to keep the dragon in melee attack range.

We can add some further cunning to `turn()`, after the sleep
check:

```
..
let lineOfFire = this.aim(me.pos,enemy.pos);
if (lineOfFire) {
  switch (r.rndC(0,2)) {
  default: break; // ignore it.
  case 0: return this.port(5,me,g);// flee
  case 1: return this.shoot(
          Spell.Breath,me,enemy,g,ss,maker
        );
  }
}
..
```

This watches out for, whether we are aligned with the player. If
so, we do three different things each a third of the time: We
either flee, shoot back, or ignore it. This means the dragon is
highly unlikely to tolerate being in the line of fire.

While we are at it, we'll rename his `didShoot` ability to
`didBreathe`, and modify it a bit. He is a dragon, after all.

```
didBreathe(me:Mob,r:Rnd,g:GameIF,him:Mob,
           ss:StackIF,maker:MakerIF):boolean {
  if (!this.aim(me.pos,him.pos)) { return false; }
  if (!r.oneIn(this.spellRate)) { return false; }
  let map = <DMapIF> g.curMap();
  if (!CanSee.canSee2(me,him,map,true)) { return false; }
  return this.shoot(Spell.Breath,me,him,g,ss,maker);
```

```
}
```

Since this leaves us with two different ways the dragon can
'shoot', we don't currently have a use for it. But if we gave the
dragon several missile attacks, this could be used for the
stronger and less frequent of them.

30.4.4 DRAGON BREATH

We've been referring an awful lot to the `Breath` spell which we
don't yet have, so let's fix that. We'll add a `Spell` enum value:

```
.. // in 29Spell.ts:
  D_Disarm,   //B
  Breath,     //U
..
```

Because of this, we should add an extra color:

```
.. // in 29Colors.ts:
 ['','taffy'],
 ['','cream'], // breath
];// 25 spells need 25 colors.
```

Then, our spell finders must match the new spell:

```
        case Spell.Breath: cmd = this.aim(
            new BreathCmd(me,g,this.ss,this.maker)
          ); break;
```

We must clone `BulletCmd` to get `BreathCmd`. We change two lines
in it:

```
..
exc():boolean {
  ..
  let sprite = Glyph.Fire2;
  ..
  let step:StepIF =
    new BreathStep(effect,next,sprite,m.pos.copy(),g);
  ..
```

..Which amounts to a different fire sprite, and another Step type.
(You could argue, that we could instead achieve it by making the
sprite and the step be parameters to BulletCmd. We could indeed,
but you might also argue the resulting coupling would be brittle.
That is, changes to either breath or missiles would then be
highly likely to affect both.)

We must also clone DirStep to get our BreathStep. We change
the step, so it doesn't clear the sprites right away. Instead, it
collects all cells it put dragon fire in. At the end, we then clear all
those sprites again. This should give us the effect of a line of
dragon breath.

```
..  // in BreathCmd
  cells:MapCell[] = [];
  excS():StepIF|null {

    ..

    // no more in ch30:
    //map.cell(p).sprite = undefined;

    ..

    let r = this.game.rnd;
    if (!done) {
      let EO = r.oneIn(2);
      // alternate fire:
      cell.sprite = (EO ? this.sprite : Glyph.Fire3);
       // remember the cells we painted:
      this.cells.push(cell);
      if (this.effect) {
          this.effect.setPos(p);
          this.effect.excS();
      }
    } else { // transfer args.
      if (this.next) {
        this.next.setPos(p);
      }
      this.cleanup();
    }
    return done ? this.next : this;
```

```
    }
  cleanup() {
    for (let c of this.cells) {c.sprite = undefined;}
  } // we remove dragon-fire at end.
    ..
```

To recap the changes: The old `sprite = undefined` clear is
disabled. As long as bullet is not done, we add each cell to an
array. When we are done, we finally clear all those cell sprites.

We also pick random sprites to mark the bullet path, with a mix
of yellow-orange-red. This may look more interesting than a
uniformly coloured line of sprites.

We could spice up our dragon breath even more. We could give
it a small risk of side-stepping to either side. The chances could
be e.g. 15% chance to stray, 30% chance to return in line, and 55%
to continue straight. This would tend to 'S' zig-zag behaviour. So
whenever it strayed, it would be quite likely to jump back. The
benefit to us, apart from it looking mightily cool, would be the
uncertainty of whether the dragon breath would hit you or not.

Another up-spicing would be if dragon breath did damage to
everything it passes. As our player is a single unit, and only the
enemy has this spell, it avails us little. But if this were one of our
own, such powerful area-of-effect damage 'nuke' spells could
really be nice.

30.4.5 You Can Win!

Defeating the dragon should make us win. How can we do that?
One way would be to integrate it with game-over. Right now, our
game-over check watches for player death. We could just make it
watch for other stuff too. We could then change the game-over
screen to watch the same thing, in order to show a 'you win!'
message.

So, we'll add a gameWon boolean to our game and game interface.
We update Builder2p to use Game6:

```
.. // Game6:
  gameWon:boolean = false;
.. // 08GameIF.ts:
  gameWon:boolean;
.. // Builder2p:
let game = new Game6(rnd,ply,this);
..
```

(all earlier game models must get gameWon:boolean = false; to
work again.)

In mobDies() in 11HealthAdj.ts, we add

```
if (m.g == Glyph.Dragon) { game.gameWon = true; }
```

In 09BaseScreen.ts, we update the over() method:

```
  over(s:StackIF):boolean {
    let over = !this.game.ply.alive()
               || this.game.gameWon;
    if (over) {
      s.pop();
      s.push(this.make.gameOver(this.game));
    }
    return over;
  }
```

We must change MakerIF here, because we want to pass the
finished game to the game-over screen:

```
// gameOver():SScreenIF;
  gameOver(g:GameIF|undefined):SScreenIF;
```

This requires fixups:

```
// 06DummyScreen.ts
s.push(this.make.gameOver(undefined));
// 06ScreenMaker_Fixed.ts
Stack.run_SScreen(m.gameOver(undefined));
```

```
// 06ScreenMaker_Dyn.ts
(sm:MakerIF) => sm.gameOver(undefined)
```

(We could have avoided these, if we had let gameOver() start out with an undefined argument.)

In 09ScreenMaker2.ts we change gameOver() to be:

```
gameOver(g:GameIF|undefined):SScreenIF{
  return new WinOverScreen(this,g);
}
```

Then we clone 06OverScreen.ts into 30WinOverScreen.ts, and change its constructor to:

```
export class WinOverScreen implements SScreenIF {
  name='wingameover';
  constructor(public make:MakerIF,
              public g:GameIF|undefined) {}
```

Finally, we can modify WinOverScreen to do this:

```
  draw(term:TermIF) {
    this.showLog(term);
    let won = (this.g && this.g.gameWon);
    if (won) {
      term.txt(1,1,' YOU WON! ', 'blue', 'lime');
    } else {
      term.txt(1,1,' GAME OVER! ', 'yellow', 'red');
    }
  }
  showLog(term:TermIF) {
    let log = this.g?.log.archive;
    if (!log) {return;}
    term.txt(0,0, 'Log:', 'yellow', 'black');
    let range = term.dim.y-1;
    if (log.length < range) { range = log.length; }
    let offset = log.length-range;
    for (let p=0; p<range; ++p) {
        let pos = offset+p;
```

```
        if (pos < 0) {continue; }
        let row = log[pos];
     term.txt(0, 1+p, `${p} ${row}`, 'yellow', 'black');
    }
  }
```

This also gives us a nice recap of what happened during the final
moments of the game.

30.5   So, Is the Game Balanced Now?

Heck no. Balancing it could even fill another book. The easiest
way to balance it would probably be to write a book about the
game, and then let the readers solve the problem of balancing it.
For example, you could change `makePly` in `30Builder2p.ts` like
this:

```
static plyHP_value=16;
makePly():Mob {
  let ply = new Mob(Glyph.Ply,20,12);
  ply.hp = ply.maxhp = Builder2p.plyHP_value*=2; //10000;
  return ply;
}
```

This way, the player would start out with 32 hit points. If he then
fails to win, he gets a new attempt with 64 hit points. Then 128,
and so on. Sooner or later - we hope - he will be able to win.
You could then use what you learned during those tests, to
rebalance the game in various ways.

To properly play the game, we should at some point disable the
'M' command, that lets the player cast any spell. But during
testing, the 'M' command is really handy to try out possible
solutions - and broken solutions - to various problems.

A solution is something that solves a problem just right, and
barely. A broken solution is something that solves it like a

nuclear bomb, being way too strong for the issue at hand. That is, it would make the game too easy.

30.6   THE END OF THE END

With this, we have reached the natural conclusion of this book. We now have levels to play on, a player, enemies for him, varied behaviours for those enemies, spells for both the player and the monsters, a progression of difficult monsters, and an item progression path for the player to gain power. Finally, we have a difficult win goal to defeat, with that accumulated power.

We could continue to add features, but what the game needs more, is balancing, all through the various stages of the game.

30.7   WHAT NOW?

As you work to extend your roguelike, keep in mind the balance between introducing features outside previously covered areas, versus extending and improving on the already included features. The latter will often serve you better, and including new areas will push the eventual completion of your game further into the future. It doesn't hurt that your roguelike continues to improve, but it hurts if it keeps it from being playable.

30.7.1   WHY DO YOU HATE GRAPHICS

I don't hate graphics per se, in fact I like graphics. Using letters has some advantages. It lets us spend 1% effort on the graphics side of things, and get on with the game. The problem with graphics is that they take work and time, especially to do properly. In comparison, if you tell a guy to 'just use the letter A', there is a high chance he'll manage to do so correctly.

It is quite feasible to hook up the game we have built to some graphics. For example, there exists a javascript game engine called `phaser3.js`, which we could connect the game to. I might write a guide on how to connect to phaser3.

There is a similar story with animation. It takes some further work, both a design for how the monsters moving ought to be animated, and of course sprite animations for actions and effects. Above all, it takes work.

30.7.2 WHERE ARE THE ROGUELIKERS

On reddit.com, they are in `/r/roguelikedev` and `/r/roguelikes`.

On the internet:

http://www.roguebasin.com

https://blog.roguetemple.com/ (Temple of the Roguelike)

https://roguelikeradio.com/ (a fantastic, huge podcast.)

http://roguelikedeveloper.blogspot.com/ (Andrew Doull)

31   FEATURES WE DIDN'T DO ..YET

(In which we consider a lot of other features our game might get)

F 31.1: Surveying the vast landscape of further features

31.1   JUST ONE MORE FEATURE, I PROMISE

Roguelikes are infamous for their countless features. For any given possible feature, it is tempting to think "of course! why shouldn't it also have feature X?" One might be tempted, for reasons like

- "All" the other (popular! well-playing!) roguelikes have it. "Surely I must include it, to also be popular, also be well-playing"
- "Logically, this should be possible", or "Logically, this should be limited"
- "This will be really clever"
- "It's always been so in other roguelikes"
- "Since I have feature X, I must also have related feature Y"

But building a game is also a bit like building a vehicle. If your "vehicle" ends up with too many parts, it will be difficult to make it go fast and handle well, and it will be prone to problems and bugs because of its complexity. Many of your separate features will interact with each other, and not necessarily in a good way.

In spite of all the traditional features we have already jammed into our roguelike, there are many more features we haven't included, but which it could be tempting to add. I will enumerate some of them here.

31.2   HUNGER CLOCK

Old-Timey roguelikes would require the player to eat food regularly, both to regain hit points, and to not die of hunger. Why did they do this? It was never really about food. It was to avoid two kinds of unwanted play style. Boring Caution was one of these styles, and Boring Hoarding was the other.

Boring Caution is when the player both moves very cautiously and continually keeps his hit points full (by always resting up to full health). Playing safe like that, leads to a boring play experience.

Boring Greed is when the player keeps replaying easy levels he has already outgrown, to stock up on spell items and ammo. Again, this leads to a boring play experience without challenge or surprises - when you carry 800 arrows and 98 health potions, you are never in interesting danger.

Hunger is a brutal fix for this: Each level doles out a limited supply of food, corresponding to a limited amount of moves before you starve to death. If you want to live, you must charge forward into danger, to find more food!

The hunger mechanic can work, but it is a beast to balance. In a lot of games, it instead ends up meaningless, sooner or later you have food coming out of your ears, and the food limit then never really guides you to behave any specific way. But now you've heard of it.

31.3 LIGHT/TORCH CLOCK

Similar to the food clock, you must manage the resource of your torches, or oil for your oil lamp. Your light can grow dim, and go out. Most that can be said for the hunger clock, goes for the light clock as well.

However, light has a few other tricks up its sleeve: You can have lighted and unlit rooms, and change the tactical situation by lighting a room (with a spell or using a torch). Enemies (or you) might deliberately extinguish the lights in a room for the same reasons, e.g. to sneak through or hide. Some things may still be visible in darkness, and some creature classes may have infra-vision, allowing them to sense some other beings in the dark, e.g. by their heat. You might also have monsters that radiate darkness, so that light doesn't work near them.

31.4   PROPER FIELD OF VIEW/VISION

Approaches similar to *Bresenham* can be employed to calculate a visibility circle/cone around a game character, to draw what can be seen (possibly in bright yellow tones), and hide what cannot be seen (either with black or subdued dark blue hues). It is a matter of taste - it can look great, and it can look flickering.

We've opted out of including it here, to instead show that simple Bresenham and a circle can achieve similar results for gameplay. You are of course free to employ full FoV, especially if your game library offers it for free. My personal take is that the effort spent on it, might be better spent first on your game loop and your play balance.

31.5   ITEM IDENTIFICATION

Inherited from dungeons & dragons, it is tradition to jam your game full of a 50-50 mix of helpful and dangerous items that look similar, and then watch in glee as your player tries to figure out whether a given item will save him or kill him. The items will have visible qualities like colors, but they will be scrambled for each fresh game, so the player must again figure out, whether a tangerine potion will heal him or poison him. It undoubtedly adds an element of terror, panic and hilarious fun, as the desperate player, surrounded by a gang of vicious kobolds, chugs down 3 different multi-colored potions, only to sprout hairs and turn violet, before succumbing to the onslaught of the kobolds. Apart from the fun, it also adds a little lottery game loop, of ferrying unidentified found items around, working to get them sorted into useful and dangerous. Personally I have always had a broken relationship with the identify systems. My problem is, that I would grow fond of a given combination of physical item attributes, and then sad having to let go of that association for the next game. I longed for a game mechanic that would allow e.g. the color attributes to persist. I'm not sure this is possible, given that the ID system is the sole reason for **including** them.

31.6 WEIGHT LIMIT EFFECTS

Inventory weight & encumbrance: It is a physical realism-inspired mechanic, intended to limit how much of what you find, you can keep to carry around.

This mechanic has plenty of aspects to love. It helps - forces - the player to prioritize what he will carry, and to not be burdened by carrying and managing an ever-growing collection of everything he finds. It forces him into interesting choices of "should I drop those two items to be able to carry **that** item?"

It lets him make a dangerous trade-off of dragging a heavy encumbering load of treasures back to town. This might cost him his life, either because his noise, or his precious treasure, attracts crowds of greedy monsters on his trek back, or because his heavy load hinders him when he tries to fight back. In the fuller version, each item is assigned a weight, and the player's strength stat will decide how much the weight encumbers him. In the light version, it could just be a simple inventory limit of "10 items or less".

31.7　SECRET TRAPS & AREAS

Traps & secrets: Again, in dungeons & dragons, your intrepid adventurers will search buried tombs and abandoned temples for hidden treasure. To make it less trivial than picking up a parcel at the local post office, and more like a treasure hunt, we may want to make things secret and difficult to access. This entails things like hidden rooms, corridors, doors, traps, and treasure. Of these, traps have the most potential for weird strange fun stuff. Still, in my personal taste, I think about the resulting game loops. We are not just designing a single hidden secret to find - if we add it to the game, typically it means we are assigning the player a repeated loop of "do this, again and again, until you fall off your chair". I was never a big fan of searching endless wall edges to find that missing hidden door that would allow me to proceed. Still, if done well (think, a bit like a well-written movie script), it can actually be sort of fun. It could be a puzzle that works a bit like 'Checkov's gun'. Of the many rooms on a given level, make **some** of them be candidates. A candidate would appear special in some way. It could be its shape, or its placement. The candidates would be those rooms that might hold secret doors. There would then also be a secret vault on the level, that you can't yet access - but it would of course still occupy space on the map layout. If the player then maps the entire accessible dungeon, that should indirectly reveal, where there are still white unexplored areas remaining on the map. Now the final piece is to combine the placement of the potential candidates with the placement of the unexplored remains, to figure out where to search for the hidden doors. So, this mechanism is definitely possible and has been done many times, but I view it is a lot of work to do, which you must really be certain about to succeed in implementing well.

I feel a bit similar about traps. Sometimes they accompany hidden treasures, sometimes they are their own thing. I tend to find them tedious. Their main gameplay effect is to herd the player into playing more carefully instead of charging ahead. If you at any point risk losing half your hit points and become confused, poisoned or blind, you are more inclined to proceed cautiously towards that next group of kobolds. Still, the trap mechanism can be used for lots of fun things - for example, the player can use them offensively, by leading monsters into them.

I am being a bit unfair to traps. The variant I don't enjoy, is the one that appears and triggers without warning. There are people and roguelikes doing great things with traps. That other style of trap is a mix of a mechanical contraption, and a puzzle. Above all, you will recognise when you encounter them: You run into something that looks weird and mysterious. It will look like it has some apparent purpose, but it will reveal itself to be more than what you see at first. Often, it will at first look like it offers you something, either beneficial or harmless, but you will eventually discover it does **something else too**. This style has a couple of advantages. One is, that it, sort of, warns you that something is fishy here. This warns you, and gives you the option of running away - "I am not going to deal with that risk". It also says, that here is a challenge, and **if** you can handle that challenge, you might get something positive out of it. Typically, is also offers a confidence risk: It won't let you test the problem safely, so the only way to win the reward, is to confidently act "I am certain I have figured out the correct action here, so I am willing to bet my character's life on it". One roguelike that employs such interesting mechanical traps with weird side-effects, is called Brogue.

I have a suggestion for how to implement the traditional trap mechanism in a reasonable way. The normal 'bad' way is to implement them as fully hidden, indistinguishable from e.g. normal floor tiles. These can only then be seen by being detected, with a skill, spell or check. My suggestion is to instead make them visible, but **only** when you are standing next to them.

You might pair this with drawing them in a similar way, e.g. a comma instead of a period. The idea here, is to achieve the original intent of traps: To encourage careful play. If you take care to observe, each time you have taken a step, you should be OK. But whenever you charge ahead with reckless speed, you will probably not notice a quickly-appearing comma before you step on it.

To make good sense, traps should best appear in 'dangerous' areas, e.g. near probable treasure vaults. The game challenge then becomes to get a good 'spider sense' for when you should switch to cautious mode.

31.8 Crafting

Crafting systems: In theory they could be very fun, allowing you to research and combine your own magic recipes, from mixed ingredients, trying to make a more powerful efficient fireball with cheaper ingredients, and less hurtful side-effects. But it is all too easy for crafting systems to turn into tedious busywork and grinding. When they work best, they might allow you to tweak and add bonuses and improvements to your existing gear, a bit like what is traditionally called 'enchanting'.

31.9 Trading & Merchants

This is a tempting game-loop mechanism. You'll allow the player some way to accumulate a resource, that will eventually allow him some sort of upgrade. It can be based on arbitrage, so the player will traffic goods back and forth between places where their prices differ. E.g. the original Elite lets the player accumulate money this way. Still, I think this should be a secondary game loop. Until you have a reasonably fun primary game loop, I believe it is a trap to build any intricate trading economy.

31.10   TOWN LEVELS

This is similar to trading. This is the specific game loop where you drag heavy found loot back to town level, to sell it for money, and to appraise it. Your proceeds are then used to buy critical or luxury goods, like spell fodder, ammunition, weapons, armour or food. It is a tempting game loop, but again, until primary the game loop feels good, it is dangerous to build too much of this.

31.11   CHARACTER STATS

Stats: Player (and monster) character properties serve a number of purposes. Like classes, they help narrow down what each player can or can't do. We can tie being really good in one area to being less good in other areas, by letting the player choose the distribution of limited resource points. If we let the player increase his stats, it can also be tied to a game loop and grind.

31.12   SKILLS

Again like stats and classes, a way to let the player be stronger in certain areas, and often tied to having to be weaker in others, for balance. Compared to classes, which are relatively rigid in their design, skills tempt with the possibility to "shape your own destiny". However, that flexibility often means, either that there will be extra limitations to achieve balance, or that the skill system can be misused in an unbalanced way.

31.13   Mana Magic

Mana magic systems: A limit mechanism on how strong and fast
magic you can use. Typically used if the player can learn innate
spells, which indicates no other factor would limit him.
Alternatives are cooldowns on spells, or item-governed spells.
Can also be used for interesting magic school systems, if the
mana is colored/flavored.

31.14   Levels & XP

Experience and level gain: A game loop or grind, that lets the
player earn to improve certain characteristics and stats. Most
notably his health pool and mana pool, but also other stats like
strength or intelligence. In its usual form, leads to a numbers
arms race, where you'll need stronger enemies, stronger attacks
and better armour, in an endless loop.

31.15   Schools of Magic

Magic school types: A tactical complication to shake up simple
"my damage numbers are higher than yours". With magic
schools, you may need different kinds of magic against different
monster types.

31.16 Resistance & Weakness

Resistances & vulnerabilities, rock-paper-scissors: Tied to magic schools. You may have enemies and creatures that have either resistance or vulnerability to certain attacks. Similarly, the player may earn protections against or suffer vulnerability to certain schools. Can be used for intricate rock/paper/scissors type combinations. It is a way to achieve more complex interesting combat. It ties into what is often called 'risk/reward' systems: Risky moves let the player run an additional risk, for chance of increased gains and attack power.

31.17 Deities

Deities and praying: Traditionally, players can earn favors from gods, and similarly incur a god's wrath by the wrong behaviour. The mechanism lets experienced players work to earn karma or credit, which can then be relied upon in dire circumstances. As gods are fickle, it's not a reliable approach. It's more a sort of 'try your luck' in situations you might otherwise not get out of anyway. I was never personally fond of the idea, but I recognize it has a great tradition and potential.

31.18 Classes

Player Classes: These are an interesting concept. They relate to balance, and the feel of playing the game. In a way, classes allow you to make your game multiple times. What would the game be like if the player could shoot fireballs? What would the game be like if the player could teleport through shadows? What would the game be like if the player lived inside the walls? The normal design of a player will give him a couple of strong spells with drawbacks, and a number of weaker spells. Whatever abilities we give the player, we must balance their combined power, to have a game and not just a nuclear weapon blasting the dungeon to bits immediately. So, if you have 10 ideas for powerful spells, you can't really give them all to the same player. Classes help solve that - each class is supposed to be a toolkit consisting of a balanced selection of spells. You don't have to do classes, but if you have many competing ideas for how the game should roll, classes can let you make this work.

31.19   Mini-Map

A lot of roguelikes sport a small radar mini-map in the corner, displaying a small overview of the parts of the dungeon you have explored. It is a nice quality-of-life feature, but it is not really required for a game to work.

31.20   Game Persistence, Save & Load

If you want games to last more than 20 minutes, you will probably want the player to be able to save and load his game progress, so he can resume his game tomorrow night. However, avoiding game state persistence can be a tactic to keep your game endeavour in coffee-break roguelike territory (that is, games of relatively short duration and scope).

31.21   TIME/SPEED MOVEMENT SYSTEMS

In roguelike games, different levels of speed have immense
balance power. If a creature can move faster than the others, they
can often 'kite' enemies, and in theory continuously deal damage
while avoiding taking any damage themselves. The simplest
naïve approach to speed will give double speed and half speed,
equal to a grotesque difference in power. An elegant way to
overcome this, is to instead use a turn queue which is based on
fractional speeds. So you might have a speed of 1.15, and your
enemy might have a speed of 1.07. This approach is much easier
to balance. This is one of the things I left out of the book. But
just by replacing our TurnQ with a queue based on fractional
speeds, our game would support this feature - this is one of the
reasons we employed the TurnQ.

31.22   DYNAMIC TERRAIN

We haven't really used terrain in this book. Instead of ordinary
floor, you can have varied terrain. You can have swamps, water,
ice, dry grass, trees, lava. You can have terrain that can burn (dry
grass) or freeze (water), or melt (lava). Terrain can change and
affect. You might flood a dry place, or empty a flooded place. You
may have gas or poisonous fumes. The terrain can be dynamic in
a number of ways. By affecting you or combat. By what you can
do to it (set it on fire). By what then happens to it (how it
changes as it burns). By simply being replaced with something
else (e.g. by flooding). Minecraft and Brogue demonstrate this.

31.23 Visiblity & Sound

You can have monsters that are invisible, or only visible when they are very close. They can be interesting to interact with, if they don't kill you before you learn anything.

Some roguelikes do great things with sound, giving you hints about what is happening outside your range of vision. It is great for mood and tension. "You hear something bad moving closer in your direction." "The shrieking intensifies".

31.24 Pets

There is a great roguelike tradition of friendly allies, such as familiars and pets, that aid you in combat and in other ways.

31.25 Artifact Weapons & Armor

In the glittering blinking shiny slot machine that our roguelikes also serve as, you will often find rare random and powerful artifacts. Legendary and epic weapons. Some inspired by D&D, by Tolkien, and the like. Weapons like Defender, or Holy Avenger, or Sting. Even when their names are fixed, their attributes may be randomized for variety. You might have fun making artifacts with procedurally computer-generated names. For extra points, tie the syllables of the random name to the item abilities. For double points, keep the random name pronouncable. Would you really want to wield an overpowered polearm named Gelaomanoepeforlaramidaragorl? Orcrist just rolls better off the tongue.

32 Just Make a Small Program?

(In which we dream about writing our game as one small program)

F 32.1: In a neat little clock you can view all the pieces at once

32.1　Maybe

Looking at the many lines of code in this book, people just starting out with programming might speculate how much code we really need. Why do we need so many lines of code and so many files? Can't we just write a small tight dense program that fits together all we need?

That is a good question. The answer is "yes - and no". In this chapter, we include a small code listing, that fits together an entire roguelike in about 64 lines of code, where you and monsters can fight and kill each other.

A crude analogy is doing maintenance work on a two-storey house. You might there ask "do we really need the effort of raising-assembling-mounting scaffolding on the building before we execute the work? Can't we just do it all from a ladder?". The answer here is yes, technically you could probably achieve it just with a ladder. However it would be more cumbersome, dangerous and slow to do it that way. Putting up the scaffolding will allow you to work easier and faster from then on.

Compressing your game code into a dense file and a single class achieves similar trade-offs. You will be throwing away a lot of the names we would have used. Your various entities will become anonymous conventions, which the programmer must instead remember and juggle in his head. Some of your data and variables will serve multiple purposes, e.g. overlapping the dungeon map model directly with the display grid. Possibly storing some state, e.g. your hit points and inventory directly in the map (e.g., the top row could display but also **hold** your current inventory).

It is also similar to the difference between casting an industrially produced item as a single piece, versus assembling it from multiple components. The latter is more complex, but allows you to replace, upgrade and service parts of the item. Which of course would not be possible, if it was cast as a single piece.

In a similar way, a lot of our lines of code concern the interfaces through which the various pieces are fitted together. All these interfaces allow us to attach or remove extra features as we develop, modify and upgrade the game. As an example, our `Game` object contains a `Bag` component and a `Worn` component. The presence of these components includes the given features in the game, and removing those components will again exclude the features. This quality of being able to include and exclude separate features is precisely possible because we separate the various features into such isolated components.

If we instead forced all those features to live together in a single class and a single file, it would be rather complex to enable or disable specific features - we'd have to manually identify the sections of the single file that concerned e.g. an inventory bag, to be certain we disable it correctly. As opposed to simply blotting out an included modular component.

Something similar happens if we want to replace or substitute a feature. Let's say we have a simple inventory design, and a complex inventory design, and implementations for both. With the code split up into module components, it is rather straightforward to switch between those two features. If we, again, instead coded everything into a single source file, trying to swap between two such inventory implementations would be rather complex and cumbersome - akin to trying to replace the roof on our house using just a ladder instead of a proper scaffold to work from.

This leads to the central point of having our isolated component files and classes. If you think of your game, your software, as a work in progress - your "workplace" where the normal state of things is that you expect to be **changing** things around every time you are active there, then the split-up into named components is the appropriate structure that makes change feasible, easy and possible.

Contrary to this, the monolithic "all the game code in one single giant class file" may be an excellent way to SHIP the final playable game. Since it is just intended to RUN, but not to be edited. (note: this is what so-called bundlers do.) But it is not a practical structure, if you believe there is still work or change to be done.

You can very well insist to work in and build your entire game in the 'compressed' format. There are people that do that, possibly because they haven't learned or tried any other approach, or because they like it. But a lot of programmers, nevertheless, have agreed on preferring 'divide and conquer your code', by splitting it up into understandable module component fragments, that can be understood and modified in isolation, without having to take the other 90% of the game code into consideration to do so.

In particular, as a program or a game grows ever bigger, the larger the benefits of splitting it up into modules. A bit like how, as you approach high-rise buildings, scaffolds become the norm, and ladders become ever less of an option.

A roguelike with enemies, combat and death, in about 64 lines of code:

(beware it is C# instead of TypeScript, but it doesn't change the point)

```
 1 class Point { public int x,y; }
 2 class Mob : Point { public bool ply; public char c;
 3   public void hurt() { if (!dead()) { --c;} }
 4   public bool dead() { return c < (ply ? 'A' : 'a'); }
 5 }
 6 class Cell { public char env; public Mob m;
 7   public char c() { return m != null ? m.c : env; }
 8 }
 9 class Engine_Exp {
10   public void run() {
11     Console.CursorVisible = false; Console.Clear();
```

```
12     buildMap(); initMobs(); loop();
13   }
14   Random rd = new Random(42);
15   int rnd(int n,int m=0){return m+rd.Next()%(n-m);}
16   static int mx = 40, my = 25;
17   Cell[,] t = new Cell[my,mx];
18   void env(Point p, char c) {
       t[p.y,p.x] = new Cell{env=c}; draw(p); }
19   void draw(Point p) {
20     Console.SetCursorPosition(p.x,p.y);
       Console.Write(cell(p).c());
21   }
22   Cell cell(Point p) { return t[p.y,p.x]; }
23   void buildMap() {
24     for (var p=new Point(); p.y < my; ++p.y) {
25       for(p.x=0;p.x<mx;++p.x){env(p,0==rnd(4)?'#':'.');}
26     }
27   }
28   List<Mob> q = new List<Mob>();
29   void initMobs() {
30     for (int i=0; i<15; ++i) {
31       var m=new Mob{x=rnd(mx),y=rnd(my),
                     ply=(i==0),c=(i==1)?'f':'Q'};
32       q.Add(m); cell(m).m=m; draw(m);
33     }
34   }
35   void loop() { for(;;) {
       var m=q.First();q.RemoveAt(0);turn(m);q.Add(m);
     }}
36   void turn(Mob p) {
       if (p.ply){ply_turn(p);}else{npc_turn(p);} }
37   void ply_turn(Mob p) {
38     char k = Console.ReadKey(intercept:true).KeyChar;
39     int N=k=='k'?1:0, S=k=='j'?1:0,
           E=k=='l'?1:0, W=k=='h'?1:0;
40     act(p, new Point{x=p.x+E-W, y=p.y+S-N});
41   }
42    void npc_turn(Mob p) {
```

```
43      int x=rnd(-1,2),y=rnd(-1,2); if(x*x+y*y<1){return;}
44      act(p,new Point{x=clip(p.x+x,mx),y=clip(p.y+y,my)});
45    }
46   int clip(int n, int L) { return (n+L)%L; }
47   bool legal(Point p) {
       return p.x>=0 && p.y>=0 && p.x<mx && p.y<my; }
48   void move(Mob p, Point n) {
49     cell(p).m=null; draw(p);
       p.x=n.x;p.y=n.y; cell(n).m=p; draw(p);
50    }
51   void act(Mob p, Point n) {
52     if (!legal(n)) {return;}
53     Cell nc = cell(n);
54     if (nc.m != null) { hit(n,nc,nc.m); }
55     else if (nc.env == '.') { move(p,n); }
56    }
57   void hit(Point n, Cell c, Mob m) {
58     m.hurt();
59     if (m.dead()){ q.Remove(m); c.m=null;
         if (m.ply){System.Environment.Exit(0);}
61     }
62     draw(n);
63    }
64 }
```

32.2 SHOULD I CODE IN THIS BOOK'S STYLE?

Not really. This book's code does a number of things you might
not normally want or need to do.

- All the local one-letter variables. They are used to keep the
  code narrow for printed book pages, and to recap the local
  context when viewing fragments of code. Use whatever
  variable identifier length your conscience is happy with.
- All those adjusted interfaces. I use these because I keep all
  30 evolutions of the game running at any given time. When

developing a game not for book chapters, you'd mainly care about your newest combination, and not need to worry about e.g. Game0,Game1..GameN at the same time.

- The `ScreenMaker` is a good example of what you don't really need for your own games.

That said, the Builder approach I heartily recommend. It should help you mix and match and experiment and recombine your game pieces, both for new content, and for easy testing.

F 32.2: Simple code making simple dungeons

33 Making better maps

(In which we take a better look at making dungeon maps)

F 33.1: Building Worlds Takes Machinery

33.1   ROOMS & CORRIDORS

We only made a single proper map generator in the main part of the book, as we wanted to get on with building the rest of the game instead. But there is a myriad of varied ways to generate strange dungeons maps, which could easily fill a book of their own.

Making generators that build weird dungeons can be immense fun, and there are many ideas to learn from and to combine. We include a selection of dungeon generators here, to wet your appetite and feed your inspiration.

Let's up our game and make some decent maps. We want rooms connected by sneaky corridors, possibly with doors to open and close. Let's get to work!

33.2   MAP-BUILDER'S WORKSHOP

We are about to build map upon map upon map - lots of them. So we will create some tools to make that easier. Our first tool is a combined map and terminal, called `MapDrawer`.

- Its main feature is to **draw** tiles immediately as we set them.
- It makes it easy to inspect the contents of a tile, by only caring about the `env` tile.
- It has integrated map rendering (of the entire map).
- It supports initializing the entire map with a specific tile (sometimes we want to start with all wall, sometimes we want to start with all floor).
- It has a `carve()` setter, which allows us to selectively draw over earlier drawn parts, without erasing e.g. earlier floors, or walls (this will be explained in detail, in context when we use it).
- Its final feature is to be a simple 'one-stop-shop package' that lets us start making maps immediately, with just a

single line.

Let's formally define its interface: `07mapgen/33MapDrawerIF.ts`

```
export interface MapDrawerIF {
  setp(p:WPoint, glyph:Glyph):GlyphInf1;
  get(p:WPoint): Glyph;
  carve(p:WPoint, glyph:Glyph, hard:Glyph):void;
  dim:WPoint;
  map:DMapIF;
  render(): void;
  fillMap(init:Glyph):void;
  legal(p:WPoint):boolean;
}
```

We can implement the map **model** parts of it like this:
`07mapgen/33BaseMap.ts`

```
export class BaseMap implements MapDrawerIF {
  constructor(public dim:WPoint, public map:DMapIF){}
  legal(p:WPoint):boolean {
    return p.x >= 0 && p.y >= 0
      && p.x < this.dim.x && p.y < this.dim.y;
  }
  get(p:WPoint):Glyph { return this.map.cell(p).env; }
  set(x:number, y:number, glyph:Glyph) {
    this.setp(new WPoint(x, y), glyph);
  }
  setp(p:WPoint, glyph:Glyph):GlyphInf1 {
    let i: GlyphInf1 = GlyphMap1.inf(glyph);
    if (!this.map.legal(p)) { throw p; }
    this.map.cell(p).env = glyph;
    return i;
  }
  carve(p:WPoint, glyph:Glyph, hard:Glyph) {
    if (this.get(p) != hard) { this.setp(p, glyph); }
  }
  render() {} // (impl below)
  fillMap(init:Glyph) {
    for (let p=new WPoint(); p.y<this.dim.y; ++p.y) {
```

```
      for (p.x = 0; p.x < this.dim.x; ++p.x) {
        this.setp(p, init);
      }
    }
  }
}
```

To make it actually **render** on the screen, we'll complete it as
`07mapgen/33MapDrawer.ts`:

```
export class MapDrawer extends BaseMap {
  term:ResizingTerm;
  constructor(dim:WPoint, init:Glyph,0) {
    let map=new DMap(new WPoint(dim.x,dim.y),init,0);
    super(dim, map);
    this.term=new ResizingTerm(dim);
    this.term.onResize();
  }
  setp(p:WPoint, glyph:Glyph):GlyphInf1 {
    let i = super.setp(p,glyph);
    this.term.at(p.x, p.y, i.c, i.fg, i.bg);
    return i;
  }
  render() { MapRenderer.renderMap(this.term, this.map); }
}
```

Which of course requires the renderer,
`07mapgen/33MapRenderer.ts`:

```
export class MapRenderer {
  public static renderMap(term:TermIF, map:DMapIF) {
    let w:WPoint = new WPoint();
    let t:TPoint = new TPoint();
    for (t.y=0, w.y=0; t.y < term.dim.y; ++t.y, ++w.y) {
      for (t.x=0, w.x=0; t.x < term.dim.x; ++t.x, ++w.x) {
        let cell:MapCell = map.cell(w);
        let i:GlyphInf1 = GlyphMap1.inf( cell.glyph() );
        term.at(t.x, t.y, i.c, i.fg, i.bg);
      }
    }
```

```
    }
}
```

We will also afford ourselves a utility class with general helper functions to aid in building maps. It starts out with a single function. `07mapgen/33MapBuilder.ts` :

```
export class MapBuilder {
  public static addFence(map:DMapIF,
                         wallg:Glyph=Glyph.Wall,
                         fill:Glyph=Glyph.Bad) {
    let p:WPoint = new WPoint();
    for (p.y=0; p.y<map.dim.y; ++p.y) {
      for (p.x=0; p.x<map.dim.x; ++p.x) {
        let edge:boolean =
          (p.x==0||p.x==map.dim.x-1
          || p.y==0||p.y==map.dim.y-1);
        let glyph = edge ? wallg : fill;
        if (glyph == Glyph.Bad) { continue; }
        map.cell(p).env = glyph;
      }
    }
  }
}
```

33.3 STARTING OUT

We will experiment a bit, and try to build some maps in the simplest ways we can come up with, to see 'how far we can get, with how little'. If it takes a somewhat complex algorithm to get exactly the map we would prefer, we *are* willing to go that distance. But before we come up with a needlessly complex way to make our maps, let's see how far simple techniques can take us. This will give us a perspective on *why* we'd want to introduce more complex mechanisms, and what we'd get out of it, or miss out on by *not* doing so.

33.3.1 SIMPLE DUNGEON IDEAS

One simple algorithm would be a set of vertical columns, with
vertical hallways between them. If we break each vertical column
in one or more places, we achieve a connected level, even with a
bit of randomness. It might be a bit boring, but it would work.

Another simple way to make a random connected maze-like
structure, is to divide the map into a matrix of tiny two-by-two
squares, and then in each square put either a vertical bar or a
horizontal bar. Such a mix of horizontal and vertical bars will
never close, so you can reach every cell.

Both of these methods, though simple to implement,
unfortunately produce somewhat boring levels. Still, it's a start
to get our feet wet, so let's try it.

33.4 BROKEN COLUMNS

Our first foray will be the series of 'broken columns', or broken
walls if you will. The idea is to build an array of vertical walls,
side by side. And then punch random doorways in each of those
walls. We will punch *two* holes. Because if you only punch a
single hole, there would only be one path through the entire
map, leaving the rest of the map as dead-ends. In other words, it
would be a map without loops - not very interesting to navigate
for the player, because he gets fewer **choices**. We reuse
`addFence()` from `MapBuilder`. This entire implementation only
takes up 4-12 lines of code, depending on how you count it. That
is rather small for building a game map.

07mapgen/G0_BrokenColumns_Algo.ts:

```
export class G0_BrokenColumns_Algo {
  run(dim:WPoint, r:Rnd, dm:MapDrawer) {
    MapBuilder.addFence(dm.map, Glyph.Wall,Glyph.Floor);
```

```
    dm.render();
    for (let p = new WPoint(2,1); p.x<dim.x-1; p.x+=2 ) {
      let a = r.rnd(1,dim.y-1), b = r.rnd(1,dim.y-1);
      for (p.y = 1; p.y<dim.y; ++p.y ) {
        dm.setp(p, (p.y == a || p.y == b ?
                    Glyph.Floor : Glyph.Wall));
      }
    }
  }
}
```

To run the broken-columns, you need a runner - `src/index_gen00.ts` like this:

```
let dm = new MapDrawer( new WPoint(41,25), Glyph.Floor );
let rnd = new Rnd(17);
var algo = new GO_BrokenColumns_Algo();
algo.run(dm.dim, rnd, dm); console.log('done');
```

F 33.2: Broken Columns method

33.5 ALTERNATING WALLS MAZE

Our next foray uses a neat trick to generate a kind of maze, with very little code. The idea is to divide the map into a grid of small squares (e.g. 2x2 tiles), and put at random a small horizontal or vertical wall in each. When the wall segments are placed this way, all floor tiles will be connected and reachable.

The exact properties depend on how the outer edges of the entire grid are treated. If you leave a rectangular open floor path on the outside, the corridors will be open too. If you close off **two** edges, e.g. the bottom edge and the right edge, you end up with a sort of tree structure (right and bottom edge will be closed off). Similarly, if you instead wall off both left and top edge, as well as bottom and right edge, you instead achieve a set of disconnected tunnels (but we don't really want that, for our current intentions).

We on purpose leave an empty rectangle-path on all 4 sides. We also deliberately choose the map dimensions to support our layout - as the small squares are 2x2, our full map dimensions must accommodate an integral number of these (e.g. with 40 x 26). Notice we only use around 5-12 lines of code for this algorithm, which again is **tiny** for building an actual maze (it's amazing).

`07mapgen/G1_HorzVert_Algo.ts` :

```
export class G1_HorzVert_Algo {
  run(dim:WPoint, r:Rnd, dm:MapDrawer) {
    MapBuilder.addFence(dm.map, Glyph.Wall, Glyph.Floor);
    dm.render();
    for (let p = new WPoint(2,2); p.x<dim.x-3; p.x+=2 ) {
      for (p.y = 2; p.y<dim.y-3; p.y+=2 ) {
        let vert = r.oneIn(2);
        let q = p.plus(new WPoint(vert?0:1, vert?1:0));
        dm.setp(p, Glyph.Wall); dm.setp(q, Glyph.Wall);
      }
```

```
      }
    }
}
```

F 33.3: Horizontal/Vertical method

And an `src/index_gen01.ts` to run it:

```
let dm = new MapDrawer( new WPoint(40,26), Glyph.Floor );
let rnd = new Rnd(17);
var algo = new G1_HorzVert_Algo();
algo.run(dm.dim, rnd, dm); console.log('done');
```

Beware that, even though it has seemingly generated a 'proper' labyrinth, there is something fishy going on with its structure. Notice how everything seems to flow from the NW to the SE, and how nothing flows in the NE-to-SW direction.

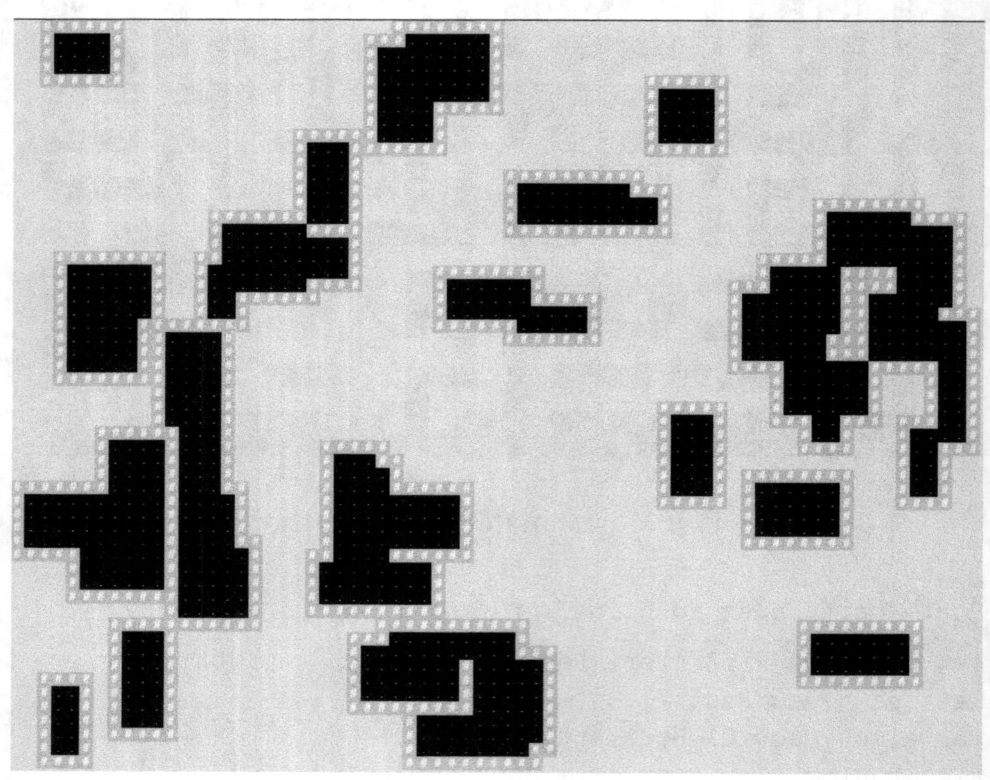

F 33.4: Randomly Placed Rooms

33.6 PLACING RANDOM ROOMS

Neither of our two first attempts contain any actual **rooms**. They are all corridor-maze-like. Let's make a fresh attempt, where we just place rooms at random. We will be a little bit clever about it: If we try to add a room that would overlap one previously added, we take care that their **walls** don't overwrite each other's **floors**. That is, wherever one of them would have a floor, we keep the floor in place, and ignore the wall one of them would want there.

To add random rooms, we must decide two things about them. One is **where** to place them, which is easy - we just place them at random (x,y) coordinates which would not push them outside the map boundaries.

33.6.1 SHAPE, SIZE AND AREA OF **ROOMS**

The other thing to decide is their **shape** - their size. For now, we'll just make plain rectangular rooms, but whole chapters could be written about rooms with other shapes. In particular, once you have decided a layout and placement of rectangle-shaped room-footprints, you could easily replace every one of them with one that is differently shaped (e.g. a cross-shaped room, an L-shaped room, an elliptical room, a moon-shaped room, a donut-room, and so on).

Our rooms should have a *goldilocks* quality - be neither too small, nor too large, and instead 'just the right size'. We can nail it down further. The most narrow a room can sensibly be, is 3 floor tiles wide. Of course, it could be even thinner than 3, but we mostly don't want 2-wide rooms, unless we see a specific need for it. A specific need could be to make *wide corridors*, to dissuade so-called conga-line combat.

We would want to increase up to a certain width, e.g. 8 or 10 or 12. But if we do that, we should maybe consider making larger values **rarer** than smaller values. Because rooms eat up **area**, and large rooms eat area **fast**. So if we let big rooms be common, we probably won't have *room* for many rooms. (We have not *implemented* big-room-protection, we have just highlighted the issue and warned about it here.)

So far I've mentioned *width*, but the same goes for **room height**. This leads to an additional issue: Like big rooms, **square** rooms take up lots of space. To phrase it another way, we can save space by using narrower rooms, and thus fit in more rooms. It is not as bad as it sounds: Instead of making the rooms **very** narrow, we'll just consider rooms to have a *longer side* and a *shorter side*. We'll pair this with randomly making rooms vertical or horizontal. So when we pick dimensions for a room, we would say e.g. "**short side** will be between 3 and 8 wide", and "**long side** will be between 5 and 12 long". This still allows us to get a few square rooms, but we won't *favor* them.

33.6.2   ROOM PLACER EXPLAINED

Our random-room-placer experiment ends up looking like the listing below here. It has quite a few lines, given what a simple task it handles. But the code is very mundane and practical, there is nothing complex going on.

O7mapgen/G2_RndBox_Algo.ts :

```
export class G2_RndBox_Algo {
  constructor(public dm:MapDrawerIF) {}
  run(dim:WPoint, r:Rnd) {
    let area = dim.x*dim.y;
    let ratio = 85; // A way to match #rects to area.
    let numRooms = area/ratio;
    console.log(area, area/numRooms)
    for (let i=0;i<numRooms;++i) { this.addBox(dim,r); }
  }
  addBox(dim:WPoint, r:Rnd) {
    let a = r.rndC(3,8);
```

```
    let b = r.rndC(5,13-a);
    let vert = r.oneIn(2);
    let w = (vert?a:b), h = (vert?b:a);
    let e = new WPoint(r.rnd(0,dim.x-w),
                       r.rnd(0,dim.y-h));
    let f = new WPoint(e.x+w, e.y+h);
    this.draw(e,f);
  }
  draw(e:WPoint, f:WPoint) {
    for (let p = e.copy(); p.y <= f.y; ++p.y) {
      for (p.x = e.x; p.x <= f.x; ++p.x) {
        let edge = ( p.x==e.x || p.y==e.y ||
                     p.x==f.x || p.y==f.y);
        this.dm.carve( p,
          edge ? Glyph.Wall : Glyph.Floor,
          Glyph.Floor);
      } // can't overwrite 'hard' == Floor
    }
  }
}
```

If we start backwards, `draw()` just draws a room-rectangle, with the inner part as floor, and the outermost edge as walls. It has the slight complication that it asks `carve()` to do an OR with respect to floors - it will never draw a new wall on top of an existing floor tile (`hard == Glyph.Floor`). We could alternatively have named it `drawRect`.

`addBox()` is the meat of the algorithm. It just picks random width and height, random horizontal/vertical alignment, and random placement for a room, as discussed above here.

The outermost part of the mechanism is a loop, which calls `addBox` N times. There is a slight trick here, the '85'. It is a manual adjustment: I experimented with different amounts of rooms for a given area, until I liked the fill ratio. After that, I calculated the ratio between full map area and the number of rooms I had added. The fill ratio of course matters. If you place too few rooms, the result will look like 'surely there is space for more rooms there!' If you place too many, you end up with a cluttered mess that looks like the aftermath of a bad city war, if it looks like anything at all.

The runner for our random-room-placer: `src/index_gen02.ts`

```
let dm = new MapDrawer(new WPoint(70,55),Glyph.Unknown);
let rnd = new Rnd(17);
var algo = new G2_RndBox_Algo(dm);
algo.run(dm.dim, rnd);
console.log('done');
```

We now have the opposite problem of the previous two algorithms, which didn't have any rooms: We don't have any **corridors**! In particular, the various rooms are not all **connected** with each other. As such, we can't immediately use our new room-placer-machine for a game map. To be able to use it, we would have to eventually make some sort of *corridor-connecter* mechanism. We will get back to that issue, but not straight away. This foray was just to remind us that to work with rooms, we will need some 'method to our madness'.

There is another way we might use it in its present shape: If we were to punch out doorway holes in the room-rectangles, it could be a crude city of random house rectangles.

33.7 Grid of boxes

In our experiment with adding random rooms, we saw the risk of cluttering and uneven distribution of rooms. We can combat this aggressively, by instead placing the rooms in a regular grid pattern. Let us whip up some code for that. First, some helpers. These will be methods in our class `G3_GridBox_Algo`.

`07mapgen/G3_GridBox_Algo.ts`:

```
addBoxAt(x:number, y:number, w:number, h:number) {
  this.draw(new WPoint(x, y),this.clip(new WPoint(x+w, y+h)));
}
draw(e:WPoint, f:WPoint) {
  for (let p = e.copy(); p.y <= f.y; ++p.y) {
    for (p.x = e.x; p.x <= f.x; ++p.x) {
      let edge = (p.x==e.x || p.y==e.y ||
                  p.x==f.x || p.y==f.y);
      this.dm.carve(p,edge?
          Glyph.Wall:Glyph.Floor,Glyph.Floor);
    } // can't overwrite HARD(floor).
  }
}
clip(BR:WPoint):WPoint {
  if (BR.x > this.maxx) { BR.x = this.maxx; }
  if (BR.y > this.maxy) { BR.y = this.maxy; }
  return BR;
}
```

It is plain code. It is an interface for adding a 'room box', a method to do the actual drawing, and a clipping helper, so we don't draw outside the map. In particular, **if** we try to draw outside the map, it will clamp our attempt, so it stays within the map area. Now to the actual mechanism built on these tools:

```
export class G3_GridBox_Algo {
  maxx:number; maxy:number;
  constructor(public dm:MapDrawerIF) {
    this.maxx = dm.dim.x-1; this.maxy = dm.dim.y-1;
  }
  run(r:Rnd, dim:WPoint, ratio:number) {
    let map = this.dm.map;
    MapBuilder.addFence(map, Glyph.Wall, Glyph.Rock);
    this.dm.render();
    let rnd_size:boolean = false;
    let rnd_offset:boolean = false;
    let avg = 7;
    let half = Math.floor(avg*0.5);
```

```
    for (let bx=half; bx < dim.x-half-1; bx += avg) {
      for (let by=half; by < dim.y-half-1; by += avg) {
        //if (!r.oneIn(ratio)) { continue;}
        if (((bx+by)%ratio)!=1) { continue;}
        let a = avg-2, b = avg-2;
        if (rnd_size) {
           a = r.rndC(3,8); b = r.rndC(5,13-a);
        }
        let vert = r.oneIn(2);
        let w = (vert?a:b), h = (vert?b:a);
        let xo=0,yo=0;
        if (rnd_offset) {
           let xr = Math.floor((avg-w)*0.5);
           let yr = Math.floor((avg-h)*0.5);
           xo = r.rndC(-xr, xr);
           yo = r.rndC(-yr, yr);
        }
        this.addBoxAt(bx+xo,by+yo, w, h);
      } // for
    } // for
  } // run.

}
```

It is quite a mouth-full, but that is because I have rolled three
variants of the same code into one (to not list it three times). In
the starting configuration, we have 2-3 disabled mechanisms:
rnd_size is disabled, rnd_offset is disabled, and ratio is
disabled. Let us see how the all-disabled variant runs. To run it,
we need an index_gen03.ts like this:

```
let dm = new MapDrawer( new WPoint(70,55), Glyph.Unknown );
let rnd = new Rnd(17);
var algo = new G3_GridBox_Algo(dm);
algo.run(rnd,dm.dim,1); console.log('done');
```

Well, that is rather.. boring. But it proves to us that our grid
code is correctly built. Let's now turn on a bit of randomness.
We turn on rnd_size, so the rooms are not all the same size:

F 33.5: Regularly Placed Rooms Grid

F 33.6: Random-Size Room Grid

```
( let rnd_size:boolean = true; )
```

That is already a kind of result. We can see some of the rooms
touching and overlapping, and being hard to navigate. But we
could probably fix that by knocking some door-holes in the
room-walls (careful - knocking down the right walls to *ensure* you
can reach every room, is **not** trivial). Let us turn off that feature
again, and instead try the random offset:

```
let rnd_size:boolean = false;
let rnd_offset:boolean = true;
```

F 33.7: Randomly Offset Rooms Grid

By itself, that looks nice. It introduces a bit of wiggle, but not too
much. We can now safely try the two features in combination.

That is, checking them in isolation gave us an idea of what might happen, if we combine them. If you were instead to combine all the things up front, you would have little idea what is going on, and which parts contribute with what. In combination now: (true and true)

F 33.8: Random Size AND Offset

This also turns out relatively nice. It is similar to the original random-size variant, but the added offset-wiggle gets rid of some of the 'too regular' flavor. We are now left with a final issue. The current map is rather dense, there are rooms *everywhere*. What if we were to leave out a few rooms? Say, half of the rooms, maybe every second room? That is why the loop contains these two statements:

```
//if (!r.oneIn(ratio)) { continue;}
  if (((bx+by)%ratio)!=1) { continue;}
```

The commented-out part is a mechanism that would **at random** only include every 'ratio' (e.g. every third, or every second) room. It is the safer, better, more robust of the two variants, but by design not regular (given that it's random).

Let us instead turn off `rnd_size` and `rnd_offset`, and try with a ratio of 2. In our `index03_gen.ts`, we need the run-line changed like so:

```
algo.run(rnd,dm.dim,2);
```

Well, that is clearly leaving out every second room.. Beware that there are many pitfalls in implementing the ratio-filter this way!

F 33.9: Ratio Grid of Rooms

The major pitfall is that we use the 'city-block-centers' (bx and by) directly, in the modulo calculation. If we want to make this more robust, we should instead introduce dedicated integer indices to track the horizontal and vertical position (i.e. numbers that count the block position as 0,1,2..N).

The problem with using bx and by directly is, that anything could happen, if we e.g. change avg_side to 8 instead of 7. Or not - the point is, we can't be sure, unless we verify it. My advice is, that if you choose to use modulo to govern this mechanism, that you then test your ratio mechanism in isolation, to make sure it behaves like you intended. If you want to be totally safe, use the rnd_ratio mechanism instead. Still, the regularity achieved with modulo makes it an interesting alternative.

Let us now try the combination of all three mechanisms: Random size, for variety. Random offset, to get rid of vestiges of regularity. And ratio, to get a reasonable mix of rooms and space.

F 33.10: Size, Offset and Ratio Together

That is a reasonable result. We have gotten random rooms, but they are now nicely evenly distributed. It is not a dungeon per se

- it looks more like a kind of city. But we could also *use* this 'machine', to knock out rooms inside *other* dungeons we'll build.

We might consider making its behaviour flags into external parameters, so we can vary how we use it from outside.

A final idea: We could instead use the methods presented here to shape the **street network**. Try to look at this layout again, where the light gray lines become the **streets**, instead of walls. This would then entail making rooms out of the black contained shapes, and you would have to either discard the gray islands, or run a post step to connect them.

F 33.11: Random-Size Room Grid

F 33.12: A Classic Maze Structure

33.8   Basic mazes

Let us have a look at 'classic' labyrinths. They are .. very dense. They may *look like* something we want, but it turns out they are 'too much of what we want'. Too dense, no macro structure, no loops.

There are many ways to construct mazes, e.g. with Prim's algorithm or Kruskal's. Let us look at one simple way: You start with a level filled with single-room cells. Then you repeatedly pick random rooms from a current pool, and knock down walls to neighboring cells. Whenever you knock down a wall to an unvisited cell, you mark that cell as **visited** and add it to the pool. If you pick a cell from the pool that has no unvisited neighbor, you just remove it from the pool without doing anything. When the pool is empty, you are done.

A different method makes you track an equivalence class ID for each cell, and track when two equivalence classes merge (then their IDs merge - you throw one of their IDs away and replace it with the 'survivor'). This approach continues until you have reached a single equivalence class - signifying that all cells are now connected and reachable. At the outset, every cell started out with its own separate equivalence class.

In the practical execution of this approach, we still employ the technique of actually knocking down walls to get a connecting doorway, between two neighboring cells from different equivalence classes.

While these ideas work, the labyrinths they build will be trees, without any loops. Let us look at some code for the first method explained above.

First, a helper class to help manage compass directions:
07mapgen/Dir.ts

```
export enum Dir {N=0,E=1,S=2,W=3}
export class Dirs {
  public static isEW(d:Dir) {
    return d==Dir.E || d==Dir.W;
  }
  public static dirs:WPoint[] = [
    new WPoint( 0,-1),
    new WPoint( 1, 0),
    new WPoint( 0, 1),
    new WPoint(-1, 0) ];
  public static ldirs:string[] =
    ['N','E','S','W'];
}
```

Then, the maze generator: 07mapgen/G4_Maze_Algo.ts

```
export class G4_Maze_Algo {
  pool:WPoint[] = [];
  constructor(public dm:MapDrawer,
              public rnd:Rnd, public dim:WPoint) {}
  run(r:Rnd) {
    let map = this.dm.map;
    MapBuilder.addFence(map, Glyph.Rock, Glyph.Wall);
    this.dm.render();
    this.addRoom(this.center());
    while (this.pool.length > 0) {
      this.processItem( this.pickPoolItem(r) );
    }
  }
  pickPoolItem(r:Rnd) { return r.rnd(this.pool.length); }
  center():WPoint {
    return new WPoint(Math.floor(this.dim.x/2),
                      Math.floor(this.dim.y/2)); }
  processItem(ix:number) {
    let p = this.pool[ix];
    let ways = this.collectWays(p);
    if (ways.length == 0) {
      this.pool.splice(ix,1); return;
    }
```

```
    let way = ways[this.rnd.rnd(ways.length)];
    this.markWay(p,way, p.plus(way));
  }
  collectWays(p:WPoint):WPoint[] {
    return Dirs.dirs.filter( d => this.free(p,d) );
  }
  free(p:WPoint, d: WPoint):boolean {
    let n = p.plus(d).addTo(d);
    return this.dm.legal(n)
        && this.dm.get(n) == Glyph.Wall;
  }
  markWay(p:WPoint, way:WPoint, door: WPoint) {
    this.dm.setp(door, Glyph.Floor);
    this.addRoom(door.plus(way));
  }
  addRoom(room:WPoint) {
    this.dm.setp(room, Glyph.Floor);
    this.pool.push(room);
  }
}
```

The basic mechanism is: Find the center of our map, and add
that as our first room in the pool. From then on, keep picking a
random room from the pool, and 'do something with it', until
the pool is empty.

And what is it we then **do**, for each random room we pick from
the pool? First, we figure out which unvisited neighbours it has,
in the directions N,S,E,W. If no unvisited neighbours exist, we
remove the room from the pool, and go back to our main loop.
Otherwise, we pick one of its unvisited directions at random, dig
a doorway in that direction, add the newly entered room to our
pool of 'active' rooms, and mark the new room as now visited.

Our visited-mark is actually the map-tile itself for the room: The
map starts out filled with wall-rock. As we visit rooms, we then
put a **floor-tile** on them, which makes sense - it makes them
walkable. We *could* instead track the room-visited status

separately in a dedicated structure. But given that these parts of
the map already follow the same logic anyway, it makes sense to
just use those directly. So a tile is **visited** if it is a *floor-tile*. We
test 'visited' status with the method `free()`. If it calms your
heart, you could call it `is_visited()` instead.

This algorithm is somewhat more complex than the mechanisms
we've built until now. But for what it does, it is actually rather
succinct and clear code. Its output looks a lot like the
alternating-walls output. But it doesn't suffer from the
'north-western wind' syndrome.

It may seem puzzling that the very simple algorithm could
produce a similar result. But if you think about it, the
broken-columns mechanism actually also achieved this. And
therein lies a hint to what is going on: Within the general kinds
of mazes, lie subsets of 'degenerate mazes', with much simpler
and less complex sub-structures. And those less complex
structures can be generated by simpler code. But because those
mazes have relatively trivial structure, they are less interesting to
look at. In other words - if you want more exciting labyrinth
layouts, you may have to tolerate more complex code to achieve
them.

To run it, we need this runner: `index_gen04.ts`

```
let dm = new MapDrawer( new WPoint(71,55), Glyph.Wall );
let rnd = new Rnd(17);
var algo = new G4_Maze_Algo(dm, rnd, dm.dim);
algo.run(rnd); console.log('done');
```

F 33.13: A Maze With Room Cutouts

33.9 IMPROVING ORDINARY MAZES

When we introduced mazes in the previous chapter, we mentioned that ordinary labyrinths appear to be 'too dense'. They have no loops. They have too many dead-ends. And they have no macro-structure, no rooms. It's a bit like eating flour raw. Well, we can fix that with a bit of work. For the missing rooms, we can simply *add* some: We just take our 'random grid of rooms' machine, and let it punch rooms into our labyrinth!

We can just do this: `src/index_gen05.ts`

```
let dm = new MapDrawer( new WPoint(71,55), Glyph.Wall );
let rnd = new Rnd(17);
var algoBox = new G3_GridBox_Algo(dm);
var algoMaze = new G4_Maze_Algo(dm, rnd, dm.dim);
algoBox.run(rnd,dm.dim, 2);
algoMaze.run(rnd);
```

Isn't that nice! First, we let `GridBox_Algo` inject random rooms into the map. Then we let our `Maze_Algo` generate a labyrinth on top of the result. It will consider the existing rooms as already-visited cells, and ignore them.

In theory, you can run the algorithms in reverse, and get similar (but not identical) results. Running them in the opposite order may actually be a bit more robust. Then the maze-builder is ensured a free empty canvas upon which to draw, without risk of the randomly added rooms somehow tripping up the algorithm (say, by making parts of the map weirdly unconnected).

Whatever you do, be aware that when you combine several algorithms this way, you must make sure that the output of one algorithm is **compatible** with the following algorithms you run after it. For example, some algorithms may expect their starting map to be all floor, and other algorithms may expect the map to be all wall. If you run afoul of this, your result may either be disappointing, or you may trigger runtime errors or even **infinite loops**!

The output already looks nice as it is. Notice that the rooms are open caves. If we wanted to, we could probably build them with walls around, and then cut a few door-holes in those outer walls. We will not do so, but have now suggested the idea.

Adding the rooms also solved another of our problems - the missing loops. We did not appreciate the tree-like structure of the graph that our initial maze described. We do *not* want a tree structure, we want loops, i.e. several ways to navigate around - alternative routes to take. And such alternatives are what we call loops.

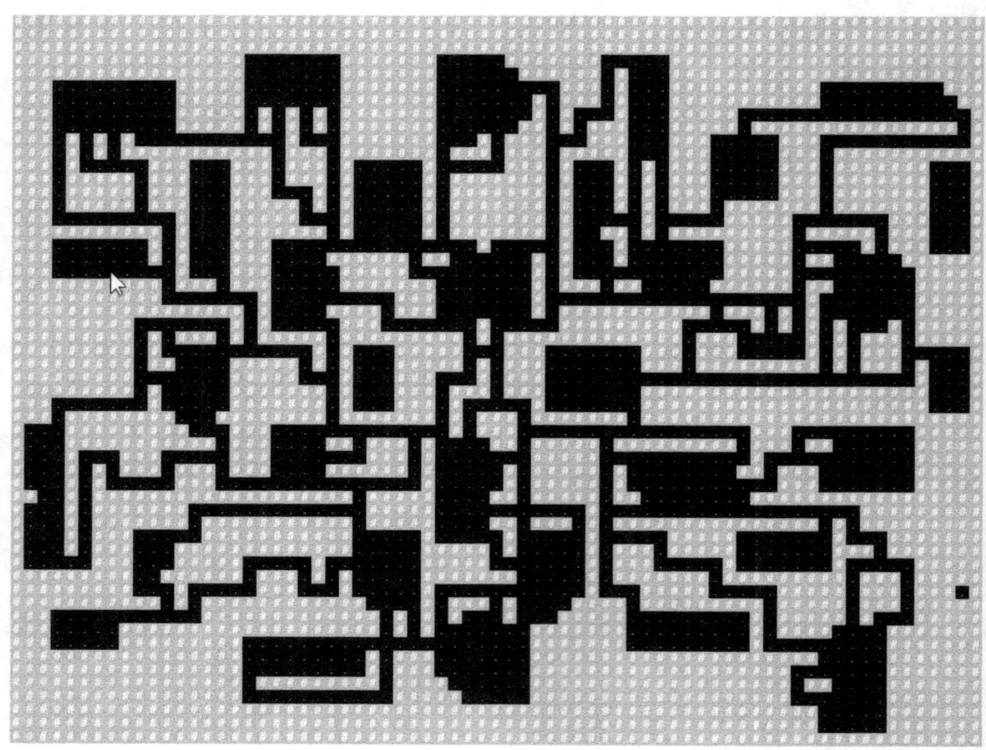

F 33.14: Room Maze With Deadends Removed

33.10 REMOVING DEAD-ENDS FROM MAZES

The maze still contains heaps of dead-ends all over the place. It is sort of too crowded. While we do like the meandering hallways in it, we don't need the full area covered with extra tunnels. We need a dead-end remover. We need some method to prune or cancel some of the tunnels, while taking care to still keep everything connected.

Consider: If you remove all dead-ends from a labyrinth, you sort of still have the same **structure** (what you might call topology). The dead-ends are like an extra layer of confusion added on top. So let us see if we can get rid of the dead-ends somehow (hint: we can).

O7mapgen/G6_CaveIn.ts:

```
export class G6_CaveIn {
  constructor(public dm:MapDrawer){}
  run(dim:WPoint) {
    let round=0;
    let count = 1;
    while (count > 0 && round < 100) {
      count = this.cave(dim);
      console.log('round', round++, 'caves', count);
    }
  }
  cave(dim:WPoint):number {
    let total=0;
    for (let p=new WPoint(1,1); p.x<dim.x; p.x+=2) {
      for (p.y=1; p.y < dim.y; p.y += 2) {
        total += this.findDoor(p);
      }
    }
    return total;
  }
  findDoor(p:WPoint):number {
    let numDoors=0;
```

```typescript
    var pdoor:WPoint, dir:WPoint;
    for (let d of Dirs.dirs) {
      let dp = p.plus(d);
      if (this.isDoor(dp)) {
        //If we have seen >1 doors,not a deadend:
        if (++numDoors > 1) { return 0; }
        pdoor = dp; dir = d;
      }
    }
    if (numDoors == 1) {
      this.closeDoor(p, pdoor);
      //numDoors += this.findDoor(
      //   new WPoint(p.x-2*dir.x, p.y-2*dir.y));
    } //(idea:when we close a door, keep chasing dir)
    return numDoors;
  }
  isDoor(p:WPoint):boolean {
    if (!this.dm.legal(p)) { return false; }
    return this.dm.get(p) == Glyph.Floor;
  }
  closeDoor(p:WPoint, d:WPoint) {
    let debug = 0;
    let doorFill = debug ? Glyph.Ply : Glyph.Wall;
    let roomFill = debug ? Glyph.Cap : Glyph.Wall;
    this.dm.setp(p, roomFill);
    this.dm.setp(d, doorFill);
  }
}
```

So what is going on here.. We have a central method `cave()`,
which will scan through every **room tile** on the map, and check if
it is blocked on 3 sides. If it is, it will then be filled in and closed
off. This consists of filling in both the **room-floor** itself, **and** the
fourth open door tile leading into it.

`cave()` also keeps count of how many rooms it has collapsed.
This explains the outer loop: We keep doing `cave()` rounds, until
we couldn't collapse any more rooms. In theory, we continue for

e.g. 100 rounds, but in practice most dead-ends are filled in by first and second pass, and all dead-ends are usually gone by the 10th pass or so. Also, we don't really care if we get rid of all dead-ends, so it could even be better for us to stop after e.g. 2 passes.

I've attempted a speed-up of the naïve algorithm. Notice the comment inside `findDoor`, where it tries to call itself. The idea is, that as you close off the fourth open doorway at the end of a tunnel, it would make sense to keep chasing back in that same direction, attempting to continue to close the remaining part of the dead-end. I have not enabled it, as the issue may be more complex than it appears at first sight.

To run it, our `index_gen06.ts` must now be

```
var algoBox = new G3_GridBox_Algo(dm);
var algoMaze = new G4_Maze_Algo(dm, rnd, dm.dim);
let caveIn = new G6_CaveIn(dm);
algoBox.run(rnd,dm.dim, 2);
algoMaze.run(rnd);
caveIn.run(dm.dim);
```

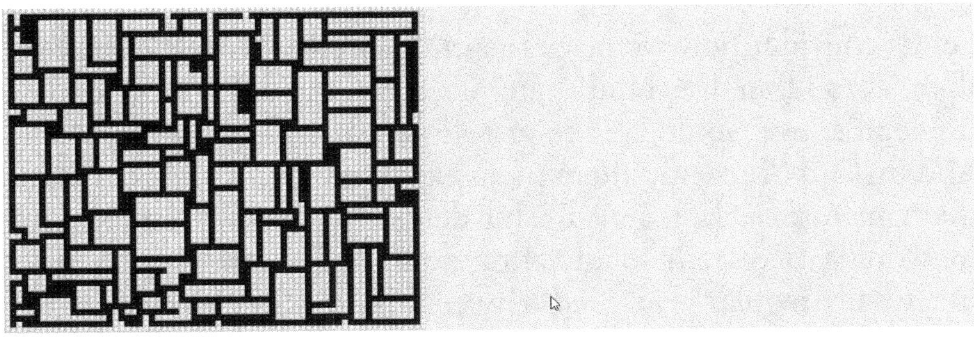

F 33.15: Growing Box Seeds

33.11 GROWING BOX-SEEDS

Another approach is to start with a floor-filled level, and scatter 1x1-tile wall seeds throughout it. We could then at random incrementally grow these seeds, in the directions of either north, south, east or west. You might view these seeds as rectangles, and one of their sides in a given compass-direction expanding in that same direction. We would then stop, whenever an expanding seed wall would hit another part.

This could be used in several ways. If we were to let the rectangles expand until they touched, we would end up with a mass of directly connected rooms. If we instead stopped just before they touched, we would form a network through their **complement**. That is, *between* all those random rectangles, a **network** of connected tunnels would form. These connected tunnels might be more interesting than the former mentioned mass of touching rectangles. After we have built such a spread of grown-out boxes, we could then hollow out their insides, and knock down a wall or two as doors, to make it possible to enter those hollowed-out rooms.

Let us consider how we place the initial seeds: Instead of placing them at random, we could again place them in an exact **grid** (remember, we would still be growing their **walls** at random). And instead of placing them in an **exact** grid, we could also place them *approximately* in a grid. This describes 3 grades: At one end, we would place seeds totally at **random**. At the other end, seeds in a totally **regular** grid. And between these extremes, seeds in a sort of grid, but a bit irregular. All three variants could be useful. The irregular grid would get both the benefits of a regular placement, and the advantages of a bit of randomness. For our attempt here, we'll stick with the totally random seed placement.

We will thus build our so-called 'box-grower'. The idea was to scatter a number of 1x1 box 'seeds' on our map grid, and then keep extending randomly chosen sides of randomly chosen boxes, until we run out of space to expand in. There will be a relatively large body of code to implement it, but most of it is mundane housekeeping without much complexity.

First up, a 'book-keeping' data structure `GA_Rect` to track our growing seeds (basically rectangles), while the algorithm runs. It contains upper left and lower right corner of the rectangle, and a list of compass directions that haven't been blocked yet. Its methods are just utility helpers, things like to provide upper right **corner**, to retrieve the end-points of a given **side**, or to **grow** the rectangle in a given direction.

As part of `07mapgen/G7_BoxGrow_Algo.ts` :

```
class GA_Rect {
  public UL:WPoint; public BR:WPoint;
  ways: Dir[] = [Dir.N, Dir.E, Dir.S, Dir.W];
  constructor(c:WPoint){
      this.UL = c.copy(); this.BR = c.copy();
  }
  UR():WPoint {return new WPoint(this.BR.x, this.UL.y);}
  BL():WPoint {return new WPoint(this.UL.x, this.BR.y);}
  removeWay(ix:number) { this.ways.splice(ix,1); }
  growDir(dir:Dir) { switch (dir) {
    case Dir.N: --this.UL.y; break;
    case Dir.E: ++this.BR.x; break;
    case Dir.S: ++this.BR.y; break;
    case Dir.W: --this.UL.x; break;
  } }
  getSide(dir:Dir):WPoint[] { switch (dir) {
    case Dir.N: return [this.UL, this.UR()];
    case Dir.E: return [this.UR(), this.BR];
    case Dir.S: return [this.BL(), this.BR];
    case Dir.W: return [this.UL, this.BL()];
    default: throw 'bad dir';
  } }
}
```

With the seed rectangle defined, the outer part of the algorithm looks like this: (still `07mapgen/G7_BoxGrow_Algo.ts`)

```
class G7_BoxGrow_Algo {
  pool: GA_Rect[] = [];
  finished: GA_Rect[] = [];
  constructor(public dm:MapDrawer, public dim:WPoint) {}
  initPool(r:Rnd) {
    for (let i=160;--i>0;) { this.rndSeed(r,this.dim); }
  }
  rndSeed(r:Rnd,dim:WPoint) {
    this.addSeed(new WPoint(r.rnd(dim.x), r.rnd(dim.y)));
  }
  addSeed(p:WPoint) {
    this.pool.push(new GA_Rect(p));
    this.draw(p,p);
  }
  run(rnd:Rnd) {
    MapBuilder.addFence(dm.map,Glyph.Wall,Glyph.Floor);
    this.initPool(rnd);
    this.dm.render();
    while (this.pool.length>0) {
      let ix = this.pickRectIx(rnd);
      this.growRect(ix, this.pool[ix]);
    }
  }
  pickRectIx(r:Rnd):number {
    return r.rnd(this.pool.length);
  }
  growRect(ix:number, rect:GA_Rect) {
    let dirIx = this.pickDirIx(rect, rnd);
    this.growSide(dirIx, rect.ways[dirIx], rect, ix);
    if (rect.ways.length==0) {
      this.removeRect(ix);
      this.finished.push(rect);
    }
  }
  pickDirIx(rect:GA_Rect, r:Rnd) {
    return r.rnd(rect.ways.length);
```

```
    }
  growSide(dirIx:number, dir:Dir, rect:GA_Rect, ix:number) {
    if (dir==undefined){
        throw `bad ${dirIx} ${rect.ways.length}`;
    }
    let grew = this.grow(rect,dir);
    if (!grew) { rect.removeWay(dirIx); }
  }
  removeRect(ix:number){ this.pool.splice(ix,1); }
```

run() places a fence around the map, and adds 160 1x1 cells to the
pool of growing seeds. It then keeps picking random seeds and
tries to grow them, until the seed pool is empty. The grow-seed
action picks a random **open** direction from the seed, and asks
growSide() to attempt to grow that side. If the chosen seed has
zero directions still open, it is removed from the pool and placed
in the finished-list. Finally, growSide() itself mainly handles
removing the direction from the seed, if we find it is blocked. The
actual side-growing action only happens in grow(), which we
haven't shown yet. So let us see what all the fuzz is about:

```
grow(r:GA_Rect, dir:Dir):boolean {
    let s = r.getSide(dir);
    let d = Dirs.dirs[dir];
    // 1 out: // c=candidate.
    let c1 = s[0].plus(d), c2 = s[1].plus(d);
    // 2 out: // b=buffer.
    let b1 =    c1.plus(d), b2 =    c2.plus(d);
    this.adjustBuffer(b1,b2,dir);
    if (!this.is_free(b1,b2) || !this.is_free(c1,c2)) {
       return false;
    }
    r.growDir(dir);
    this.draw(c1,c2);
    return true;
}
```

Before we explain the nitty-gritty here, let us explain it on a conceptual level: We get hold of the coordinates of the seed side - s - we intend to expand, and then calculate the areas next to it, and verify whether they are unoccupied. If the area is free, we grow the seed into it, and draw it.

Now in detail: First, we get the chosen side of the current seed - the side we intend to grow and expand. We get it as a top left and bottom right end-points of that side. Even though it is a kind of rectangle, it is also just a line - either 1 cell wide, or 1 cell high.

Then we add the expand-direction (as a vector) to both those points. This has the effect of translating the entire line segment exactly in the expansion direction. With this we have the coordinates of the new line segment we intend to add ('candidate', i.e. c1, c2). Thus, we can call `is_free()` to check whether some of its points are already occupied.

But we do more than that: We offset the line segment one further time, into b1,b2 ('buffer'), and we also check if the **buffer** is occupied. This way we avoid our seeds growing to line up exactly and touch corners - instead we'll leave a 1-tile wide empty hallway between all seeds.

For this to work, it's not enough to just offset in the expand-direction. That is why we also call `adjustBuffer()`, on the buffer. It extends the buffer sideways too, so it becomes 1 tile longer in those directions (we might have named it `extendBuffer` instead). It is a small but important adjustment, to achieve our neat corridors. Without it, nearby seeds would often block off the corners of the hallways and make them impassable. If you are unsure what this achieves, you can try turning it off, and see the sad effect.

Let us show the implementation of the final bits used above: `is_free()` checks the rectangle for any non-floor. `draw()` fills a rectangle with walls. And `adjustBuffer()` extends the two end-points of a side-segment.

```
is_free(e:WPoint, f:WPoint):boolean {
  let dm = this.dm;
  for (let p = e.copy(); p.y <= f.y; ++p.y) {
    for (p.x = e.x; p.x <= f.x; ++p.x) {
      if (!dm.legal(p)) { return false; }
      if (dm.get(p) != Glyph.Floor) { return false; }
    }
  }
  return true;
}
draw(i:WPoint, j:WPoint) {
  for (let p=i.copy(); p.y <= j.y; ++p.y) {
    for (p.x = i.x; p.x <= j.x; ++p.x) {
      this.dm.setp(p, Glyph.Wall);
    }
  }
}
adjustBuffer(a:WPoint, b:WPoint, dir:Dir) {
  switch (dir) {
    case Dir.S: case Dir.N: --a.x; ++b.x; break;
    case Dir.W: case Dir.E: --a.y; ++b.y; break;
  }
}
```

The box-grower is one of the larger algorithms, it ticks in at around 80 lines of code. But it is not because it holds much complexity. Most of the code is just mundane book-keeping. Some of it is caused by handling 4 cases of compass directions. With different implementation abstractions (e.g. to avoid the compass cases), it might be expressed simpler. Some of the lines are spent on not having `is_rect_occupied()` and `draw_rect()` available as library primitives (this is a deliberate choice, to avoid our algorithms polluting each other). We also use up some space for keeping a distinction between an item and said item's **position** in a container. I believe this distinction is important to

have, because the random or not-so-random positions we pick,
influence how our algorithms behave (e.g. the shape and
structure of our labyrinths). So better not use containers that
offer built-in random pick and automatic item removal.

To run it, we can use this `index_gen07.ts`:

```
let dm = new MapDrawer( new WPoint(70,55), Glyph.Floor);
let rnd = new Rnd(17);
var algo = new G7_BoxGrow_Algo(dm, dm.dim);
algo.run(rnd);
```

Why are we placing 160 seeds? The area of our map is 3850, so
160 is 4% of that. A better way to find the number of seeds,
would be as a percentage of the map area. We could make a
method that does so:

```
calcSeeds(dim:WPoint):number {
  let area = dim.x * dim.y;
  return Math.ceil(area*0.04);
}
initPool(r:Rnd) {
  let seeds = this.calcSeeds(this.dim);
  for (let i=seeds;--i>0;) { this.rndSeed(r,this.dim); }
}
```

Note that there is nothing magical about 4%. You simply get
different kinds of layout, with larger or smaller percentages. For
example, 20% would get you a very granular maze-like layout, and
1-2% would get you large city blocks. If you make this percentage
an external parameter to the algorithm, you can reuse the
generator to make varied stuff.

In its current state, it is yet just a tunnel-network builder - we
will have to do something on top of it, to turn it into a full 'map
with rooms and corridors'.

We could use the property `finished` on the container as a
starting point: It will contain a list of all the grown seeds, and

their exact coordinates, once the algorithm has run to completion. So we could iterate through its rooms, and flesh them out with walls, doors and interiors.

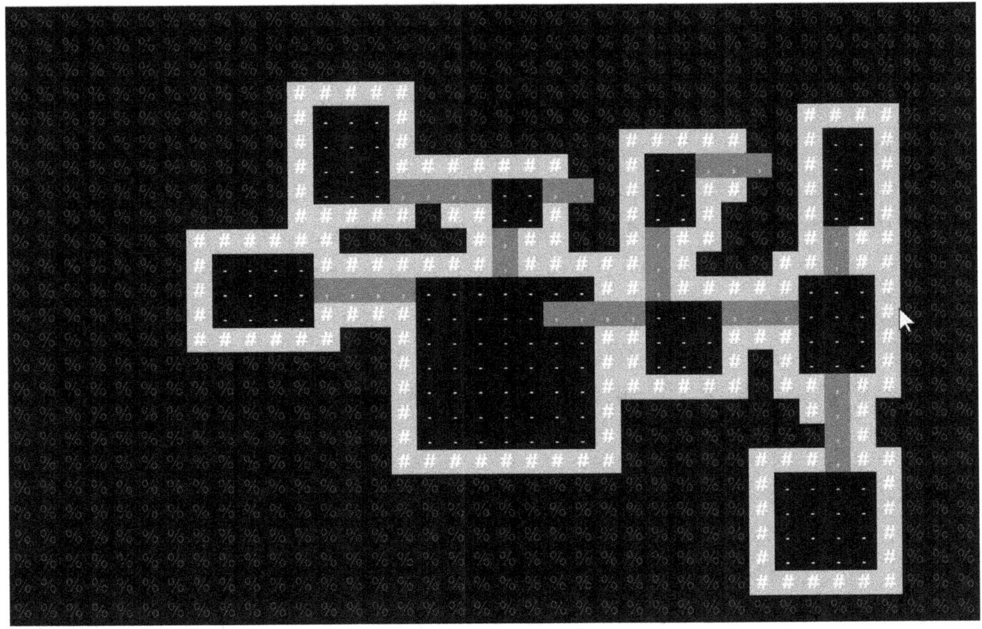

F 33.16: Sprouting-Box Method

33.12 SPROUTER

The 'sprouter' method starts from a single room, and then continually sprouts short corridors with new rooms at the other end. It will then continue to try to sprout from those *new* rooms. Whenever it fails to sprout in a blocked direction, it will give up on that direction (sort of). It will keep on growing until it has exhausted space in whatever confines it was placed in. For it to be great, we must ensure it also adds **loops** somehow, probably in a separate later stage.

The technical way it operates is: Keep a pool of rooms under construction. Start by putting a single central room in that pool.

For each room, we will track a list of 4 initial random compass directions (duplicates are allowed, so a room might even contain east 4 times!). Those are the 4 directions the room might branch off into. Now, repeat a loop that goes like this:

Pick a random room. From that room's list of possible directions, extract and *remove* a single random direction. Try to *suggest* a **corridor** in that direction. If the corridor is not possible because of collision, skip out to next iteration of the outer loop. If it *is* possible, try to then *suggest* a new random **room** at the end of that corridor. If both corridor and room are possible, dig the tunnel, then the room. Add that new room to our pool. When any given room runs out of possible directions, remove the room from our pool. Keep repeating the loop, until the room-pool is empty.

A detail to clarify: I mentioned the algorithm would take note when a direction is blocked off, to not try it again. This just means that **this** attempt is removed from the room's possible-directions list. If that list contains e.g. 4 instances of east, the remaining 3 'east' attempts still stand. They might still work, because each corridor-attempt is chosen at a random offset, so even though one attempt at going east failed, another east-attempt at a different offset might succeed.

The walkthrough may sound a bit convoluted, but it's actually quite simple: "Repeat branching out in a random direction from a random room, until you exhaust all attempts". With the caveat "remember which combinations you have tried, so you don't repeat them."

This method has a limitation with regards to our goal: It builds a tree-shaped labyrinth. Tree-shaped means there are no **loops**. Tree-shaped networks are not very fun shapes to do combat in, because 'no loops' is a another term for 'a heap of dead-ends'. We would prefer a hallway structure that includes loops. There are many ways this could be achieved, but a simple method is to remember all the *succeeded* tunnels that failed when trying to add the room (remember, if we couldn't add the room, we abandoned the attempt).

If we note the failed attempts, we can do a second stage where we revisit some of them to add extra tunnels. We can trace along their intended direction, to try to connect them up to other rooms. It is important we only draw and connect the extra tunnels *after* we have finished adding rooms. If we were to try to add the tunnels too early, we would swiss-cheese our map-level full of unfinished tunnels, without leaving any area free to sprout further rooms.

We'll make a tool class with some useful primitives, to help us implement the sprouter algorithm. We want it to have the following methods: `07mapgen/SurfaceIF.ts`

```
export interface SurfaceIF {
  tunnel(s:WPoint,e:WPoint, tile:Glyph):void;
  box_empty(s:WPoint,e:WPoint):boolean;
  box(a:WPoint,b:WPoint, wall:Glyph):void;
}
```

`tunnel()` draws a line between two points, with a cell type. `box()` fills a rectangle with a cell type. `box_empty()` checks whether a given area is clear or occupied. We can implement it like this: `07mapgen/Surface.ts`

```
export class Surface implements SurfaceIF {
  constructor(public s:MapDrawerIF,
              public rnd:Rnd) {
    this.dungsurf = new MapSurf(s);
  }
  tunnel(s:WPoint,e:WPoint, tile:Glyph) {
    let mid = this.rnd.rnd(2) ? new WPoint(s.x,e.y)
                              : new WPoint(e.x,s.y);
    let overrideYes = true;
    if (!this.box(s,mid, tile)) { return false; }
    if (!this.box(mid,e, tile)) { return false; }
```

```
      return true;
    }
    box(a:WPoint, b:WPoint, wall:Glyph):boolean {
      let dx = (a.x < b.x ? 1: -1);
      let dy = (a.y < b.y ? 1: -1);
      var inside:boolean;
      var charToSet:Glyph;
      for (let xi=a.x;  ; xi+=dx) {
        for (let yj=a.y;  ; yj+=dy) {
          inside = (xi != a.x && xi != b.x
                  && yj != a.y && yj != b.y);
          // (INSIDES <- FLOOR, BORDERS <- WALL.)
          charToSet = inside ? Glyph.Floor : wall;
          let wantWall:boolean = (charToSet == Glyph.Wall);
          if (!this.overrideCell(xi,yj,charToSet,!wantWall)) {
            return false; // Wall may not override floor!
          }
          if (yj==b.y) { break; }
        }
        if (xi==b.x) { break; }
      }
      return true;
    }
    overrideCell(x:number, y:number,
                 tile:Glyph, override:boolean) {
      let p = new WPoint(x,y);
      let canWrite:boolean =
      (override || this.s.get(p) == Glyph.Unknown);
      if (canWrite) { this.s.setp(p,tile); }
      return canWrite;
    }
    box_empty(s:WPoint,e:WPoint):boolean {
      let p = new WPoint();
      for (p.x=s.x; p.x<=e.x; ++p.x) {
        for (p.y=s.y; p.y<=e.y; ++p.y) {
          if (this.s.get(p) != Glyph.Unknown) {
            return false;
          }
```

```
      }
    }
    return true; // no walls found.
  }
}
```

The core of the algorithm looks like so:
`07mapgen/G8_Sprouter_Algo.ts`

```
export class G8_Sprouter_Algo {
  q:Queue = new Queue();
  dim:WPoint;
  surface:SurfaceIF;
  constructor(public s:MapDrawerIF,
              public rnd:Rnd) {
    this.dim = s.dim
    this.surface = new Surface(s,this.rnd);
  }
  run() {
    this.addFirstRoom(this.dim);
    while (!this.q.empty()) { this.step(); }
  }
  step():boolean {
    let i_room = this.q.rndIx(this.rnd);
    let room = this.q.q_[i_room];
    this.growWay(room);
    if (!room.hasWays()) { this.q.remove(i_room); }
    return !this.q.empty();
  }
}
```

To figure out what it's doing, we'll need to look at growWay, and its helpers suggestLeg and suggestRoom:

```
growWay(room:Room) {
    let way:Dir|undefined = room.ways.pop();
    let L = this.suggestLeg(way, room);
    let outside = L.e.outside(this.dim);
    if (outside) { return; }
    let r = this.suggestRoom(L);
```

```
    if (this.surface.box_empty(r.a, r.b)) {
        this.addRoom(r);
        this.drawTunnel(L);
    } else {
        let quickLoops = false;
        if (quickLoops && this.rnd.rnd(3)<2) {
          this.drawTunnel(L);
        }
        this.collisions.push(L);
    }
}

suggestLeg(way:Dir, room:Room):Leg {
  // Propose random corridor out from room.
  let len = this.rnd.rnd(1,4);
  let EW = Dirs.isEW(way);
  let offset = this.rnd.rnd(1, EW ? room.w()-2 : room.h()-2);
  let s = new WPoint();
  switch (way) {
  case Dir.E: s.x=room.b.x;          s.y=room.a.y+offset;break;
  case Dir.W: s.x=room.a.x;          s.y=room.a.y+offset;break;
  case Dir.S: s.x=room.a.x+offset;s.y=room.b.y;          break;
  case Dir.N: s.x=room.a.x+offset;s.y=room.a.y;          break;
  }
  let d = Dirs.dirs[way];
  let e = new WPoint(s.x+d.x*len, s.y+d.y*len);
  return new Leg(s,e,way, d, len);
}
suggestRoom(L:Leg):Room { // make room at end of tunnel.
  let w=this.rnd.rnd(3,6); let h=this.rnd.rnd(3,6);
  let noff = this.rnd.rnd(1,h-1); // Push inwards.
  let roff = (h-noff);
  let south = L.d.rotateCW();
  let r = new Room(this.rnd);
  r.a.x = L.e.x + south.x*(-noff);
  r.a.y = L.e.y + south.y*(-noff);
  r.b.x = L.e.x + L.d.x*w + south.x*roff;
  r.b.y = L.e.y + L.d.y*w + south.y*roff;
```

```
    return r.normalize();
}
```

For these to work, we must extend `WPoint` with a few helpers. The method `outside()` checks if a point is outside the specified dimensions - i.e. negative or too large. The method `rotateCW()` rotates a point 90 degrees clockwise. For justice, we'll also give it `rotateCCW()`.

```
rotateCW() :WPoint {return new WPoint(-this.y, this.x);}
rotateCCW():WPoint {return new WPoint( this.y,-this.x);}
outside(dim:WPoint):boolean {
   return (this.x<0||this.y<0||
           this.x>=dim.x||this.y>=dim.y);
}
```

`growWay()` has a disabled `quickLoops` feature: It would add the loop-tunnels straight away, but as we explained, this would sabotage our work to scatter rooms around the map. We had better instead build a later-phase mechanism that works off the `collisions` list.

The rest of `G8_Sprouter_Algo` is

```
addFirstRoom(dim:WPoint) {
   let c = new WPoint( Math.floor(dim.x*0.5),
                       Math.floor(dim.y*0.5));
   let ex = new WPoint(4,4);
   let f = new Room(this.rnd);
   f.a = c.minus(ex); f.b = c.plus(ex);
   this.addRoom(f);
}
addRoom(r:Room) {
   this.q.add(r);
   this.surface.box(r.a, r.b, Glyph.Wall);
}
drawTunnel(L:Leg) {
   this.surface.tunnel(L.s, L.e, Glyph.Floor);
   // (Supporting walls only needed for longer halls.)
```

```
    if (L.len<=1) { return; }
    let RH = L.d.rotateCW();
    let s0 = L.s.plus(L.d);
    let s1 = s0.plus(RH);
    let s2 = s0.minus(RH);
    let e0 = L.e.minus(L.d);
    let e1 = e0.plus(RH);
    let e2 = e0.minus(RH);
    this.surface.tunnel(s1, e1, Glyph.Wall);
    this.surface.tunnel(s2, e2, Glyph.Wall);
  }
  collisions:Leg[] = [];
```

And that is not all, we also need the helper data structures: (still
`G8_Sprouter_Algo.ts`)

```
class Leg {
  constructor(public s:WPoint, public e:WPoint,
              public dir:Dir, public d:WPoint,
              public len:number) {}
}
class Queue {
  q_:Array<Room> = [];
  empty():boolean { return !this.q_.length; }
  rndIx(rnd:Rnd):number { return rnd.rnd(this.q_.length); }
  remove(ix:number) { this.q_.splice(ix,1); }
  add(r:Room) { this.q_.push(r); }
}
class Room {
  a:WPoint = new WPoint(); b:WPoint = new WPoint();
  ways:Dir[] = [];
  constructor(rnd:Rnd){ this.addRndDirs(rnd); }
  hasWays():boolean { return !!this.ways.length; }
  addRndDirs(rnd:Rnd) {
    for (let i=0; i<4;++i) {this.addRndDir(rnd);}
  }
  addRndDir(rnd:Rnd) { this.ways.push(this.rndDir(rnd)); }
  rndDir(rnd:Rnd):Dir {
    return [Dir.N,Dir.E,Dir.S,Dir.W][rnd.rnd(4)];
```

```
}
w():number {return this.b.x-this.a.x;}
h():number {return this.b.y-this.a.y;}
normalize():Room {
  if (this.a.x>this.b.x){
    var s=this.a.x;this.a.x=this.b.x;this.b.x=s;
  }
  if (this.a.y>this.b.y){
    var s=this.a.y;this.a.y=this.b.y;this.b.y=s;
  }
  return this;
 }
}
```

Phew, that is a lot of code. It is around 110-140 lines. Once again, not because it does anything particularly complicated. It just takes a lot of manual book-keeping and coordinate wrangling.

Its runner is `index_gen08.ts`:

```
let dm = new MapDrawer( new WPoint(70,55), Glyph.Floor);
let rnd = new Rnd(17);
var algo = new G8_Sprouter_Algo(dm,rnd);
algo.run();
```

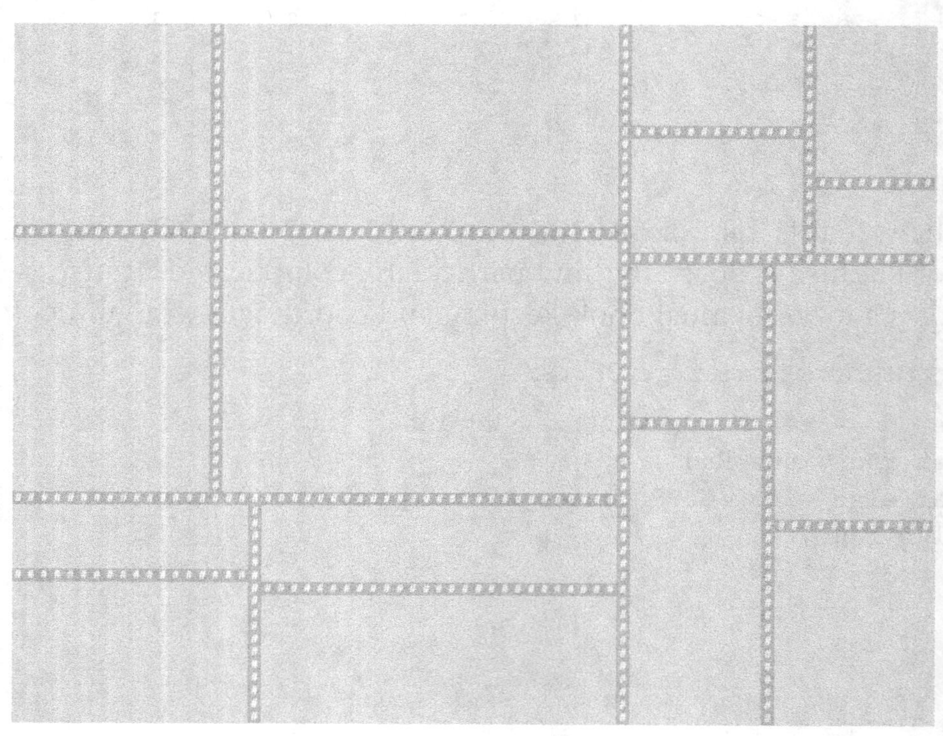

F 33.17: Binary Space Partition

33.13 BINARY SPACE PARTITION

Binary space partitioning, or BSP for short. It consists of
splitting a given space in random halves, then continuing to split
those **new halves** in a similar way. To get a balanced result, we
should alternate splitting horizontally and vertically. By itself,
the result is not that interesting. It will resemble a series of
intersecting streets. But with offset in the set of divided areas it
provides, you can generate interesting structures from it. For our
purposes, it may help to think of it as defining a street network,
and delimiting the house blocks on which you can then erect
rooms or buildings.

We will therefore post-process the BSP output, by putting
room-walls on the inside of the rectangles, by using the original
splitting-lines as corridors, and then finally knock a few holes in
those room walls as doors to enter by. The core of the algorithm
looks like this - a recursive `divide()` which keeps calling itself,
and stops when rooms get too small:

`07mapgen/G9_BSP_Algo.ts`

```
class G9_BSP_Algo {
  constructor(public dm:MapDrawer, public rnd:Rnd) {}
  run(dim:WPoint) {
    MapBuilder.addFence(this.dm.map, Glyph.Rock);
    this.dm.render();
    this.divide(true, 0,
      new WPoint(1,1),new WPoint(dim.x-2,dim.y-2));
  }
  divide(vert:boolean, level:number, a:WPoint, b:WPoint) {
    let c=this.split(vert?a.x:a.y,vert?b.x:b.y,this.rnd);
    if (c < 0) { return this.room(a,b, this.rnd); }
    let e = new WPoint(vert ? c : b.x, vert ? b.y : c);
    let f = new WPoint(vert ? c : a.x, vert ? a.y : c);
    this.draw(f,e,Glyph.Floor);
    this.divide(!vert, level+1, a, e);
    this.divide(!vert, level+1, f, b);
```

```
  }
  split(c:number, d:number, r:Rnd):number {
    let dist = d-c; // 10 and 11 is quite different.
    if (dist < 11) { return -1; }
    let range = Math.floor(dist*0.4)+1;
    let offset = -(range*0.5) + 0.5*(c+d);
    return Math.floor( r.rndC(0,range) + offset);
  }
```

33.13.1 DIVIDE

Let's see what `divide()` does: a and b are the upper left and lower right corners of the area we want to divide. `vert` says whether we will divide horizontally or vertically. `divide()` calls `split()` to pick a random position at which to split. If `split` returns a negative number, we abort the split because the area was too small to split. Otherwise, we calculate the end-points of the splitting line. Then we call our own `divide()` function again, this time on each of the two split halves.

There is a detail in how we describe the split areas: As the code is written above, we include the dividing line as part of the split-areas. You might consider this a bug.. or rather - we should try out what happens if we explicitly exclude the dividing line from the two half-areas.

33.13.2 SPLIT

The `split` function does a few things we should explain. We have a distance threshold at 11 (or 10). This means if the range to split is narrower than 11, we abort the split. This is because our tiles work with integer sizes, so there are limits to what we can fit inside. Inside a successful split, we need room for:

- One dividing line
- Two divided rooms
- Four exterior walls for those rooms

- Some interior floor for both those rooms

The sum of these necessary parts are 1+4+2 = 7. That is, 7 would be the bare minimum, and would render ridiculous rooms with just a single floor tile. For this reason, we set the limit at 10/11 instead.

Other than that, our original starting dimensions influence how the smallest rooms turn out (since the smallest rooms are a result of dividing the original area by 2, N times). For this reason 10 and 11 give such different results: Accepting size 10 allows us one further subdivision, than we would get with size 11. Because of this, size 10 will appear to give us rooms half as large as size 11. But beware this can fluctuate a bit.

Then we have the range. We were about to split an area in two parts. But we want those areas to be similar in size, not e.g. 10% and 90%. A 10% part would essentially render one part useless. Instead, we want to split near the middle, in a range of e.g. 40% of the full range - that is what the 0.4 is for (the further +1 is a rounding-up, to avoid cases where our range would otherwise end up as zero).

We then want to distribute our 40% range evenly (half and half) around the midpoint average of our [c;d] range - that is what `offset` does.

33.13.3   FINISHING WITH ROOMS

That explained the core of the algorithm. But we must also account for the mysterious method `room()`. It is

```
room(a:WPoint, b:WPoint, r:Rnd) {
  let l=this.one;
  let a1=a.plus(l), b1=b.minus(l);
  if (!this.legal(a1,b1)) {return;}
  this.draw(a1, b1, Glyph.Wall );
```

```
    let ex = b1.minus(a1); let size = Math.min(ex.x, ex.y);
    if (size < 4) { return; }

    let a2=a1.plus(1), b2=b1.minus(1);
    if (!this.legal(a2,b2)) {return;}
    this.draw(a2, b2, Glyph.Floor);
    for (let k = r.rndC(1,2); k-- > 0; ) {
      this.knockDoor(a1,b1,r);
    }
  }
}
one:WPoint = new WPoint(1,1);
legal(a:WPoint, b:WPoint){ return a.x<=b.x && a.y<=b.y; }
..
```

The premise is, that if we give up splitting an area because it's too small, we'll instead build a walled room in it. We do this in two stages. In the first stage, we determine the inner dimensions, and paint them as a rectangle of **walls**. We do a sanity check on the dimensions: If they are so small the rectangle overlaps itself, i.e. inverts, we bail out.

In the second stage, after the wall-filling, we then find the smallest side of the room. If the room is narrower than 4, we again bail out: We'll then just leave the area as filled-in wall, since there is not enough space for a proper room. Otherwise, there *is* room for a floor inside, so we find the *next* inner region, and fill that with **floor**. Finally, we call knockDoor() once or twice, to get some doorways into the room.

draw() and knockDoor() are implemented like so:

```
knockDoor(a:WPoint, b:WPoint, r:Rnd) {
  let rx=r.rndC(a.x+1, b.x-1), ry = r.rndC(a.y+1,b.y-1);
  let vert = r.oneIn(2); let side = r.oneIn(2);
  let door = new WPoint(
     vert ? (side?a.x:b.x) : rx,
    !vert ? (side?a.y:b.y) : ry
  );
```

```
  this.dm.setp(door, Glyph.Door_Open);
}
draw(a:WPoint, b:WPoint, g:Glyph) {
  if (!this.legal(a,b)) { throw [a,b]; }
  for (let p = a.copy(); p.y <= b.y; ++p.y) {
    for (p.x = a.x;p.x <= b.x ; ++p.x) {
      this.dm.setp(p, g);
    }
  }
}
```

`draw()` just fills a rectangle. But beware it relies on b being below and to the right of a. Or rather, *not* left of or above (it would cause an infinite-loop bug). For our own protection, we throw an exception if that should happen.

`knockDoor()` randomly chooses whether the door should be on a vertical or horizontal side. It also randomly chooses which of the two *sides* it should be on. Within a side, it then picks a position in the wall, which is between the two end points - it must avoid the corners, as those would not work as doorways. There is no sanity check when placing two doors - sometimes they will be e.g. side-by-side.

To run it, we'll have `index_gen09.ts` :

```
let dm = new MapDrawer( new WPoint(70,55), Glyph.Bad);
let rnd = new Rnd(17);
var algo = new G9_BSP_Algo(dm, rnd);
algo.run(dm.dim);
console.log('done');
```

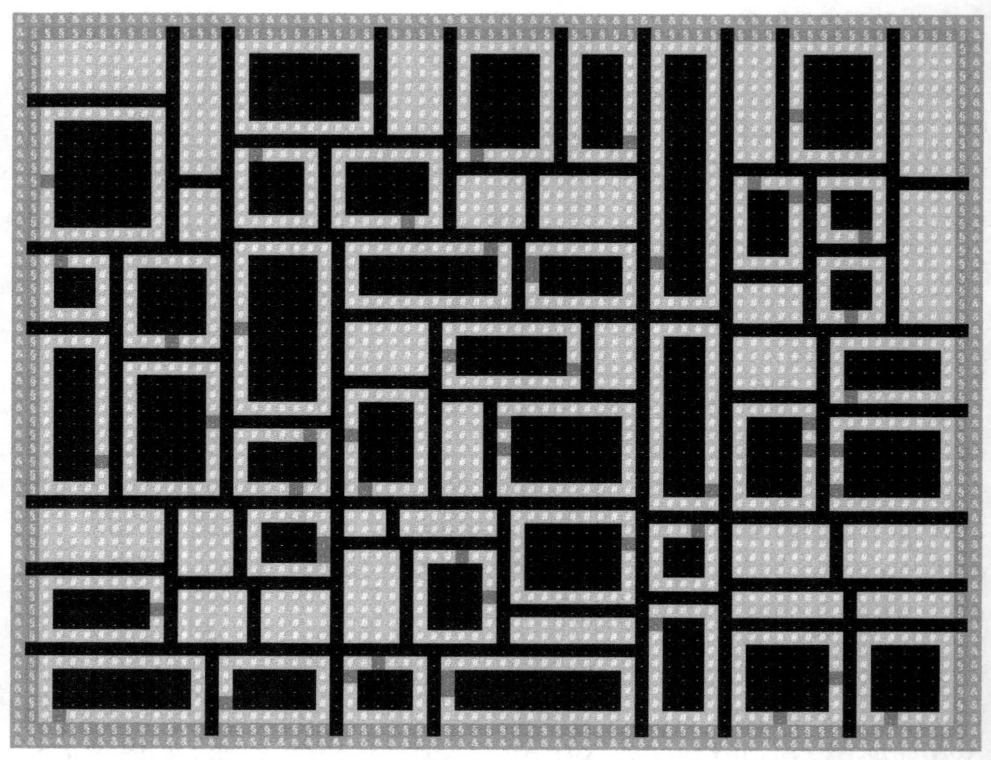

F 33.18: Binary Space Partition Improved

33.14 Thoughts on Making Dungeon Layouts

We can consider some general and approximate qualities of the kinds of dungeons and dungeon features we are interested in. We know we want **rooms** and **corridors**.

33.14.1 Corridors, Halls, Tunnels

As with rooms, we have views on which kinds of **corridors** we would like. The Goldilocks principle again: We'd like them just right - neither too long nor too short, not **too** winding or branching, but neither too little. The basic corridor would **connect** two rooms. Corridors may also branch or contain crossings.

33.14.2 Dead-Ends

For variety, it wouldn't hurt that some corridors instead wind up as **dead-ends**. This would for example mean, that it would be dangerous to flee out of a room away from a monster, without knowing whether you were fleeing into a dead-end, with the monster still chasing after you.

33.14.3 Loops

Loops in a way are the opposite of dead-ends. Whenever a corridor turns out to be a dead-end, it certainly forms no loop. As mentioned elsewhere, we are fond of (some degree of) loops, because they offer the player alternative route choices.

33.14.4   QUALITY OF CONNECTEDNESS

For playability and fairness reasons, we prefer all areas of a dungeon level to be **connected**, so the player can reach every room or hall tile from every other tile. We may renege on this. Until such time, we instead need ways to check and fix whether all parts of a dungeon are connected.

33.14.5   DELIBERATELY UNCONNECTED

Some fun might be had by having secret extra parts of the dungeon that the player would have to figure out were present, and figure out how to reach. Such a 'feature' could quickly instead be considered annoying, as the player eventually realizes the dungeon parts don't connect at all, and may feel he has no way to figure out what the parts are and how to reach them. We might deliberately introduce some mechanism to find, discover, and navigate to, such sealed-off areas: Locked and hidden doors, keys, and teleports.

If we intended such secret parts, we would probably want to deliberately hook them up with secret doors that could be found. Maybe the player could have a pick-axe to dig through rock, and maybe missing connections could be made of softer, recognizable rock ('quartz vein').

This suggests that, even if parts were not visibly connected, the computer program still needs to know about their eventual connection. That is, we might try to hide it from **the player**, but our program still needs to maintain and know about that connection it decided to hide.

33.14.6   ORDER OF CONSTRUCTION

There are many ways to go about assembling a dungeon, and which **order** to do things in. There are advantages both to making the corridors first, and to placing the rooms first. An argument in favor of **rooms first** is the *'stone and sand in a bucket'* principle: If you must fit things in a bucket, you place bigger items (rocks) first, then later add the smaller sand to fit in the crevices between the bigger rocks. However, this argument does not always work for our artificial rooms. If the rooms were *fixed up front*, yes it would make sense (because we would have to fit their exact sizes). But for our levels, the *corridors* could actually instead be considered the fixed-size items to fit: Namely, our corridors mostly must be 1 tile wide, so you need to account for that needed space in your level generation and placement of rooms. In some regard rooms & halls appear to be equally important.

33.14.6.1   ROOMS THEN HALLS

Let us consider some arbitrary approaches, as incremental stages for eventual algorithms. You could start by placing a sensible or intended amount of **random rooms**, all over the level. Just carving them out of an all-rock map, either with *overlap checks* in your placement, or even ignoring and *allowing overlap* (that would instead just cause specially shaped rooms). Our initial random room-placer behaved like this.

With the room-placing as such a separate stage, we'd then next need a **corridors-stage**, that would carve connecting tunnels between the rooms. Those tunnels could e.g. be random path-finds, or even just crude L-shaped connections.

The way we earlier combined our maze generator with the box generator, was one way to do something like this.

In one strategy for adding corridors, we might track which

rooms are closest together, and connect those first. We could then progressively keep connecting closest unconnected rooms, until everything is connected.

If we do it like that, we would also like a way to add **loops**. We don't want the level to just be connected like a tree - that is boring. A strategy for loops might still involve closest neighbours: After first connecting up everything, we might continue to connect some rooms to their second-closest neighbours.

33.14.6.2 OR, HALLS THEN ROOMS

You might instead start with a network of connected tunnels and corridors, after which you then start to inflate rooms into various places on that tunnel network.

33.14.6.3 OTHER STYLES

So far, we have focused on **rooms**, **tunnel** connections between them, and **loops**. This is a just a style choice: You can have other map styles with wide open spaces, or intricate tunnels without rooms, or a labyrinth purely of adjacent rooms with zero tunnels. We are just here exploring rooms & tunnels.

33.14.7 MAKING A CONNECTION, OVERVIEW

Luckily for us, there are established ways to ensure connectedness, termed **graph-algorithms**, that excel at verifying, finding and making connections. So-called **equivalence classes** can be used to track whether the parts of a graph network are connected. The idea is that you consider all parts that are connected to each other, to belong to the same *equivalence class*, say 'equivalence class #17'. If you count your equivalence classes, and note their number to be higher than .. 1, you know your parts are not connected.

Starting from your unconnected equivalence classes, you can use so-called **path-finding**, to connect unconnected parts. The idea in path-finding is, that you pick a random spot inside, or on the edge of, one of your parts. Then you search outwards from that spot, to find possible paths that would reach other parts of your map belonging to a *different* equivalence class. The route you took as you searched, is then one possible path (hallway) to connect these two until-now-not-connected parts. Each time you add such a found path to make a connection, you then update your existing equivalence class notes, to say 'class 17 and class 23 are now joined to both be class 17'. Then you keep looping, until your count of equivalence classes is reduced to 1, meaning everything has been connected.

A neat trick when you search outwards for connecting paths, is to change the distance metric used for your map. Normally we are used to distances to travel a cell to be equal to one. That is, it takes one kilometer or one litre of fuel to travel across each cell. But if you instead associate a small random number with each cell (say, 1 to 5), magic happens: Instead of the shortest path automatically being a straight narrow line, it would now be a meandering winding path. You might think of it like traversing mountains, valleys and swaps - travelling 1 km through mountains takes longer than through a flat valley.

33.15   CONNECTING CORRIDORS, BASIC ALGORITHM OUTLINE

One of the simpler ways to connect N rooms goes like this. We divide our rooms into two parts. The has-been-**connected** set, and the so-far-**unconnected** set. For our connected set, we will track its distances to each unconnected room.

We start out as follows. Our unconnected set is initialized to be the entire set of rooms. We remove a random room from the unconnected, and, like the UK, declare it to now be connected (to itself). As part of this, we build the list of its distances to all the unconnected rooms.

With this, we can begin the loop. We remove the next candidate from the unconnected - this will preferably be the **closest** unconnected, which our updated distance-list helps us find. We **note** that we will connect it with a corridor (details on that later).

Then we must update our distance list. This entails checking the distance between the **candidate** and every other room. Anywhere the candidate is closer than our previously connected were, we update our connected-distance to be that of our new candidate. At this point, we can repeat our loop, continuing to extract unconnected candidates and make them connected. This process by itself does not ensure loops, So any loops must be added separately, e.g. by connecting up second-closest neigbours.

The distance matrix can be calculated once in $O(N^2)$, and stored in a two-dimensional (or triangular) array.

We left out one detail to explain: How to connect up the corridors. Naïvely, we might just do so by ramming in an L-shaped connecting corridor between room A and room B, e.g. by connecting their centers. This requires some clarification. For the very first room, we can obviously do this. But as our connected-pool becomes a fuzzy cloud of multiple rooms, it is no longer as obvious how you 'just connect a corridor to it'. One way we can solve that, is when we update our current list of closest distances: Each time we update a noted closest distance to room Z, we can also note down **which room** supplied that closer distance. E.g. if we are adding candidate K, and K has a new closer distance 17 to Z, we will then note, that this 17 was supplied through K. Later, if we try to use this connection, we will then connect the corridor to K at one end.

For the distances our algorithm uses, we are not picky. You might use socalled 'taxi distance', or classic euclidian distance.

33.16 CONNECTING CORRIDORS, ADVANCED ALGORITHM OUTLINE

This is a somewhat complex approach to generating corridors.

Let's say we have some engines that spit out interesting configurations of rooms, but they don't know anything about making connected structures. This means that, instead of generating a single connected structure, they'll generate $N>1$ isolated structures, and our goal is to somehow connect these N structures, until they can all reach each other.

We have a secondary goal of creating **loops**. Though we should be satisfied if everything is connected, we would prefer an approach that aids us in adding loops. We can guess at ways this could work: If our approach presents us with a list of (sorted?) candidates, we could choose to include more than one of each candidate, to achieve loops.

Here our approach: We do a sort of crystal growing on each equivalence class. On the border of e.g. area 37, we randomly add '#37' markers to the empty cells outside, so they are now included in the area 37 subset. We can continue to grow crystals outside these again, and so on.

Each crystal area will gradually reach **other** areas. Whenever an area reaches another area, we note this meeting, in a sorted list - (one list for each area), which thus keeps track of "area A has now reached area B". We also note the **point** where B was reached. Note that we **don't know** the point where it connects to A, since A at this point is a kind of flood fill source.

This way, for every area, we have a sorted list of its approximate 'closest neighbours' - at least, the ones it reached first.

We can improve this: As we fill each growing 'crystal', we can **also** tag it with its summed distance back to the origin area.

(There is a detail in updating those summed distances: Each time we check the neighbours of an active cell, we should compare if we found a new shorter distance: If the cell east of me has been visisted with a distance of 21, but I am now at distance 17, then I should revise that neighbour to now be 18, as I represent a shorter route to that place. There is a possible complication there: I may have to update transitively, since **other neighbours** of that 21 might now **also** be closer.)

We can then do something cool for the next step, by combining the accumulated distances and the sorted lists of nearest neighbours: Our nearest neighbour list already knows the arrival point at the neighbour. We lack is the route back, and the starting point at the start area.

For this, we can exploit the accumulated distances: They can help us search backwards, by continually moving backwards in the direction of the lowest sum. Since the sum is guaranteed to always decrease by at least one, and because it describes the distance back, eventually we will reach a cell with distance zero, which means we have traced back to the start area! It doesn't matter if several routes offer the same distance - we just need one of them, any one of them.

And there is that final trick we can combine this with: Naively, we would assign the distance '1' to moving between any two cells. But we could instead assign (and remember) a random travel cost of e.g. 1-5 for each cell. If we do this, we will get twisting tunnels instead of straight lines as shortest paths (you might think of it like picking the shortest route through a hilly landscape).

To use these paths to connect up our rooms, there is a detail to be aware of. For a given isolated floor-room, we have grown a 'crystal' of nearest paths around it (think of it like the flesh around a fruit core). But we have grown such crystals around **every** room. This means, that none of the room crystals reach the other rooms directly. Instead, it is the room crystals that reach each other. What this means for us, is that we must combine each connecting path, out of two halves: The first part goes from room A to its crystal edge, where it meets the crystal edge of room B. Thus, at the edge, we must pick the other path part, going from edge to room B. To achieve loops, you could connect paths to a second or third neighbour.

The technique we described here, is a variation of what is traditionally known as **Dijkstra Maps.** Apart from using it to build maps, it can be used in many other ways. For example to let monsters track where the closest base or gold pile is.

33.17   USING BUILDERS IN MAPBUILDER

With all these fancy new builders, we can make an updated version of our dungeon builder. First, a new class in `O3build/LevelMaker33.ts` :

```
export class LevelMaker {
  constructor(public rnd:Rnd){}
  make(level:number,dim:WPoint,
       dragonLevel:number): DMapIF {
    let m:DMapIF = new DMap(dim,Glyph.Unknown,level);
    let s = new BaseMap(m.dim,m);
    switch (level%10) {
    case  0: this.genMap0_brokCol(s); break;
    case  1: this.genMap1_horzVert(s); break;
    case  2: this.genMap2_rndBox(s); break;
    case  3: this.genMap3_grid(s); break;
    case  4: this.genMap4_maze(s); break;
    case  5: this.genMap5_both(s); break;
    case  6: this.genMap6_caveIn(s); break;
    case  7: this.genMap7_boxGrow(s); break;
    case  8: this.genMap8_sprout(s); break;
    case  9: this.genMap9_bsp(s); break;
    }
    return m;
```

```
  }
  genMap0_brokCol(s:DrawIF){
    new G0_BrokenColumns_Algo().run(s.dim,this.rnd,s); }
  genMap1_horzVert(s:DrawIF){
    new G1_HorzVert_Algo().run(s.dim,this.rnd,s); }
  genMap2_rndBox(s:DrawIF){
    s.fillMap(Glyph.Wall);
    new G2_RndBox_Algo(s).run(s.dim,this.rnd); }
  genMap3_grid(s:DrawIF){
    new G3_GridBox_Algo(s).run(this.rnd,s.dim,2); }
  genMap4_maze(s:DrawIF){
    new G4_Maze_Algo(s,this.rnd, s.dim).run(this.rnd); }
  genMap5_both(s:DrawIF){
    this.genMap3_grid(s); this.genMap4_maze(s); }
  genMap6_caveIn(s:DrawIF) {
    this.genMap5_both(s); new G6_CaveIn(s).run(s.dim); }
  genMap7_boxGrow(s:DrawIF){
    new G7_BoxGrow_Algo(s,s.dim).run(this.rnd); }
  genMap8_sprout(s:DrawIF){
    new G8_Sprouter_Algo(s,this.rnd).run(); }
  genMap9_bsp(s:DrawIF){
    new G9_BSP_Algo(s,this.rnd).run(s.dim); }
}
```

We can then clone `30Builder2p.ts` to `33Builder2q.ts` , and
change `makeDragonMaps()` to be this:

```
makeDragonMaps(rnd:Rnd, level:number,
               dragonLevel:number):DMapIF {
  let dim = WPoint.StockDims;
  return new LevelMaker(rnd).make(level,dim,dragonLevel);
}
```

And finally a runner, `index33_mapmakers.ts`:

```
ScreenMaker2_Fixed.Gfirst(new Builder2q());
```

34 About

I can be contacted at smakuda@protonmail.com regarding the book.

I may be able to assist with issues related to the code in the book, depending on the nature of those issues.

The code is intended to be runnable, but as javascript, TypeScript, webpack and web browsers continue to evolve, eventually some adjustments may be needed.

I make no guarantees on what the code may or may not be suited for. It is above all intended as learning material.

This is the first revision of this book. Dated 2023-february-12.